C. H. Spurgeon

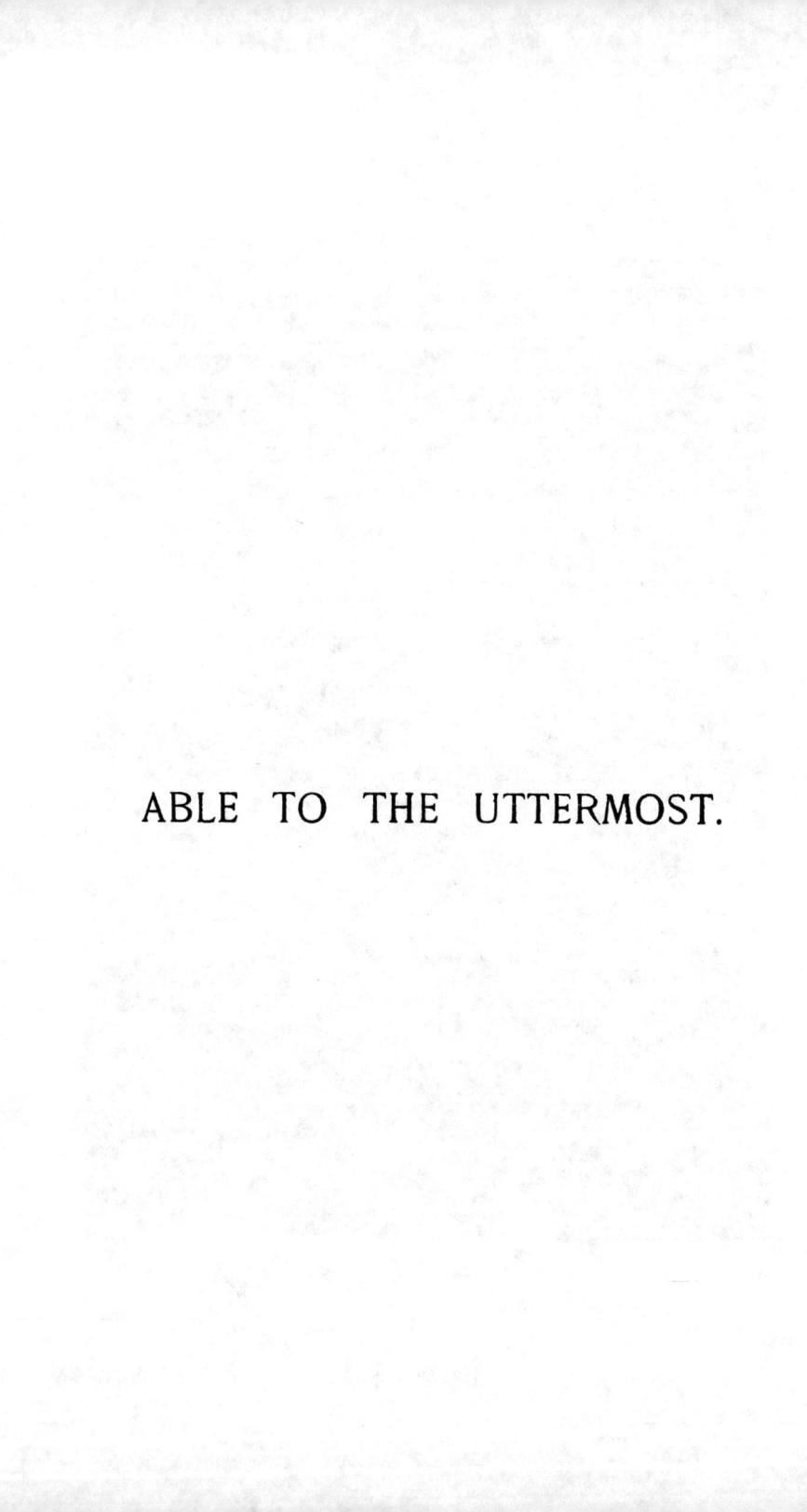

ABLE TO THE UTTERMOST.

Able to the Uttermost

TWENTY GOSPEL SERMONS

By

C. H. SPURGEON

Selected from his hitherto
unpublished Manuscripts

Publishers of C. H. Spurgeon Titles:
New Park Street Pulpit, Metropolitan Tabernacle Pulpit,
and other Original Works

 **Pilgrim**
PUBLICATIONS

P.O. Box 66
PASADENA, TEXAS 77501

1985

THE TREASURY OF DAVID

Original Passmore and Alabaster Edition (below)

For years this set has been available, but to our knowledge no publisher has reproduced the original Passmore & Alabaster (Spurgeon's publisher) edition in a clothbound, seven volume set. It has been published in a 3-volume format and in a 7-volume paperback set, and we have nothing against the content of these editions; but our edition is in the original format, clothbound, matching the format of the *Metropolitan Tabernacle Pulpit.*

In the summer of 1980, we finished the 63-volume *New Park Street and Metropolitan Tabernacle Pulpit* sermon series -- the largest set of books by one author in Christian history. Now we rejoice in the republication of the most famous work ever issued on the Psalms.

We believe that every owner of this set will cherish it, and we suggest you recommend it to others. Pastors, Evangelists, Teachers, Churches and Schools will want this original set for their libraries.

CONTENTS.

CONTENTS—*continued.*

FOREWORD

Charles Haddon Spurgeon not only pastored the largest church in the world, he founded an orphanage, a pastors' college, operated 21 mission halls, and led in other great ministries to the poor of London. He also published more sermons and wrote more materials than any other English-speaking evangelical preacher of his day, or since.

His 135 books (plus another 28 which he edited) total about twenty-three million words, or the equivalent of the 27 volumes of the 9th edition of **Encyclopedia Britannica**! About 4,000 of his sermons remain in print today and are still among the best-selling volumes by any religious author, living or dead. The majority of these are in the magnificient **New Park Street Pulpit** and **Metropolitan Tabernacle Pulpit**, recently reprinted by Pilgrim Publications.

But he must have preached at least three or four times as many; he was busy throughout the week outside of the Tabernacle, and preached there twice on Sunday and once during the week, while only one of these sermons was usually published in the weekly **"Penny Pulpit."**

The publishers were able to keep selecting one hitherto unpublished sermon from the many manuscripts left behind each week right up into 1917, 25 years after his death.

This collection, **Able to the Uttermost**, is a further twenty sermons which may right be called the **Forgotten Sermons of C. H. Spurgeon**. They were printed in 1922 from hitherto unpublished manuscripts after the final official one was issued on May 10, 1917.

Here then we have a slightly enlarged view of the great preacher. His presentation, insight, warmth of spiritual realism, and uplifting of the substitutionary atonement are in view on almost every page.

It is fitting that such a volume should be re-issued soon upon the heels of the sesquicentennial year of his birth (1834). Some 500 more 'Forgotten Sermons' have recently been discovered which have never yet been published in volume format. Our hope is that the reception given to this volume may be such that publication of these will also be encouraged.

Craig P. Skinner, Ph.D.
Professor of Preaching
Golden Gate Baptist Theological Seminary
Mill Valley, California

Author of **LAMPLIGHTER AND SON - The Forgotten Story of Thomas Spurgeon and His Famous Father, C. H. Spurgeon;** Broadman Press, 1984 - (Sesquicentennial Edition).

𝔐etropolitan 𝔗abernacle 𝔓ulpit

◇

𝔗he 𝔑ew 𝔓ark 𝔖treet 𝔓ulpit

◇

Spurgeon's sermons were preached at New Park Street Chapel (1855-1860) and the Metropolitan Tabernacle (1861-1892). They were recorded by stenographers and published yearly, as follows:

NEW PARK STREET PULPIT: Volumes 1-6, Years 1855-1860

METROPOLITAN TABERNACLE PULPIT:
Volumes 7-63, Years 1861-1917

The entire series consists of 3,561 numbered sermons. This is a publishing record for number of sermons, consecutive weekly issues, consecutive yearly volumes, and number of volumes in a sermon series.

Wilbur M. Smith called it "the greatest sermon set in the English language." **B. H. Carroll** said the sermons "constitute a complete body of systematic theology." **Dr. W. A. Criswell** says, "Never have I read anywhere or in any literature anything that compares to the sermons of C. H. Spurgeon."

The Pilgrim reprint edition of Spurgeon's sermons is **complete, unedited,** and **unabridged.** All other sets or selections of Spurgeon's sermons are excerpted from the 3,561 we are publishing.

See your local book dealer about this set; if there is no dealer in your area, write to the publisher for a price list for this set and other Spurgeon books which we publish.

I.

ABLE TO THE UTTERMOST.

Wherefore He is able to save them to the uttermost that come unto God by Him, seeing He ever liveth to make intercession for them.—(Hebrews vii. 25.)

THERE is great power in advocacy. Many a man has no doubt escaped from the just sentence of the law through the eloquence of the person who has pleaded for him; and let us hope that far oftener justice has been obtained, where otherwise it might not have been, through the clear and earnest pleadings of the advocate before the bar. There is a remarkable instance in Holy Scripture of the power of pleading. Benjamin and the rest of Joseph's brethren had gone away from the Egyptian court. On their road home to their father Jacob they were overtaken by Joseph's steward. He charged them with having stolen Joseph's silver cup. This was, of course, denied, and an offer was made that the sacks of corn should be searched. Beginning with the eldest, the steward continued his search till he came to Benjamin's sack; and there it was. There was no denying the evidence. The fact was proved. They themselves were all unwilling witnesses that the charge was true. The stolen goods were found upon Benjamin. They go back; they are brought into the hall of Joseph, whom they think to be the governor, and do not know to be their brother. He charges them somewhat severely with their ingratitude. They had feasted at his table; he had sent them away with provisions; and the only return they had made was that they had stolen his cup.

Now, as it seemed to them, there was a clear case against them. Benjamin must be kept a prisoner. They make an offer all of them to stop and to be bondsmen, but Joseph says, " No, the man with whom the cup is found, let him lie in prison." And then it is that Judah rises and begins to plead, and marvellous was the effect of his pleading. He did not attempt to urge that there was innocence in the case of Benjamin. It appeared to him very clear that the cup was there : therefore he did not attempt that plea. But he described his father at

B

home, and the love that the old man bore to this, his youngest, son. He said there had been two by his father's favoured wife, but one is not, and this is the only one that is left. He declared that if this child was taken from him he should see his father dying of grief; he should bring his grey hairs with sorrow to the grave. And then he went on to plead that he would be willing to stay and be a slave instead of Benjamin. Substitution was his argument. "Take me," said he. And then he mentioned that he had made a covenant with his father Jacob, and had said, "My life for the lad's life. I will be a surety for him." And with all his might he pleaded his own suretyship engagement; he pleaded his willingness to fulfil it by becoming a substitute, and begged that Benjamin might go free. Such seemed to have been the effect upon Joseph that he could no longer restrain himself. He had played his part well up to that moment, but suddenly he bade the Egyptians begone, put every stranger out, and then, bursting into a flood of tears, he cried, "I am Joseph your brother. Doth my father yet live?"

Perhaps he might have continued a little longer the part he had assumed, but Judah's earnest-hearted eloquence prevented all this, and the soul of Joseph poured itself forth in love. It was a faint type, this, of the power of the advocacy of our greater Joseph, the shepherd of Israel. He pleads for us His brethren, guilty as we are. He does not deny our guilt, but He pleads that He is a surety for us. He brings forward the ancient covenant engagements into which He entered with His Father when He put His life for our life; and there He stands, even now, pleading also His own substitutionary sacrifice—not only that He is willing to be bound for us, but that He has been so bound—not merely that He is willing to take our guilt and be regarded as the guilty one, but that He has been numbered with the transgressors and has borne the sin of His people. No wonder that the love of God is shed abroad in our hearts by the Holy Ghost, which is given to us. No wonder that e'en the Father pours forth His love in plenteous streams of benediction upon the souls for whom the Saviour pleads.

Now, for a very short time this evening I have to call your attention to the advocacy of Christ, and you will notice in the text that there are three points worthy of your careful observation. The first is that the participators in the benefit are mentioned—"they that come unto God by Him." Secondly, the benefit itself is mentioned, and the extent of it. "He is able to save unto the uttermost." And then, thirdly, concerning the benefactor, we have a teaching with regard to the source of His power to save: " Seeing He ever liveth to make intercession for them." Briefly, then, upon each head.

I.

It is a very important enquiry for all here present, who are the participators in the intercession of Christ.

Not all mankind, certainly, for our Lord has expressly said it. " I pray for them. I pray not for the world, but for them also which Thou hast given me." And, if you remember, there is a sort of enlargement of that, but it does not alter the case. He says, " Neither pray I for these alone "—who were already around Him and were saved—" but for them also that shall believe on Me through their word " ; so that this intercession is for His people, and for those who shall be His people. Or, to put it in the words of the text, to which we will keep, " He is able to save them to the uttermost that come unto God by Him." Here, then, are the people for whom He pleads. He maketh intercession for " them that come unto God by Him."

What is coming to God? Now, every man, every reasonable man, who sincerely desires to exercise worship, wishes, when he worships, to come unto God. When I pray I do not wish my words to die on the air, but that they may come to God. When we sing, if we are at all thoughtful, we are not satisfied with catching the melody, but we want our praises to come up to God. Worship is a sort of coming to God. There is a coming to God for the supply of our needs. We are sinful. The only way to get pardon is to come to the offended God for it. Besides, being sinful, we need to be purged from the propensity to sin. The way to get holiness is to come to the holy God for it. Whenever we have any need or any want, he that knows that all good things are of God will come to God in prayer for the supply of his need. Coming to God means seeking pardon and desiring to be reconciled to Him. By nature we are going away from God, and that is the place where the sinful heart wants to be—farther and farther from God; but when the Holy Ghost touches us, then we desire to come to God to seek pardon, that the obstacles between us may be removed, and to seek holiness that we may be like God and able to have communion with Him. To come to God is for the spirit to approach the great unseen Spirit, whatever it comes for—whether to pray or to give thanks—whether to seek pardon or to seek sanctification.

Now, there are some in the world who try to come to God, but they do not come by Jesus Christ. Such persons are excluded from the benefit of the Saviour's intercession. " He is able to save them to the uttermost that come unto God by Him." *By Him.* Some will come by an earthly priest. They believe that he has a power which they have not, which is a delusion and a lie—a very fit lie for men to teach who wish to gain power over their fellow-creatures, but of which an honest man would be utterly ashamed. Every Christian is a priest unto God, but no man is more a priest than any other man. Each believer is one of the chosen priesthood, but none above the rest of Christians. Christ will have nothing to do with you if you come unto God by a human priest, for the human priesthood is ended. There is but one priest, even Jesus, who is " a priest for ever," as we read just now, " after the order of Melchisedek." All that intrude into that office now are simply thieves that come not in by the door, but climb up some other way.

There are some who try to come to God without any mediator at all. They speak of addressing the Deity themselves. This would have been proper enough before the fall, but now the great scriptural truth is given out : " No man cometh unto the Father but by Me." You may think you are approaching God, but you certainly are not. There is a presumptuous familiarity about such an approach which is rather a dishonour than an honour to God. " There is one God and one Mediator between God and man, the man Christ Jesus " ; and to attempt to approach God without the Mediator is to insult His Son and so to provoke the Most High. Alas ! there are some foolish enough to attempt to approach God on the footing of their own goodness. Let them beware lest the pure and holy God break forth against them, for this is a terrible provocation of His fiery holiness, for the uncleanness of man to talk of holy things—for sinful man to speak about worthiness—for guilty man to dream of merit. Who art thou ? Get thee back to Thy place among the lepers. Cover thy forehead and cry, " Unclean, unclean ! " What hast thou to do to come unto the temple of the Most High, for " all our righteousnesses are as filthy rags." 'Tis all God thinks of thee, and His thoughts are true.

But, beloved, there are men in the world, and they are not a few, who have been taught by divine grace to come unto God by Christ. They have sought pardon for the Mediator's sake, and found it. They seek every blessing now in Jesu's name, and they obtain it. They live now in dependence upon the Son of God, and their life cannot die. This is the way to come to God—trusting in Jesus, pleading His merits, acknowledging our own unworthiness ; and Christ will stand by every man and save every man to the uttermost who comes unto God in that way by Him, for this is the appointed way. God bids you, sinner, come to Himself through Christ. "There is none other name given under heaven among men whereby we must be saved." Come through that door which is marked by the blood of the atonement, and you shall be admitted. Attempt any other entrance, and you shall be driven away as breaking through the laws of God. It is the appointed way, and, thank God, it is a most fit way. We can come to Jesus, for He is a man. He can go for us to God, for He is " very God of very God." The blended natures of the human and the Divine make the Lord Jesus a suitable medium between man and God. All the wisdom in the world could not have devised a more excellent plan than this. The son of Mary and the Son of Jehovah! O thou blessed Saviour, with Thy right hand grasping the Deity, and with Thy left hand laying hold upon the infirmities of manhood! Well may we come unto the Father by Thee. Thou art the ladder that Jacob saw, and the rounds are so placed that we may readily climb by Thee into heaven. Thy foot doth rest on earth: Thy top reacheth unto the excellent glory of the Godhead.

Beloved, since we have, then, a way of coming to God that is appointed by God, and that is so fit a way, let us also be glad that it is so available a way. Any soul here that wishes to come to God by Christ may come. There is no embargo in Scripture against any man's coming. " No man cometh unto the Father but by Me " ; but whoever will come that way may come, and he may come as he is. He may come without any other help than that which God has provided. That is a sweet thought. You do want a mediator between your soul and God, but you do not want any mediator between your souls and Christ. You cannot come to God except through the intervention of another, but you may come to Jesus just as you are, whoever you may be, and in whatever state of heart you may be. If God the Holy Ghost do but give thee the will now to come, and thou desirest to approach to God like a poor prodigal, saying, "Father, I have sinned," come along the blood-stained way of the Redeemer's sacrifice, and there shall be no lion there to stop thee, but all along it the sweet bells of Heaven shall ring, "Come and welcome! Come and welcome! Come and welcome!" Every soul may come that cometh to God by Jesus Christ. That is the limit; but come by Him, and those that come unto Him He will in no wise cast out.

Thus we have described the persons. Oh, happy is the preacher if he can hope—if he *could* hope—that all came to God this way. May he hope that some will be led to-night to come unto the Father through the crucified Son.

II.

Now, the second interesting point of our text is this— the benefit which Christ the intercessor is prepared to give, and the extent of it. "He is able to save to the uttermost" —or, as the margin puts it, "He is able to save evermore"— "them that come unto God by Him."

First, He is able to save them. Now, there are some that come to God or desire to come, and they say, "Oh, that I might be saved, but my sins! my sins! my sins!" His precious blood is pleaded before the throne, and it can put away all sin. "But my sins," saith one, "far exceed those of any other man. My sins, they are many, grievous, aggravated. They clamour against me. Like Abel's blood which cried against his brother Cain, my sins cry out against me." Yes, and thou art like Joshua of old, who stood in the vision in filthy garments, and the angel of the Lord said, when he was accused of Satan, "Take away his filthy garments from him." Jesus saith the same to thee. If thou comest to God by Him, He is able to take all thy filthy garments from thee, and to make thee now pure. Believe it; it is His own gospel. He is able to make you as though you had never sinned. If you have had a long course of sin, in a moment He can blot out those sins, and set you in the sight of God as though you had never once transgressed. The pardon which Jesus brings is perfect and complete, making a clean sweep of all iniquity, so that if the sins of the pardoned be sought for they shall not be found, for He will pardon those whom He reserves in this respect—in having power by pleading His blood before God. He is able to save from sins, and from the uttermost sins, those that come unto God by Him.

Oh, that blessed word, " *to the uttermost* "—because there are some that seem to have gone to the uttermost. There are persons who appear to have sinned as far as ever they could. They have flung the reins upon the necks of their fiery steeds, and then they have lashed them to see how fast they could go. We see some who seem to defy all laws, human and divine. They sin with both hands greedily. In the ways of transgression they seem to have wings to their heels as they run along the dangerous pathway. Well, but if thou wilt stay in thy course and come to God by Christ, thy sins, which are many, are forgiven thee. Though they be red like scarlet they shall be as wool : though they be as crimson they shall be whiter than snow. Glory be to God, we have a Saviour not for little sinners, but for great sinners—ay, the greatest sinners that ever lived. " This is a faithful saying, and worthy of all acceptation, that Christ Jesus came into the world to save sinners, of whom," saith Paul, " I am chief."

Yes, but there are some who, when they are coming to God by Christ, not only find sin in the way, but they find Satan in the way. " Oh," saith one, " I have such horrible thoughts. Ever since I began to seek a Saviour I have felt blasphemies rising within me, to which I was a total stranger before. I am forced to clap my hand to my mouth for fear sometimes I should say these frightful things." Well, do you hate these things ? If so, they are none of yours ; they are Satan's injections. Press forward to God by Jesus Christ, for the living Intercessor is able to save you from Satan. " He hath desired to have you, that he may sift you as wheat," but Jesus has prayed for you that your faith fail not. " Resist the devil, and he will flee from you," because he sees Christ behind you, and he is always afraid of Him. " Ah, but," saith another, " it is not only that. I have such an evil nature, and ever since I have been seeking God through Christ my nature seems to be more evil than ever it was. Whether it is worse or not I cannot tell, but it seems so to me. Why, when I try to pray I find rebellious thoughts. I get up and go to my business with a solemn resolution that I will live near to God, but at the close of the day I seem to have drifted farther away than ever. ' When I would do good evil is present with me.'

Snatches of old songs come up when I am trying to praise God ; and recollections of old sins come and haunt me just when I desire my mind to be most in union with the purity of Heaven." Ah! we know what that means. What a mercy it is that Christ is able to save to the uttermost them that come unto God by Him from their besetting sins, from their con-stitutional sins, from these inward temptations, from their tendency to evil. Christ killed on the cross not merely our actual sins, but our original sin, too. While the blood made atonement for the guilt, the water which streamed with the blood presented cleansing from the power and the defilement of sin within us. Continue still to come to God through Christ, poor soul, however hard thou be beset, for surely He lives who will intercede for you.

I wish I could depict—if it were possible I would—the souls that have gone to the uttermost. Perhaps there is one here driven to desperation. He has come to God by Christ, and yet feels he cannot come. He believes that everybody else might be saved, but not himself. He feels that he, of all men, bears a mark like Cain upon his brow. It may be that once he was a professor, and he thought he walked with God. Now he has lost all hope—not only all the comfort, but, as he believes, all the life of true religion in his soul. He believes himself to be the most hopeless case that was ever laid at the feet of the great Physician.

Oh, my dear friend, I am glad of that—not glad of your sorrow, but I am glad that now there is opportunity for Christ to show how grandly He can save. What renown it brings to the Saviour when He saves to the uttermost! Why, when He has fully saved you, you will sing louder than anybody ; you will work for Him more than any. You will be like the woman who broke the alabaster box: you will love Him much because you have had much forgiven: and when you get up yonder, where all the singers meet, you will want to lie the lowest at His dear feet, and yet to sing the most sweetly to the praise of His grace. I am glad I have met with you. I only trust the Master may meet with you now, and prove that " He is able to save to the uttermost them that come unto God by Him." Oh, if you do but come to God by Him, He can, He will, save you, far as you may have gone, and des-perate as your state may be.

I seem to hear somebody say, " I am afraid of death." Oh, then, how this text ought to cheer you! He is able to save to the uttermost. A man has lain long upon his bed, and grown very faint: the bones are coming through the skin. He has a difficulty to breathe ; sleep forsakes him. Now comes the trial hour. The death-sweat lies cold upon his brow. He can scarce pray : his thoughts are distracted by his pains. He cannot listen now to good advice. The mind has become feeble. Ah! even in those last moments he that has come to God by Christ need be under no alarm. He is able to save when we are not able to pray ; able to save when we are not able to think. Do not think that the Lord will let the safety of His people depend upon their happening to be conscious when they come to die. Oh, no ; we are in the hand of Christ. A lifeboat saves the man that is in it, though that man may be fainting and unconscious while he is there. So will Christ bear into Heaven, I doubt not, many a soul that shall be too faint to know the moment of its departure ; and it shall come back from its swoon and find itself no longer on the pallet that grew hard in its long sickness, but there with a crown upon its brow praising the Lord. Well, if there be any fear of anything after death Christ is able to save to the uttermost, for after death comes the judgment, the resurrection, the standing before the throne, the sheep as well as the goats. Ah! in—

> That day of wrath, that dreadful day,
> When heaven and earth shall flee away,

before the Judge's face—in that dread hour beneath the wings of Him who is messenger of the eternal covenant we will cower down and rest in safety. "He shall cover thee with His feathers, and under His wings shalt thou trust. His truth shall be thy shield and buckler." Unto the uttermost He will save us. Thoughout eternity He will still live, and, living, He will still be able to save them that come unto God by Him.

III.

Now the third point—though upon all these things we might profitably enlarge—the third point is the source of this remarkable power which rests in Jesus Christ our Saviour.

Why is He "able to save them that come unto God by Him"? It is because "He ever liveth to make intercession for them." Notice the terms: "He ever liveth." Under the old law, when a priest died there might be an interregnum before the next took his office; at any rate, there might be some time elapse during which the worshipper or penitent might bring his sacrifice, and there would be no one to present it. That case can never occur with us. He ever liveth. I think I have told you the story which Robby Flockhart, who used to preach in the streets of Edinburgh, was accustomed to tell sometimes about the usefulness of a living Saviour as well as a dying Saviour. He said that when he was a soldier one of his comrades was condemned to die. Calling in his friend Robby, he made his will, and left him what little money he had; but on the day appointed for the shooting of the soldier he was pardoned. " So," says Robby, " he lived, but I lost my legacy, for a testament is not in force while the testator liveth." Jesus, the great testator, is dead. There is no fear about that; therefore the testament of His love is valid. It would not have been unless He had died. " Well," said Robby, " another time a person left me a small legacy, and I did not get it, for some rogue of a lawyer got a hold of it, and I never saw a penny of it. And," said he, " I used to say, ' Ah! if he had been alive he would have seen me righted; he would have got his old friend Robby the money.' But being dead he had no power to see his will carried out. Ah," said the good old preacher, " Jesus Christ lives to see His own will carried out. He died on the cross; that made it valid. He lives again to see it carried out, so that every blessing in His will, in the covenant of grace, is sure to all those to whom it belongs "; and those are known as those who come unto God by Him. What a mercy it is to have a dying Saviour! What a mercy it is to have a living Saviour! Oh, to confide in Him who hung upon the cross, but who now sits upon the throne! Here is one great rock upon which to build our hopes, and we need never fear that the foundation shall fail us at any time. " He ever liveth."

But do notice the words. " He ever liveth to make intercession for them." We say sometimes of a man, " Why, that man lives for pleasure." We mean that that is the great object of his life. Another man seems to live for his children. Very well, the text says, He lives to make intercession, as if He had nothing else to do but that—as if he lived for that, threw all his life into that—to make intercession for those that come unto God by Him. Do I strain the text when I put it so? I think I do not. He lives to reign. He lives to come again. He lives for many objects; yet is it fair to say that all the force of His life seems to run in this channel. He lives to make intercession for those He bought upon the cross; that is " for those that come to God by Him."

O may we all come to God that way! May we come to God through a crucified Saviour. May He be our channel of communication with the Lord, for, if so, the intercession of Jesus goes up for us—goes up for us continually. Why is there such power in the intercession of Christ? It is because Christ is what He is—God and perfect man. It is because Christ did what He did : He suffered, and He kept the law. His merits and His miseries put power into His plea. His nature and His office and the covenant make His plea effectual. It is this that keeps us in the favour of God. If the Lord should hide His face from His servants Jesus stands in the gap and says, " Remember that they are Thy people, that they are bone of My bone and flesh of My flesh. Accept them for My sake." And once again the Father takes away the cloud, and His unchanging love shines on His people. And when His people are in great need, then Jesus comes again, and saith, " My Father, all things are Mine. Give to My people what they need. Give the Holy Spirit yet again to them "; and it is done. And in temptation Jesus comes unto the Lord, and says, " Thy enemy assails My people. He accuses and vexes them. Deliver them." And deliverance is sent. You do not know, dear brothers and sisters, what you owe to the pleadings of Christ. If you could only put your ear, as it were, to the keyhole of heaven's palace and hear Jesus pleading there, oh, what notes would you hear! —not sighs and cries, 'tis true—

> For with authority He pleads,
> Enthroned in glory now.

It is a royal pleading, not a pleading with bloody sweat as in the garden of Gethsemane, but it is effectual pleading, and wins for us everything the Saviour seeks for our good.

What shall we say, then, to all these things? Why, that happy are those that come to God by Jesus Christ. Let them be happy. Christ is able—and we are sure He is willing—to save them to the uttermost. Go and be glad. Go your way. Eat the fat and drink the sweet. Let your head lack no oil, and your face no ointment. " Rejoice in the Lord always, and again I say rejoice." " Be glad in the Lord, ye righteous, and shout for joy all ye that are upright in heart."

But if you have never come to God by Christ, you have no intercessor; you have no share in His blood. You are lost; you are dead in sin. What then? The voice of the Gospel speaks even to you, and it says, " Believe in the Lord Jesus Christ, and thou shalt be saved." May the Spirit of God go forth with that Gospel, and may you be made to live by the power of the Holy Ghost, that you may then believe in Jesus, and find salvation in Him!

The Lord bless you! And may we meet in Heaven for His, the Intercessor's sake! Amen.

THE SORROW THAT LEADS TO REPENTANCE.

And there followed Him a great company of people and of women who also bewailed and lamented Him. But Jesus, turning unto them, said, Daughters of Jerusalem, weep not for Me, but weep for yourselves, and for your children.—(Luke xxiii. 27, 28.)

THOSE who beheld the Saviour were mainly women. Women had ministered to Him of their substance, and now, when they could not show their bounty, they showed their sympathy. It is remarkable that in the whole history of our Saviour no woman behaved badly to Him. He might be deserted, or betrayed, or slandered, or put to death, but this was left for men. It was contrary to the Jewish law for any person to show sympathy with a condemned individual. We have every reason to believe that that was the law of the time. It became the traditional law. We are told it was the law then. But the women braved the law, defied it, and showed their sympathy with this man who was being taken forth, like a malefactor, to be put to death. His disciples, who were men, fled like women, and the women were as bold as men. *They* played the man who might have been expected to be feeble, and those who ought to have been strong became weakness itself.

Our Saviour did not think lightly of the compassion of these women. It is recorded in Holy Writ that He bestowed upon them His last acknowledgment. I know He spake afterwards before He died, but, they were rather cries than words—they were grief's ejaculations, but His last speech on earth, I may say, was made in acknowledgment of the tender sympathy of these bold but sorrowing women, who clustered around Him on His way to His death.

I wonder who they were. Would it be wrong to suppose that they had heard His speech, that they had been charmed by the gracious things that dropped from His lips? Had it been more than that; had some of them been healed? Were those there who had felt His mighty touch, and had gone their way restored after years of suffering and infirmity? Probably there were some. Or were there those there who had had their children healed, their friends and relatives restored, and who felt gratitude to Jesus for making those who had been the objects of their anxiety to become once again the objects of their delight? I know not what may have been the miracles that bound these women to the Saviour, but certain I am that it was not mere pity for a person about to be put to death, for they do not appear to have wept for the other two who were taken out to execution. The Saviour did not say, " Weep not for us," but He recognised that the weeping was about Him, and Himself personally, and He said, " Weep not for Me, but for yourselves, and for your children."

It was not because they saw a man about to die that their tender hearts flowed over in their eyes, but because they recognised in Him something more than an ordinary man. They did not look upon Him as a criminal about to be executed; there was some tie of love and gratitude between their hearts and Him. It seems to me that it would be better to die amid the tears of sympathising women—better to die amidst the multitude who wept and bewailed your death than it must be to live as some men will have to live for years to come, amidst the lamentations of many and the accusations before the throne of God of others against them as men that made war against the human race and caused thousands to be slain. Better to die with Jesus, than to live with emperors and kings who make war. Curses thick and heavy fall upon all who shed human blood, but, let the curse fall upon the Saviour, as it did, it comes amidst the bewailings and lamentations of those who have sympathy with Him in His grief.

I shall now invite your attention to our Saviour's speech to these women when He said, " Weep not for Me, but weep for yourselves, and for your children."

I.

Notice, first of all, our Lord's disinterestedness. He was in a condition when one would have thought He would have was in a condition when one would have thought He would have courted compassion. He had a heart of tenderness like ours, and He needed human sympathy, but yet He put it away. He bade them not weep for Him, not because He despised the sympathy, for, as I have shown you, He loved it; but He was so little selfish that He would not have them spent their sorrows upon Himself. And this was no unusual circumstance in the life of Christ, for Him to be altogether oblivious of Himself, and only thoughtful for other people. This, indeed, is the whole secret of His ever being in this world at all. Had He thought of Himself, He had never left yonder shining throne and the courts where seraphim sing. It was because He thought not of Himself but of us that He came down to earth to be born of a woman, to live in suffering, and to die in shame. All through His life we constantly see Him putting off everything that would give Him comfort—that would give Him honour—that would give Him ease—that He might do good to the sons of men.

To go through the whole of that it would require rather a series of discourses than the little conversation we are able to hold in the few minutes we have at our disposal this evening. I would just take you to the table where He sat with His disciples at the last supper. It was the last meal that He would eat with them before His death; but He does not ask for pity. There is no cry like that of Job, " Have pity upon me; have pity upon me." He pities them, and comforts them, and His speech is somewhat on this wise : " Let not your hearts be troubled "— not asking for sympathy from them, but even putting that aside and giving all His thoughtful consideration for their weakness and future trials. Instead of asking them to comfort Him, His thought is all for them and nothing for Himself. It was just so when He came to the garden, and when the passion there began. When the bloody sweat was falling upon the ground He did look to them for sympathy, but when He found them asleep, how readily He made excuse for them. " The spirit," said He, " is willing, but the flesh is weak. Sleep on, now, and take your rest." He had looked to have some tenderness from them, but when their sorrow overcame them, and He received none, He had no bitter reproving words; and when they came at last to seize Him, while the traitor's kiss was still upon His cheek, and they who bare the lanterns and torches laid hold upon Him, He did not for a moment think of Himself, but He said, " If ye seek Me, let these go their way." The shepherd thinking only of the sheep, ready to lay down His life for them, making no terms or conditions for Himself. He touches the ear of Malchus, he who has been wounded by Peter. He could heal others, but He makes no reservation of good things for Himself. It was a true word though spoken in bitterest irony and sarcasm. " He could save others " (and He did everywhere) " but Himself He could not save." His love would not let Him; He was too disinterested to make any provision for Himself.

We see just the same thing on the cross. There where His throes were at their worst and His agony was at the highest He has a thought, but the thought is for His murderers: " Father, forgive them, for they know not what they do." He has another thought, and it is for his mother, and He says to the favoured disciple : " Son, behold thy mother," and to His mother, " Woman, behold thy son "—all disinterestedness from beginning to end.

And so it was in the case of the text which lies embedded like a precious gem. " Weep not for Me," saith He, when most He would have prized their tears, " Weep not for Me, but weep for yourselves, and for your children."

Now, in this great disinterestedness of our Saviour, there is surely something for us who are His disciples to learn. Our highest condition will be, when we are like our Master, and our best rule in life is in all things to copy Him. When we are in much grief, we are often very covetous of human sympathy. It is natural that we should desire it and be affected and cheered by it. But sometimes the natural may be allowed till it reaches a point beyond the right and the noble. Let me remind you that there is a higher thing than the reception of what is pleasant for us. It is sometimes a higher thing to put it away, and, thinking of other's griefs, to ask sympathy to show itself elsewhere, rather than upon us. You will find it often, I think, as Christians, to be a right thing and a strengthening thing for yourselves, to bid the sympathy which awaits you go and reveal itself to others. " It is true," you may say, " I feel sorely sick, but there are others that have greater sickness than I and less of comfort to alleviate their sorrow. It is true I am poor and you may pity me, but there are some poorer than I am. If you have help to give and pity, help them first."

It was a noble act of the dying soldier—the dying captain— when they lifted up to him some water. He was dying very fast, but he noticed a poor soldier nearer death than himself turn round with longing eyes, as if he wished he could have a drink, and the captain let the cup pass from himself and let the soldier drink. And it is often the grandest thing we can do when wanting much we are content to want because there are some that want still more—when we can say, " I am thankful to you for your compassion that weeps for me, but there are worse griefs than mine." " Daughters of Jerusalem, weep not for Me." Why, in the act the mind grows stronger. That act of self-denial will do more to console you than the consolation itself. You have gotten more than you received; you have girded up your loins with a strength which otherwise you would not have gained. What nobility it confers upon us, when our self-denial can be carried out even in bitter times and in seasons of dire distress! Do you tell me it is more than can be expected of man? I grant you it is, and therein is the glory of divine grace, that it can produce what nature cannot: it can make Christians do what, as mortal men, they could not think of doing—it can make them look unto Him, who, being man, is set before us as our great example, and whose infinite perfections it is our joy to seek. I cannot say more, I feel I speak unworthily of such a theme, but I commend it to your thoughtfulness—the disinterestedness of Christians carried out to the last hour.

II.

But now, in the second place, I must direct your attention to our Lord's clearness of judgment. The clearness of Jesus, I think, is seen in this. There was cause to weep on His account and His being put to death, but with impartiality He judged that there was greater cause to weep for something else. Putting Himself, therefore, quite out of the question, by His disinterestedness, He impartially judges that there was a deeper and bitterer cause of grief for these women than the fact that He Himself was about to be put to death. The sin of which their nation was guilty, the overwhelming judgment which was soon to come upon them, and which their children would soon have to suffer—these, He conceived to be in His supreme judgment, a direr cause for grief than His own death. Is it not one of the most sorrowful things on earth that there should be anything that should be graver cause for sorrow than the crucifixion? I think I may stand here and say that grief for the dying Saviour ought to be matchless.

> Alas! and did my Saviour bleed?
>   And did my Sovereign die?
> Did He devote that sacred head
>   For such a worm as I?
>
> Well might the sun in darkness hide,
>   And shut his glories in,
> When God th' Almighty Maker died,
>   For my, the creature's, sin.
>
> Well might I hide my blushing face,
>   While His dear cross appears;
> Dissolve my heart in thankfulness,
>   And melt my eyes to tears.

C

Is not this the first cause of all grief, the greatest source of all sorrow? "No," we have to reply, "it is not." There is a greater reason for grief than this. We have the Saviour's authority for it. If He saw us to-night weeping before His cross, with sorrow for His suffering, He would say to us, as He said to these women, "Daughters of Jerusalem, weep not for Me, but weep for yourselves and for your children." It is a pleasant sight in some respects to see a congregation moved with the story of the Redeemer's suffering. When one has been describing the cross of Christ, and all the griefs He suffered there—it has seemed right, and we have thought it also a holy thing that hearts should be affected, and that tears should flow, but there is something that ought to be wept for more than this. There is a grief that lies deeper than this, though this seems to reach even to the abyss—it is sin. It is sin for which the daughters of Jerusalem were to weep, sin that would destroy them. And Christ to-night seems to tell us that sin is more to be wept for than even His death.

Now let me show you how this is. In the first place, if we weep for what He suffered, but mourn not for sin, we mourn the effect, but forget the cause, for it was sin that lay at the bottom of all that He suffered. In the garden where the bloody sweat fell, what made the cup so bitter, so overflowing with the death draught? It was your sin and mine. There were the transgressions of His people made to meet on Him. At Pilate's hall and at the bar of Herod, it was not so much the spitting in the face, nor the mockery when they made Him King with a thorny crown; it was the real shame of sin that was laid upon the Saviour. He had never sinned, but He stood in our place, the place of shame, the place of dishonour. It would have been very little for Him to have been made little of and to be despised and rejected; He could have borne that well enough, but His face was darkened because God "made Him to be sin for us who knew no sin, that we might be made the righteousness of God in Him." And when He went to the tree you must not think that the cruel nails that pierced His hands and feet or the agonies of thirst were the intensity of His sufferings. Each of your sins became a nail that pierced His soul, and unbelief a spear that went through His inmost heart. His suffering there arose from the hiding of His Father's face from Him, and that hiding was the result of our sin. It pleased the Father to bruise Him. He hath put Him to grief and made His soul an offering for sin. The

Lord hath made to meet upon Him the iniquity of us all.
"Why hast Thou forsaken Me?" That awful question which
the Son asked of the Divine Father has all misery condensed
into it, but the bottom of it is sin, sin, sin! It is not, then,
the effect that can ever be so much to be wept over, as the
cause, and therefore wipe your eyes as you behold the bleeding
Saviour, as you see Him scourged, or mark Him crucified—
drop not the tears of sorrow there—but look further, and see
your sins that caused it, and bow your heads in bitterness,
too. And yet, sweetest grief, I can say,—

> My sins, my sins, my Saviour,
> How sad on Thee they fall!
> Seeing Thy heart's dire anguish,
> I ten-fold feel them all.

"Weep not for Me," but for your own sins weep.

Think again, and here is another reason for weeping—that
sin has reigned in this world and still reigns in it, that this
very Saviour, whose precious death is the source of our salvation, is still rejected. I have sat in my chamber and thought
over the griefs of my Lord till I have felt my soul melted
within me, but if I have gone forth and met with a penitent
heart, and pointed that soul to the cross, and faith has been
given, and that soul has looked to Christ, I feel that Christ
has seen of the travail of His soul, and I have felt what I know
He feels when He remembers no more the travail for joy that
a soul is saved—a brand plucked from the burning. But, go
out of your quiet room after you have mused upon the subject,
go down one of our streets and listen to the oaths and blasphemies, stop opposite that corner where the lights flare so
brightly and the cups flow so freely ; see those who go in and
out with bloated faces ; mark the signs of vice from yonder
theatre, the harlots in their hordes at eventide ; think of all
this, and ten thousand times more than this which my lips
cannot utter, and which your ears must not hear—and all this
going on in a city where Christ is preached! and done by
people who know about the Saviour—many of them! That
drunkard was in a Sunday School ; that fallen woman had a
godly mother ; those that curse and swear at least know the
name of Christ. Hear how they use it! How they trample it
in the mire! Oh, this it is that you may weep over.

Women of London, weep not for Calvary ; but weep for
your own city and the iniquities which the moon sees and which

the sun beholds. Here, that Christ should be preached, that the Sabbath should be set apart for the telling out of the matchless story of man's redemption, that man should be prayed for at the mercy-seat, and yet sin should run down our streets and God should be blasphemed—oh, weep for that.

I think I know something worse, and that is this. This house is thronged almost as often as ever the Word is preached —thronged by hearers—these aisles, these seats all full, and Jesus Christ talked of, and I can say very simply, very plainly —you have no difficulty in understanding what I have to tell you—and I may say also very affectionately and earnestly that my heart goes—I am no deceiver in that respect—with every word I say. I would God I could preach Christ better, but I do preach in the best style I can, and I would be willing to go to school to begin to learn to preach if I could but hope that I could have more effect. But there are persons who come and listen and hear the way of salvation, but won't follow it. They hear of pardon being freely presented to them, but they will not have it. They hear of hell, and they will go to it: they hear of heaven, but they will turn their backs upon it. Oh, say you, " They are people that come in by chance now and then—they only hear it once or twice, or three or four times, and go away and forget it." Ah! if it were so I would be grieved, but these are not the people I now allude to. They are those that are always here—if not always here on week-days, always here on Sabbath days. And they are attentive hearers, too, and they have a great love for the minister, and they don't forget his sermons, and they talk about what they hear ; but they will not love the lovely Saviour, nor will they come and lay their burdens down at His dear feet, but year after year and year after year, they hear it, but they hear it not. The charmer charms, but they are deaf adders to His charms.

III.

And it is not the preacher only that has this disappoint-ment. Some are in classes, where earnest Christian men and women speak to them. Some of them have had godly parents, mothers in heaven, and they themselves were on the road to heaven. They were brought up amidst influences of the most holy kind from their earliest childhood. What will ever affect them ? What means can be devised to reach them, for they seem as though they were covered with iron and with steel, with armour of metal impenetrable.   They hear, I say, but they hear not ; they see, but they see not.   Their hearts seem heavy till I fear they have so long neglected Christ that He in His justice has said, " Let them alone ; I will give them up ; they shall see their own delusion."   Oh, here is something to weep about.   You that are inclined to think of the cross and of the Saviour's body taken down all gory from that cross, and wrapped in linen and laid in the grave, put away your tears and think of these that lay in the caves of sin till they become corrupt, and God puts them out of sight.

Once more and let me follow this course of sin a little further, and I think you will hear the blessed Master say more emphatically than any words of mine can say, " Weep not for Me, but weep for yourselves and for your children." Hearers of the Gospel, you will not be always the hearers of the Gospel.   The hour of your departure out of this earth draweth nigh.   There are some, I fear, at this moment, who used to hear the Gospel at this very place, who are now where they will never have another warning and another invitation.   Dare your thoughts follow them ?   Dare you think of them as shut up for ever in outer darkness where there is weeping and wailing and gnashing of teeth ?   Dare you remember the words of judgment, " These shall go away to everlasting punishment " ? Can you think of that dire expression, " Where their worm dieth not, and where the fire is not quenched " ?   Oh, it is not Calvary to be wept for, but hell, souls lost, lost, lost, souls that heard of salvation, souls that were invited to the Saviour— lost, lost for ever !   Angels might weep here.   I say the very seraphs might bend from their golden thrones to weep over spirits cast away by that dire sentence, " Depart, ye cursed, into everlasting fire in hell, prepared for the devil and his angels."   Daughters of Jerusalem, weep not sentimental tears, but shed tears of real grief for souls that are passing away into this destruction, destroying themselves by rejecting the Saviour's love.   I wish I could speak more on that, but I cannot, I can only put it before you in that rough way, and may God touch your hearts.

But the last thing is, I think I see in this text our Lord's practicalness.   You see, I have given you His disinterestedness, His clearness, and His judgment, and now I will speak of His practicalness.   He never would have had what was not of practical use.   If they did weep, He could not help it—He must die. All the tears they shed were of a sympathy too feeble to be of any service to Him. But, "weep for yourselves," said He, "and for your children," as if there were something practical here.

Let me observe that weeping for sin is a much more practical thing than weeping for the Saviour, for, first, tears for sin—would God I could see them in every eye—betoken some degree of spiritual life. Those that mourn their sin, that regret and lament that they have transgressed—surely there is something trembling in their souls that gives me hope. When it can be said of any man, " Behold, he lives without sin," though he may not yet have found the Saviour, yet is there much encouragement in his case. When I speak of tears I do not mean those that flow from the eyes only, for some could not weep tears—I mean tears of the heart, the repentance of the soul. Where these are I say there are signs of some life, and it is through these in God's hands when we get life that we reach to something higher. I believe that when a soul has love to Christ, and has found perfect pardon, the continuance of repentance is the grand means of attaining to a still higher condition. To continue still to mourn sin is to continue to grow in grace. Tear drops are blessed watering for the flowers of grace. Though our sins are forgiven, yet now we mourn them more than ever we did, and by mourning for sin we reach from the lowest state of spiritual life to a higher one.

Let me add that the way from the higher state to the very highest is very much a road that is watered by tears. I do not believe any man will ever come to be an advanced Christian except by sorrowing much for sin. If your spiritual life has nothing of the dew of repentance about it it is a poor thing—I am afraid it is a fiction. Well, I must judge no man, but I would stand in doubt in my own case if mine were such. " Rejoice in Christ Jesus."

But there comes the rest, " Rejoice in Christ Jesus, and have no confidence in the flesh." Where there is no confidence in the flesh we have a good deal of sorrow and mourning over sin. Rowland Hill used to say it was the only thing about heaven that he regretted—that there would be no repentances. " Those eyes like the eyes of doves by the rivers of waters "—those eyes of repentance let me never lose them. Let me weep for nought but sin, and none but Thee and then I would, oh, that I might! have none but Thee! There is something practical here.

And, did you notice, our Saviour said, " Weep for your-selves " ? But He also said " Weep for your children." We are all anxious that our children should be saved, and God will grant us that blessing probably whenever our anxiety is deep. I do not believe in weeping parents that will have all their days godless children. Or if the weeping parent does not live to see his children saved, yet his prayers will be registered in heaven, and God will bless his children even after the parent has gone to heaven. At any rate, can any of you think of your sons living a godless life or of your daughter unsaved—can you think without feeling your bowels yearning over your own offspring ? The Saviour bids you exercise that natural emotion and give to it a spiritual tongue—exercise your love to your children by pleading for them before God for Christ's sake, and then there will be something practical in your weeping which there would not be in merely weeping for Christ. If you weep for yourselves, weep for your children, and then grace will come of it and salvation will come of it, and God will be glorified and you will be blessed.

The Lord in His infinite mercy give us all to hide beneath the cross of Christ, and then may our dear children come there too for Jesus' sake. Amen.

III.

IN THE PLACE OF GOD'S CHOOSING.

As a bird that wandereth from her nest, so is a man that wandereth
from his place.—(Proverbs xxvii. 8.)

WE have here the wisdom of Solomon. This will mainly
concern human affairs, for a great many of his proverbs are
not intended for the spiritual eye, but to be of literal service
to us in the business of life. But I believe a greater than
Solomon is here, for he wrote under divine inspiration, and
therefore we may take a passage like this to have some other
meaning than we shall find in the mere letter of it, and the
principle which it involves may be carried into a higher sphere
than that of human business. I shall endeavour to blend the
two. There is no less Solomon here because we have the Holy
Spirit, neither is there any less the Holy Spirit because we
have a Solomon. Let us believe that we have something of
both, and find the meaning which may be conveyed in the
text from both the human and the divine side.

I.

First, I think the principle of the text may be applied to
a man in his place in providence. As a bird that wandereth
from her nest, so is a man that readily, constantly, hastily
wandereth from his place. There are times when a man may
remove, and remove very far, very much to his own advantage,
and also very rightly. It is always difficult with those who
love their native land and the associations of home to bring
them to emigrate, and yet from the day when God came down
to see the tower of Babel, it has been His policy that the whole
earth should be replenished with inhabitants, and He intends,
by some process or other, that men shall be scattered from
dense centres of population, and that the whole earth should
be peopled. Had all our ancestors stayed at home, had it
been wrong for them to leave their land, where would have
been the vast populations that now are teeming in the other
world across the Atlantic? And Australia might still have

had but a few wild savages and wild beasts roaming over the place. It is not, therefore, wrong for people to move from their places. There are times when it is eminently right that they should do so.

When is it right, then, for a man to move? I answer that he does not contravene the spirit of this text if he wanders from his place, having no nest from which to go away. A bird wanders from its nest, but when a man has no nest, when he is in a land where he cannot earn his daily bread, when he cannot maintain his children, when he finds that the comforts of home are not his, that he cannot obtain them by any legitimate or lawful calling, then he cannot be said to be a bird that wanders from his nest because he hath not any nest to wander from. Let him wander till he can find a nest. You will see the rooks at this season of the year. They try one tree, and if, after they have laid a few sticks, it does not suit, they leave it and go on to another. And very right, too! It would be foolish to proceed in an impossibility ; and sometimes a man is foolish for sticking in one place where it is not possible for him to provide things honest in the sight of all men.

A man, again, does not contravene the spirit of this text if God breaks up his nest for him, for if the nest be broken by a superior hand, the bird must fly. And so, if God in providence evidently makes the present position of any Christian man to be untenable, he may not be afraid to venture, though it should be to the utmost ends of the earth, to rivers unknown to song. If God bids him go, he may go safely enough ; he is no wanderer ; for when God saith " Go," then we do not wander from our home. Whenever the cloud moved in the wilderness, Israel moved. They would have been sinful to have moved without the cloud: they would have been equally sinful to have stood still when the cloud had led the way. If you can feel that God's providence is directing you to change your position, to change your habitation, to change your trade, to change your place ; if you can feel that you are doing so with a single eye to God's glory, do it ; and the God who was with Abraham when he went out of Chaldea and came into Canaan will go with you. The God who has bidden His servants wander hither and thither, and been with them in their wanderings will be with you. You need not fear. Go, and the Lord go with you.

But the text comes with full force to those persons who are of a restless disposition. There are some who are always wandering from their home. They cannot settle to anything. They are everything by turns, and nothing long. They are here, there, and everywhere. Such persons cannot prosper. A tree that is often transplanted is not likely to bear much fruit. Our English saying is that three removes are as bad as a fire, and you may rest assured that they are so, that constantly moving means constantly losing, and that changing and changing means constantly having a discount taken after all from your comfort. God deliver us from that spirit that cannot be content. Having food and raiment, let us be therewith content. Do not let us be always sighing for new scenes— fresh scenes and pastures new.

The text condemns those, again, who change out of mere motives of avarice or ambition. Because they shall get more, though they have enough, they will break up all the comforts of their abode. To desire gain is not sinful. There is a limit up to which it is lawful, beyond which it becomes covetousness, which is idolatry, but to be always looking after this world's goods and hoping that you shall be rich and able to get into another condition is not to be seeking first the kingdom of God and His righteousness, but seeking the world, and they that seek the world shall find that it will deceive them. I have no right to move a step simply out of selfishness. I ought to have a far higher motive than that. With the Christian the first thing in life is to do good—to glorify God by doing good, and when he feels, " I can do good there which I cannot do here, and yonder is a wider sphere, and a sphere more suited to me, where I may hope to bring more honour to my Lord and Master," then he may go ; but to go from restlessness or to go from selfishness is to go like the bird that wandereth from her nest : it shall not be blessed of the Lord.

II.

And so, too, if our removing comes out of cowardice or indolence. There is many a time a man runs away from the battle : he does not like it. Instead of fighting through it bravely like a soldier of the cross, he tries to get where none of the shots can reach him, where he need not strike a blow. Many a person, without being quite conscious of it, has been guilty of cowardice in this way. He has said, " My temptations in a certain condition are very great ; therefore, I will exchange my condition." Are you sure that that is right? If the temptations are great, grace also is great. May it not be that the fighting with those temptations will be to God's glory and to your own advantage, and are you right, therefore, in going? Many a man changes his temptations for the worse. I should be very much afraid of shifting any of mine ; for those I have I begin to know a little about, but if I had a batch of new ones, I do not know how I might endure them. Our temptations are very much like the mosquitoes of which they tell you when you are travelling, that you had better let the old ones stop on, for if you drive them away there are some new ones hungrier than the others that will come, and you will be worse off than before. The temptations of poverty you do know, my brother, but you do not know the temptations of wealth. The temptations of the family you know, and you propose to run away from them into solitude. You do not know those temptations, and you might not be able to withstand them. God has fitted the burden to the back, and the back to the burden. Of all the crosses in the world, your own cross is probably the easiest cross for you to carry. If you had somebody else's cross you might well bewail yourself that you had made so sad an exchange. Tarry where you are, and be not cowardly, neither seek your own ease. It is not the first thing in life to be easy and to be happy and to be merry and to be rich and to be admired and to be prosperous. There is something nobler than that. It is often a far grander thing to know nothing of what rest means in life, except rest in God, to know nothing of ease, to know nothing of prosperity, except prosperity of soul, and through much tribulation glorifying God in difficulty and finding your way to eternal bliss through it. The gist of the whole matter is in the matter of providence. The God who has appointed the bounds of our habitation has been wise in the appointment. It is sometimes wise for us to move : let us take care we do not move till it is wise. Let us not be like those who are as the will-o'-the-wisp, constantly flitting, but remember that as a bird that wandereth from its nest, so is a man that wandereth from his place.

Well, now we shall get a stage higher than this. So far it is Solomon, and savours of the world ; but, in the second place, the text may very well be applied to the man who wanders from his place in the religious world—his place in the

Church. There are times when a man does well to leave the Church with which he has been connected, when he could not do a better thing than sever the connections of his youth. Besides, if I am in a Church, and am persuaded that the doctrines taught are not the doctrines of the Scripture, the sooner I enter my protest against them the better. If I have been brought up in a Church and even have been converted in a Church, and have been edified in a Church in which I see that some other authority is acknowledged than the authority of Christ and some other teaching than the teaching of the Holy Ghost in the Word; if I am convinced of the error of that Church, from that moment I shall be guilty, I shall be an accomplice in the Church's sin if I remain in it. The voice of God to my conscience ought to be, " Come ye out from among them! Be ye separate. Touch not the unclean thing." It will be one of the happiest days in your life, though it may involve you in much trouble, if you can come right out and bear a protest for the truth as it is in Jesus.

Sometimes, again, a man may well change his place in a congregation for the sake of being better fed, really better instructed, or instructed in a way in which he shall derive more profit from the instruction. One man will not edify all. If one man did, where would all be able to be put to hear him? It is a great mercy that, while ministries that are truthful agree in what they teach, yet there are different modes of teaching suitable to different dispositions. The Old Testament speaks of the sheep feeding after their manner, and I have no doubt different sorts of sheep have different manners of feeding, and that God appoints different under-shepherds for different orders. The men that can hear one man and be profited may not be able to hear another, and could not bear a third. Yet the first, second and third shall be all equally good and equally useful men. It is wrong for us to say which is better—Paul or Apollos. It is wrong for us to be disputing about this divine, or that, or the other. God has appointed the men who will suit His servants, so that they may all be fed; and if I find upon the whole that I cannot hear a certain good man (without uttering one unkind word about him, or thinking one hard thought) without laying all the blame to myself because I am not edified by him when I see others are, it may, perhaps, be the wisest thing I can do to go where my soul is fed and there to settle down. But I must hesitate and ask myself about it, and not be as some spiritual vagrants that I know of who are sometimes here, then there, and then somewhere else, and nowhere long, and are about as useful to the Church as vagrants are to the nation, that is, they are an encumbrance to it, instead of being any ornament or assistance.

No doubt, too, a man may very well change in the religious world his position from one congregation to another for considerations that have rather a regard to others than to himself. The wife, perhaps, says, " I heard the other day with great delight such and such a minister; but then, my husband would not go there. He would go anywhere sooner than go there. But he would come to such and such a place, and therefore I desire to join that Church in the hope that my husband will attend there and may get a blessing." Sometimes you may say also, " Well, now, I should, perhaps, personally be best under such and such a pastor, but then, I can help the school in another place," or " They are weak and they need strengthening, and I shall cast in my lot there and remove from the stronger to the weaker, not for myself but for the sake of other people—that I may do good." Now, I believe that this text would not at all apply to such a case as that, and that that dear brother or sister would be right and wise in thus wandering from their place—in fact, it would not be wandering from their place but would simply be finding their right place and going into it.

III.

But now, when is it that this text comes home to a man's heart or ought to do it ? It is when a man is constantly going from one Church to another, and from one ministry to another, from love of novelty. There is a new star in the East, and we have come to worship it. Behold, a new voice is lifted up, and our ears are itching, and we must needs go and hearken to that voice and to none other. Oh, it is childish ! It is trifling with the ordinance of preaching. It is, I would almost venture to say, profaning the Word of God to make our hearing it merely an opportunity for the gratifying of our curiosity. Curiosity may be gratified in a measure without sin, but for a man to go, and for the crowd to go simply because such a person is spoken of—oh, let it not be so among us, for as a bird that wandereth from its nest, so is a man that in that way wandereth from his place. Many a minister's heart has been almost broken by the conduct of some who have acted thus childishly.

Some, too, shift their place religiously from a desire of greater respect. They are not thought quite enough of in the congregation where they are: they will try and find a place where they shall be more highly esteemed. Dear friends, you probably would not confess to such a motive; but I would have you sometimes question your heart (which is deceitful above all things) whether that motive may not come in in shifting your place from one Church to another. The highest respect that any one of us deserves is very little indeed, for the shoe-latchet of Christ we are not worthy to unloose, and if we get as good a position as we are likely to adorn, if we get a menial service for Christ, it will be quite high enough. There ought to be more scrambling after the lower places in the Church and less desire after the higher ones, and there would be if there were more Christianity among us. Some I have known who would attend a place of worship when they were poorer, when they had a little business—who used to go to a place of worship where they were much at home and much enjoyed the society of Christians and communion with Christians. They got on in the world, and now there is not a sufficient number of persons of their rank and station in life. They have become so elevated and dignified that the Christian people who were good enough to be their companions once are now their inferiors. If I called the wandering from curiosity childish, what shall I call this? I will not insult children by using such a word as that. It is degrading altogether for a man to be caring about such things. How dwelleth the love of God in a soul that is moved by such motives?

We have known, too, some who have shifted their place in the Church from some little petty discontent, and these are as birds that wander from their nest. Some insignificant trifle, something that might readily enough have been explained, some pure misunderstanding may have led them to feel uneasy, and they have gone elsewhere. I remember hearing of a man who was much displeased with his pastor, and when enquiry was made it was found that his pastor had actually gone by him in the street without acknowledging him. He harboured anger in his heart for some time about that, and he was much surprised when his minister said to him, " Do you know, I am so short-sighted that, if I had not my glasses on, I could hardly see 10 or 12 feet from my nose." Then he began to see how foolish he had been to set down to anger, or want of affection, what was purely caused by infirmity. But little things as small as that have often caused the foolish minds of this generation to go shifting from place to place as a bird that wandereth from her nest.

I am almost tired of talking of these things, and therefore will only mention one more. There are some who will wander from Church to Church, and from ministry to ministry, simply because others go. It is a strange thing that when people cannot get into a place they are always wanting to come in, and if there is room in any place they won't fill up the room. If other people will come, they will come, and if other people will not come, *they* will not come. There is so much of that— because others go. Now, my brethren, let every man judge for himself. Are you happier? Does your soul rejoice in God? Do you see that the ministry is a ministry of truth? Is the Holy Spirit upon the preacher? Is he anointed of God? Is he made a blessing to the souls of your children? Do you feel you can go there with a hope that by his teaching you can serve God the better? Then go, if nobody else goes. If you are the only hearer, be honest to the man and to your own self. But don't go merely because others go. We do not do so in our ordinary dealings. We judge of goods for ourselves, and we will not buy simply because others buy. And so it should be with the things of God. We should find out for ourselves where Christ is best preached, where Christ is most honoured, where His Spirit is most at work, and there, if that be our place, let us abide. Let others go where they will, as for us, let us say with Dr. Watts:—

> Here would I find a settled rest
> While others go and come;
> No more a stranger or a guest,
> But like a child at home.

Well, now, we shall get a step higher, and get a little more out of Solomon and a little more of spiritual truth. The text is most applicable, in the third place, to those persons who wander from their spheres of usefulness. There are such. I take it for granted that every Christian has something to do for Christ. I liked a remark which I met with the other day, that a Christian man ought not so much to try to find arguments why he should be a minister, why he should be a preacher of the Gospel, as to think it needful to find reasons why he is not a preacher of the Gospel. I believe there is truth in that, that we have all of us, if we have any ability whatever, a call to tell out the Gospel of Christ, and that our only excuse for not doing so must lie in our not having ability to do it, and as we all have some ability of some sort for propagating the Gospel, we are every one of us bound to be doing it. But there are persons who are quite willing to do something for Christ, indeed, they are very hasty in desiring to do it, and they commence at once, and what a rate they run at. No wonder they soon get out of breath, and then they discover that the form of service they have undertaken is not suitable and take up another, and with a mighty dash they go to work at that and pull up just as suddenly and discover that after all there is a third mode of serving God better than the other two, and they go at this. Ah, and with what zeal! But with what suddenness do they again stop there! They are this, they are that, they are the other, but they never succeed in any. And alas, there are some Christians who, if they have been successful for a time in some good work, will all of a sudden give it up. Either they get discouraged because they have not present success, or else they have a notion that they have done enough, and that it is time to rest. Dear brethren, if the husbandman should give up his farm because, after he has been ploughing in October and November he has not any harvest in April—if he should give up his lease and resign his farm as soon as May began, where would be his reasonableness? Yet is it so with some; they cannot continue in well doing. They seem to want to reap at once, forgetting that we shall reap if we faint not, but that we shall only reap " in due season."

Some have given up their work because, as I have said, they think they have done enough. It is a strange reason for any Christian man to give. If the same reason were to apply to nature what a sad state we should be in! The sun might say, " I have shone enough "; the moon might say, " I have cheered the night enough "; the sea might say, " I have gone to and fro like the pulse of life in the universe and done enough "; the earth might shut up its stores of bread and say, " I have yielded harvest enough "; and God Himself might say (and oh, how well and justly might He say!), " I have done enough for this ungrateful generation!" My brother, if you have only one more breath to breathe, breathe it out for God. If you have grown grey and become decrepit in the Master's service, serve on and take no furlough, but persevere until the last atom of life is gone, like John Newton who, when he could hardly get up the pulpit stairs of St. Mary Woolnoth, and had to be helped up and carried up and almost laid on the foot-board and was persuaded not to preach any more because he was too old for it, answered, " What, shall the old African blasphemer cease to praise God and preach Christ as long as there is breath in his body? No, never!" We must still continue to labour for the Lord. For, dear brethren and sisters in Christ, you that are working for the Master, I want you to notice two or three things. Those that change their spheres and modes of usefulness are like a bird that wandereth from her nest because they lose the adaptation which they have been slowly gaining. The bird gets fitted for her nest by sitting on it. It becomes a suitable nest for her. A Christian worker begins to be used to his work, and, if he wanders, he loses that. I cannot get the art of teaching children at once. I must by degrees work into it. Well, if I renounce that work and begin another, I have got to begin at the beginning again. I am like a person who learnt a trade, and after two years gave it up and had to begin an apprenticeship to some other employment. It is a pity to lose aptness for any service. But worse than that, he that changes his labour loses very much : he loses the result of what he has done, and we want every single stone we lay for Christ to keep its place. A man who begins a house and does not finish it loses what he has spent upon the foundations and the walls. He that sows, but will not stop to reap, loses the seed that he has cast into the furrows. Don't leave that class of boys : stick to them. You have taught them so many Sundays, you have prayed for them so many times—stick to them till you see them converted. Don't leave that little station in the back streets. You have got a few people together. Work on; don't lose what you have wrought. Feel " I cannot throw all that away—these months, these years of service; I will stand to it till God establishes my work and gives me some success in it." Don't lose the labour you have already spent.

IV.

Besides, such a man shows by his moving from service to service that he is of an unstable spirit. You know it is written, " Unstable as water, thou shalt not excel." No man excels who lacks in perseverance. And, brethren in Christ, I do pray that all the members of this Tabernacle may excel. I would have you to be not ordinary Christians, but Christians of a special sort. If we cannot all attain unto " the first three," yet let each one of us be a man of valour for his Lord and Master.

D

Further, I am persuaded that any man who leaves the service of his Lord, leaves it not for another sphere, but wanders from his place, is pretty sure to get into a world of trouble. I would gently pluck a brother by the sleeve who has been tempted to give up work for his Master, and I would whisper one word in his ear, and that word should be "Jonah!" If he asked me for an explanation I would say to him, Was not Jonah bidden to go to Nineveh, and he would not go? But he went where he never expected to go, as the result of it! Jonah would never have had to cry out from the bottoms of the mountains with the reeds wrapped about his head if he had gone where God sent him. If we will not do as God bids us do, but try to run away to Tarshish, we shall find that God has a will, and though, perhaps, He may bring us up on dry land, as He did Jonah, we may find that He will leave us in deep troubles because we left His service. Let us not so false or faithless prove as ever to shun the service of God. It will sometimes come across the most earnest Christian in times of faithfulness, "Oh that I could get out of this! I am not doing my Master's work as I could wish. Not seeing the prosperity I desire I cry out with Elijah, 'Let me die! I am no better than my fathers!'" May God cure us of this sickness! And I know of no better cure than for him to let us see the crucified One with the thorn-crown about His brow, working on and on through shame and suffering and rebuke, and never relinquishing His life-work till, giving up the ghost, He at the same moment said, "It is finished." May we set to it till it is done, being "stedfast, unmoveable, always abounding in the work of the Lord, forasmuch as we know that our labour is not in vain in the Lord."

Now, fourthly and lastly, we mount to our highest point. As a bird that wandereth from her nest, so is a man that wandereth from his place in matters of soul, spirit, life and grace. For where, dear brethren, is our nest? Where is our place? I answer, it is at the foot of the cross. We have no safe resting-place but there. Sinners resting in a Saviour, guilty, pardoned through the blood, lost, rescued by the hand of the Redeemer, there is our place. The temptation is to get away from that, like the Galatians, who, having begun in the Spirit, thought to be made perfect in the flesh, They had walked by a simple faith in God at first, but they hoped that their works and circumcision and other ceremonies would make them perfect. Oh, poor little bird half-fledged, if you have fallen from your nest, what must you do? And you are a picture of my poor half-fledged spirit. It will never grow to perfection, and never be able to take a flight to heaven except it shall abide within the nest of the atonement, covered with the wings of everlasting love. There is no growing place, no place of security, no place of comfort for a poor sinner but in Christ—in Christ alone.

Are any of us to-night tempted to go anywhere beyond that? Are we so looking for sanctification as to forget that He is made of God unto us sanctification? We knew ourselves to be sinners once, and we have begun to think we are great saints. Now, have we got a notion that we are angels, or something very wonderful? Oh, let us get out of that! We are nothing of the kind. When we mistake ourselves for somebody very good, we had better look in the glass. If we only make a little self-examination once more, we shall soon discover that " in us, that is, in our flesh, there dwelleth no good thing." As an old ploughman often has said to me, " If you or I get one inch above the ground we get that one inch too high, for down, down, down is our place, flat before the cross." Having nothing, yet possessing all things; being less than nothing, we find our all in Christ.

Beloved, the same may be said of our place as Christians as to our belief, our creed. Now, there are certain great truths taught in Scripture, as I think, very plainly—the doctrines of grace they are commonly called. And there are some of us who have known these truths for twenty years, and the more we know them the better we love them. There are others who are ready to believe in new-fangled notions. Something starts up as another discovery. What a many discoveries there have been during the last twenty years, and nearly all have been exploded, and so will the rest that remain in the course of a few more years. They come and go like crops of Jonah's gourds; they come up in a night, and perish in a night. It will be well for us if we do not prove like birds that wander from their nest. As for me, my flag is nailed to the mast; it neither runs up nor down. Wherein I have learned Christ, I will abide and so—

> Let all the forms that men devise
> Assault my faith with treacherous art,
> I'll call them vanities and lies,
> And bind the Gospel to my heart.

There is something taught in this Book, after all, and it is not a Book that we cannot understand if we seek God's Spirit to enlighten us. There are certain truths which have been burnt into our inmost experience. We do not believe them now merely because they are here, but because they are written on the fleshy tablets of our soul. We could not give them up. They are not matters of choice with us as to whether we will hold these doctrines or not; God has taught them to us, and interwoven them into our very being, so that we must and will hold them. God grant we may not wander from our place in any of these things.

But, once again, let the Christian take heed of turning aside from his place of walk and fellowship with God. The Christian's place is to live with Jesus. We have each one of us our work to do on earth ; but our true calling is a heavenly one. When they asked Jonah in the storm, "Of what occupation art thou?" do you remember his answer? He said, "I am an Israelite, and I fear God." That was his occupation. And the Christian's true occupation is the fearing of his God. Oh, that every day we might have the Lord before us and never wander from Him! For if we do, we are just like the bird that has left her nest : we shall flutter hither and thither and not find peace. Noah's dove is the true picture of the believer. He may fly the whole world over, but there is only one place where there is rest for the sole of his foot, and that is in the ark with Noah—in salvation with Christ. If you have lost your fellowship, beloved, pray God to bring you back again. If you are beginning to be lax and unspiritual, if you have neglected prayer, if you have lost a sense of pardon, if you have got far off from God, don't be merely mourning that you are far off and wondering how you have got there, but say, "I will return unto my first husband, for then it was better with me than it is now." "Return, ye backsliding children, for I am married unto you, saith the Lord." And oh, beloved, I hope we may never wander from one other place, and that is the place of supreme love to Jesus —complete consecration to Him. Have we ever got there? Some Christians have not. They love Christ, but not after the model He would set before them. They do not seem to love Him above all things else. But if we do, if he be our life, our soul, our all, if we live for Him, if in whatsoever we do, we do all to His glory, if we have striven to rise to the point of being completely consecrated with the blood mark on the

ear and on the foot and on the hand and on the heart—all
Christ's and all for Christ, if we eat and drink and sleep
eternal life, oh, let us never come down from that mount.
May God grant we may never descend from that place, for
if we do, we shall smart for it, and be as a bird that wandereth
from her nest.   Those that never were there—well, they shall
not have so much sin as we shall if we have been once elevated,
and then go back again to the beggarly elements.   That head
that once leaned on Christ's bosom, if it be content with any
other pillow, is not worthy of Him.

Well, all this is concerning those that wander from their
nest.   But, alas! there are some here to-night that have not
any nest to wander from.   They have not any Christ; they
have not any Saviour; they have not any home.   A poor child
sits down at night upon a doorstep.   The policeman comes
up and says, "Move on!"   "Where shall I move to?" he
says.   "Go home, child."   "I have not any home."   "Go
to your bed."   "I have not any bed."   Well, now, that can
be got over.   We can find the child a house: we can get the
child a refuge somewhere, poor little thing!   But supposing
in eternity, when the day of grace is over, you should have
to sit down, as it were, upon the doorstep, and you should
have no home, and the angelic messenger should say, "You
cannot stay here: you must move on.   Go to your home."
"Oh," you say, "I have no home, and it is too late for me
ever to find one, for the Master of the house has risen up
and shut to the door, and He will never open it again.   I would
not enter when I might, and I cannot enter now."   Ah, then
you won't have to ask where you will have to move to, for
the dread certainty is this—if you have no home in Christ,
you must make your bed in hell.

God grant that you may never have to do that, for Christ's
sake.   Amen.

IV.

FROM SORROW TO JOY.

Your sorrow shall be turned into joy.—(St. John xvi. 20.)

OUR Lord was very honest with His followers when any enlisted beneath His banner. He did not profess that they would find an easy service if they took Him to be their leader. Over and over again He stopped some young enthusiastic spirits by bidding them count the cost ; and, when some said they would follow Him whithersoever He might go, He reminded them that though the foxes had holes and the birds of the air had nests, yet He had not where to lay His head. He never duped any man. He told all the truth to them, and He could honestly say to them, " If it were not so, I would have told you." He kept back nothing which it was needful for them to know in enlisting under His name.

In this verse He reminds His people that they will have sorrow. Let no Christian forget that. Be he old or young, sorrow is an appointed portion for all mankind. And there is a sorrow which is the especial benediction of the saints. They shall have that sorrow if none others do. Oh, young spirit, you have just found a Saviour, and your heart is very glad. Be glad whilst you may, but expect not that the sun will always shine. Reckon for days of rain and days of frost and days of tempest, for come they will, and I tell you of them now lest when they come they should be strange to you and overwhelm you with confusion. And oh, child of God, you have for many years been prospering ; you have walked in the light of God's countenance, and the Lord has made a hedge about you and all that you have, till you have prospered in the land like the Patriarch of Uz. Remember that evil days will come even to you as they did to Job, and expect them, for " in the world ye shall have tribulation." This part of the inheritance of children, namely, the rod, will be quite sure to fall to your portion if you be one of the sacred family.

Our Saviour, in the verse before us, not only tells His disciples that they will have sorrow, but He warns them that sometimes they would have a peculiar sorrow. When the world was rejoicing they would be sorrowing. "The world shall rejoice," saith He, "but ye shall weep and lament." Now this is sometimes hard for flesh and blood. We cannot read this riddle—God's people sighing and God's enemies laughing—a saint on the dunghill with dogs licking his sores and a sinner clothed in scarlet and faring sumptuously every day —a child of God sighing and groaning, chastened every morning, and an heir of hell making the world ring with his merriment! Can these things be so? Yes, they are so, and we must expect them so to be ; and if we read this riddle by the eye of faith, we shall understand it. Yet we shall see God working even in these mysterious circumstances, and dealing out the best to the best after all, and giving still the worst to the worst in the long run.

Now, our Lord, in order to sustain His servants under the ill news of sorrow and of special sorrow, gave them two thoughts. The first He put into three words—"a little while." And here is a whole mint of golden consolation here —"a little while." When things are only temporary, we put up with them. If we are travelling, and we come to an uncomfortable inn, we are off to-morrow, and therefore we make no great noise about it. A painful operation has to be performed, but, when the surgeon tells us it will only occupy a second or two, we submit to it. "A little while"—it takes off the edge of sorrow. If it be but a minute, and then afterwards there shall be never-ending blessing coming out of it, oh, then we glory in the tribulation, and count it not worthy to be compared with the glory that shall be revealed in us. Afflicted child of God, I commend to you those three words, "a little while." I beseech you to roll them under your tongue as a sweet morsel when your mouth is filled with the wormwood of sorrow. "A little while," and after that little while is over then it shall be "for ever with the Lord."

The other reflection which He gave them for their comfort is that which is furnished by our text, "Your sorrow shall be turned into joy." May God the Spirit give us comfort while we think over these words.

I.

And first, brethren, this language was strictly true with regard to the remarkable sorrow which was then coming upon them when our Lord spake. You know the chapter. The

Lord had been telling them of His death.   They had been sitting around the table, and He had revealed to them the fact that He was about to be delivered into the hands of wicked men and be crucified, and that this would make them weep and lament ; but concerning this He says, " Your sorrow shall be turned into joy." *We* have also another sorrow coming out of that, namely, the sorrow that our risen Lord has gone away from us, has risen from Olivet and left His Church a widow ; yet that sorrow, too, is turned into joy.   Let us speak, then, about those two things.

You will soon see before you, brethren, a sacred feast. We are preparing to-night to come around the table on which we have the bread and wine which celebrate our Saviour's death.   Now, it is a very pleasing thought that to celebrate the death of Christ we have not an ordinance that is full of sorrow.   There is no rubric which tells us that we are to come clothed in mourning, that we are to come together as to a funeral, that dirges are to be sung, that violet colours, or such as represent sorrow are to be used.   On the contrary, the ordinance which commemorates and shows the death of Christ is one of joy, if properly used.   We come around a table, and sit there at our ease and eat and drink, for the death which was so sorrowful is turned into joy, and the memorial of it is meant to set it forth not as it was on the sorrowful side, but as it is to us on the joyful side.   Our sorrow is in the symbol turned into joy.

Now, let us think of the sorrow of Christ's death a moment. It was great sorrow to see Him suffer, sorrow unspeakable to see Him die.   You mothers who love your sons, what a sword would have gone through your hearts if it had been your son who was nailed to the tree !   Ye brothers who love your brothers, what pangs would have rent your spirit if he had been your brother who was hanging there.   We would, if it had been possible, have spared Him the thirst, have spared Him the shame and spittle ; we would have spared Him the nails and spared Him the crown of thorns.   We can never think of His sufferings without smiting upon our breast with grief and saying—

> Alas ! my sins, my cruel sins,
> His chief tormenters were.

And as we look on His sufferings we ask :—

> Oh, why should man offend,
> And make the Lord his Saviour die ?

Bitter ought to be our regret that ever we should have wandered from the path of right and made it necessary that our wanderings should be laid upon the Shepherd's head. Woe, woe, woe unspeakable, that the elect of God should thus have multiplied their transgressions and have compelled their Saviour to be smitten even to death for their sakes !

We sorrow, too, from another thought that in the death of Christ, sin for a time appeared to get the mastery over goodness. There He was, the perfect Man, the advocate of all that was true and God-like ; but His self-righteous foes, His cowardly enemies hunted Him to the death, and they could not be content till they had washed their hands in His blood. When I see Him upon the cross, I seem to feel as if Satan, the old serpent, had bitten the heel of truth and poisoned it. I begin to tremble for truth and righteousness when I see thus the pure and perfect One laid low in the dust, but all these three sorrows put together, for His sufferings, for our sins and for the temporary triumph of evil, are at once turned into joy when we know that now the Saviour has finished the atoning work, that He is accepted of His Father, that He has crushed the old dragon's head, that He has given to sin and death and hell a total defeat.

Brethren, there is nothing to sorrow for when we look at the cross now, for Jesus is again alive ; He has glory about Him that He had not, and could not have had, if He had not stooped to conquer and bowed His head to death. The man Christ Jesus now sits at the right hand of the Father exalted far above principalities and powers, and every name that is named. He sees of the travail of His soul, and He is satisfied, and instead of mournful dirges we say, " Bring forth Miriam's timbrel yet again, and let us sing unto the Lord, for He hath triumphed gloriously ! The horse and his rider hath He cast into the sea. All the host of His enemies hath He drowned in the Red Sea of His atoning blood."

Moreover, brethren, we are gainers now. It is true our sin crucified Him, but our sin is gone. The last act of sin was sin's own destruction. It pulled down the house upon itself like Samson, and there it died. Our sin is put away by the death of Christ. He has " finished transgression, and made an end of sin." And as for truth and righteousness, they are gainers, too. Now, on the cross the crisis of the great battle comes. Now is the prince of this world cast out. Now do righteousness and holiness and truth win the day, and that for ever. Glory be unto God, we come to the memorial of the death of Christ as to a festival. Our sorrow is turned into joy.

And as to our Lord's going away from us into heaven, it does at first sight wear a very sorrowful aspect. We should be glad if He should occupy that chair to-night and say, " Take, eat ; this is My body." Oh, what a happy crowd would you all be who love Him, if He stood in this pulpit to-night and showed you His hands and His feet. We would stand at the posts of His doors by the week together to get a sight of Him. If He had His throne in Jerusalem this day, what pilgrimages would we make if we might but come anywhere near His blessed person, and might kiss the very dust He trod upon ! For what a precious Lord was He ! Oh, in our times of sorrowing, if we could but once see His face, those dear lustrous eyes that seem to say, " I know your sorrows, for I have felt the same," that blessed countenance that would speak consolation, though it said not a word, and would say to every mourner, " I will help thee. I have borne thy burden of old "—would not it be a joy to see Him ? Surely I should be glad enough to cease my ministry, and you might be glad enough, however useful you might be, to give up your work as the stars hide their diminished heads when the sun rises.

II.

But, brethren, there is no cause for sorrow. I am talking idly for the moment now, for our sorrow is turned into joy. It is a great gain to us not to have the Saviour here. And see ye how it is? He said, " If I go not away, the Comforter will not come unto you." Now, it is a nobler thing to have the Spirit of God dwelling in us than it would be to have Jesus Christ dwelling upon earth. For, as I have hinted, if He were on earth we could not all get at Him ; He could only be in one place at a time, and how would the poor be able to get where He is? And if He perambulated all the world yet in the natural order of things, it is only now and then He could come to one place, and so some of us would have to be pining all our lives to see Him. But now the Holy Ghost is here. The Holy Ghost is wherever believers are. " Know ye not that He dwelleth in us for ever ? " And whereas we see nothing, this is all the better for us. A life of sight is for babes ; a living by feeling is for poor puny infants, but the life of faith is for men in Christ Jesus, and ennobles us by taking away anything that is to be seen and giving us to walk after the unseen. " Though we have known Christ after the flesh," says the apostle, " yet now after the flesh know we Him no more." We have not Christ among us after the flesh, and we are glad of it, for now our faith is exercised and God loves faith, and faith makes men into true men in the sight of God, and ennobles them and makes them friends of God. For who was " the friend of God " like Abraham, who believed God ? Faith, then, being so much more for our good than the most delightful sight, we have reason to thank God that Jesus is gone and that the Spirit is given.

Besides, beloved, Christ can serve our turn better where He is than He could here. What is He doing for us yonder in the unseen land ? Why, know ye not He has gone to take possession for us—gone ahead that He may say, " This heaven belongs to My people; I am come here as their legal representative." The moment that He put that pierced foot of His upon the golden streets He said, " These streets belong to all whom I have redeemed with My blood, to all whom My Father gave Me, and they shall possess this, for lo ! I take possession of it." And inasmuch as there was something to do to make heaven fit for us—I do not know what it was—what a joy it is to hear Him say, " I go to prepare a place for you." Why, brethren, heaven was not fit for us any more than we were fit for heaven till He went there, and He is getting it ready, so that when we come home we shall find our house furnished and all prepared.

When God made Adam, He did not make Adam first and suspend him in the air till he made Eden for him to live in, but He made the garden, fitted it for Him, and then He made the man and put him in it. And so our great Lord is gone to make heaven fit for us, and He will come again and take us unto Himself that where He is we may be also. Now for this cause we are glad that He is not here. We comfort one another with these words, and we see how true was this promise of His, " Your sorrow shall be turned into joy." Sorrow at His death, sorrow at His departing out of the world—these two sorrows are now " turned into joy."

We pause awhile and change the subject. I see before me still the preparation for the feast—for the supper, and therefore let me remind you that in coming to that table we experience a transmutation of spiritual emotions with regard to Him. I will show you what I mean. Some time ago, the Lord made us hungry and thirsty after righteousness. We could not any longer be satisfied with the world. We came to feel ourselves miserable. Our heart was pining for something. We had once been quite content with present joys, but, on a sudden, we were dissatisfied and felt a craving we had never felt before. Are you not glad of it, because when you come to the table here you see that there is bread to eat and wine to drink, emblems of the body and the blood of Christ? Do you know, when I sit down at a good table, what I feel thankful for? Two things, if I have got them. First, for what is on the table; but, secondly, for an appetite. For a feast is a poor thing without an appetite. So, see you, the hunger and thirst which God has given us after Christ are turned into joy when we come to see Christ, for now we say, "How glad I am, how thankful I am that I could no longer remain content! How happy am I that God gave me a distaste for all the joys of the world, for now I am the man that can enjoy a crucified Saviour. Now I can eat His flesh, which is meat indeed, and drink His blood, which is drink indeed!" Well, at the same time when we felt our hunger we had another sorrow, namely, that hungry as we were, we had not a crust in the house: we could not satisfy our own hunger, do what we would. We went about the world to try and find something to satisfy our need, but we could find nothing whatever. The husks that contended the swine would not content us. We wanted something more. I know at that time I had not a pennyworth of merits, though I had a mass of sins. I tried to pray, but my prayers could no more fill my soul than wind could. I tried to be diligent in hearing the word and doing good, but there is nothing to stay a hungry soul in all that we can do. But now to-day, to-day in the sight of that table and remembering this bread and wine, to picture Christ crucified the food of the soul, I am glad that I had not got anything to eat, because now I was driven to feed on Christ. Oh, what a blessed thing is an empty cupboard when it brings a soul to the Saviour! Our sorrow is turned into joy, and we call it a blessed famishing, a blessed emptiness, when we can have the emptiness and famishing removed by feeding upon an all-sufficient Saviour.

So, you see again, our sorrow is turned into joy. And on the table of fellowship to-night we see the wine-cup, and while it represents to us our Saviour as our refreshment, it also reminds us that we were once foul and needed to be washed in His blood. Now, it was a great sorrow to feel ourselves foul; it was a horror to discover that we were soiled from head to foot with scarlet sins. But, for my part, now that I have washed in the fountain filled with blood, I have forgotten my sorrow about sin. It is turned into joy. Oh, the blessedness of being made clean in Christ Jesus! Why, I think if I had been Adam, and had never sinned, I should always have had some little fear that perhaps I had come short somewhere if I had to depend on my own merits, even if I hoped I was perfect. Now, sinner that I am, I entertain no fears, for I know Christ's righteousness is perfect; I know His death cleanseth from all sin; and so the sorrow about sin is turned into joy in the sense of perfect pardon and complete righteousness which belong to us through the precious blood of our dear Lord and Saviour. Oh, when you come to the table, my dear brethren and sisters, lay aside all your griefs, whatever they may have been. Feel that if you must bring them with you they are transformed and transmuted on the road; for your sorrow since you have believed on Jesus is turned into joy.

III.

Now, for a moment or two, let me remind you that this truth will hold good of all believers' sorrows. Your sorrow shall be turned into joy. It shall be good of some of them to-day. God will make your present sorrows to be turned into joys. Do I address one person to-night who has been persecuted for Christ's sake? Do I speak with one young person whose parents treat her ill because she follows Jesus? Brother, sister, your sorrow is turned into joy, even now, for, if ye be persecuted for righteousness' sake, happy are ye. Not, happy *shall* ye be, but happy are ye. Even now ye have a great honour put upon you: you are counted worthy not only to believe on the Lord Jesus but to suffer for His sake. At the thought of Him, then, that sorrow is turned into joy. Perhaps I address some who are under very severe afflictions. Beloved brother, if the Lord shall reveal Himself in your afflictions, you will be very sorry to be rid of them; you will feel that they are even now turned into joy. Constantly, in reading Rutherford's letters you meet with the expression of his wonder that his enemies should be so kind to him as they were. He speaks in a sort of holy sarcasm. They banished him, sent him away from where he was wont to preach the Gospel, but he said, " I find my Lord lives here and they have sent me into His arms. They would not let me preach," he says, " and now my Lord doth make up for my dumb Sabbaths, for, whereas I may not speak, He speaks to me and cheers my soul," and it seems from his letters that, the more his enemies persecuted him, the more deep, the more high his joy became.

I, too, know such a thing as that, that pain can come upon you and grace can come with the pain, so that you feel thankful for it. I have heard saints of God say that they have had great losses, but that the love of God has flowed into their soul so that their losses they have reckoned to be their gains. We have heard of one that said, " Let me go back to my bed again; let me go to my pain again, for I had so much of Christ there that I would fain rather be always sick than lose the sickness and lose the love of my Lord."

Yes, beloved, He can, at this moment, turn your sorrows into joys. If you have a great lump of sorrow, you will have a great lump of joy, for He turns it all into joy. One touch of His finger can turn the granite stones into gold; bring them to His feet; ask Him to do it, and you shall be rich in joy to-night. Well, if it is not done at once, it will be done ere long. It sometimes takes a little time for a sorrow to turn into a joy. It is rather an odd figure of Cowper's, but it is a true one :

> The bud may have a bitter taste,
> But sweet will be the flower.

It takes a little time for our bitters to bloom out into sweetness, but they will. If you are praying for your dear child, praying for his conversion but do not see it, yet pray on, for your sorrow will be turned into joy. If you are in great trouble about your husband, or your brother, or your friend, whose conversion you are seeking, strive on still, for it will come. One day you shall have the joy of your heart, and your sorrow shall be turned into joy. And that trial you are labouring under just now—don't faint under it; wait a little. It is a rough wind, but it is blowing you towards the port. It is a rough wave, but it is washing you on to the rock. It is not to-day that you will see it, nor to-morrow; but afterwards, and by-and-bye it will bring forth the comfortable fruits of righteousness, and you will rejoice.

And, mark you, if never in this world, yet in the blessed country " on the hither side of Jordan " your sorrow shall be turned into joy.   It will be among the delights of heaven, I do not doubt, to look back on the sorrows of life and to see how they ministered to our meetness for the better land.   There we shall make songs out of our sighs and music out of our mournings; only let us wait and be patient.   The people of the world have the laughter to-day and we have the sighing; they shall have the sighing by-and-bye and we shall have the laughter.

God is like a certain great man who had in his house two sets of cups.   Those cups were for his friends, and these were for his enemies; but they might take which they would.   He knew his friends were wise; his enemies were fools.   Now, these cups which were for his foes were very sweet; they sparkled on the brim; they flashed.   The wine was red, and it moved itself aright.   But they were warned that whosoever drank these cups would find that the dregs were full of death. And his foes came in and drank and drank and laughed, and said the good man of the house loved them best, for he had given them the sweetest wines.   But on the other table stood the cups that were ready for his friends, and his friends were wise, and they went to them, and the cups were very bitter— very bitter!   Ah, how they set their teeth on edge and filled their mouths with wormwood!   But they knew that these were health-cups that would purge them of all disease and fill their frames with a vitality and force which magic could not give; and therefore these friends of his drank the cups with joy and thankfulness, for they knew that he had prepared them in love; and while they heard his enemies laughing at them they bore the laughter with composure, for they knew what the end would be.

To-day the saints and the sinners in the world are like two armies on the eve of battle.   You go through yonder tents.   On the left side you will hear the sound of revelry; you shall see them enjoying the dance.   Full bowls they quaff, merrily.   Say they, " We go forth to battle and to victory to-morrow!" That is the camp of sin and of the enemy.   Here you see the other camp; and the soldiers there make not merry.   They are men of sober stuff.   They have a solid joy within them, for they expect to win to-morrow; but they boast not.   Each man is looking well to his buckler, seeing that his harness is complete and his sword well-sharpened; and you will hear at intervals the prayer, the cry to God, " Make strong our arms, and send us like thunderbolts upon our foes." Now, by to-morrow's eve, I wot, ye shall know what has become of them, for yon gay and haughty cavaliers, with all their mirth, shall strew the field, and their carcases shall be given to the dogs and to the fowls of heaven. But yon suppliant hosts there, though they be reviled as Puritans, shall dash through the hosts of their foes and shall lead their captivity captive.

In which camp would you wish to be? I have taken my choice, and I pray my brethren to take theirs, and may the Spirit of God rule their choice that they may take the bitter cups that are full of health and that they may go with the sober prayerful camp whose song of victory shall turn their sorrows into joys.

Brethren, if the saints' sorrows are turned into joys, what are their joys? If their bitters are sweet, how sweet are their sweets! And if the finger of Christ touching the things of life can make them sweet, how sweet must Christ Himself be! If He turns the water into wine, how rich must He be! And if He turns on earth our sorrows into joy, what can the joys be where there are no sorrows, but where the joys are unalloyed and undiluted and last on for ever! Blessed sorrows, blessed joys! Who would not be a believer when even his sorrows shall be turned into joys?

IV.

But lastly, this little text is a Gospel. I think it is a Gospel for all my hearers to-night. Your sorrows shall be turned into joys. Whosoever among you shall come to-night to those dear feet that were pierced by the nails, and will come and trust in Jesus Christ to save him, shall have his sorrow turned into joy. Are you sorrowing for sin? It shall be pardoned, and in a moment joy shall fill your spirit. Do you sorrow because you are afraid you are not one of the elect? Come and trust in Jesus, and you shall make your election sure, and the doctrine that was so horrible to you shall be full of consolation. Are you mourning because you are unfit to come? Come with all your unfitness, and you shall thank God that you were saved from making a fitness and were enabled to come as a sinner to Christ. Do you mourn because you have a hard heart? Come and trust Jesus, and He will give you a heart of flesh and you shall bless His name that you were another instance of His Almighty power to change the hearts of men.

I would to-night that you would try my Lord and Master. I have known Him now more than two and twenty years. Two and twenty years ago, last Friday, I avowed my faith in Him in baptism, and I would not give Him a good character if He did not deserve it. I would not lie even for Him, I trust. But, oh, there was never such a Lord as He is! Sorrow He told us we should have, and we have had it, but He has always turned it into joy, and up to this moment I can say of Him, if I had to die like a dog and there were no hereafter, I would prefer to be a Christian; and if there were no joy about religion but the present joy which it gives to a believing heart, let me have it beyond all the joys of wealth, or fame, or honour. There is none like Christ. I would that some of you would come and take Him.

May His Spirit guide you and may you to-night become His disciples, and your sorrow shall be turned into joy. The Lord grant it for His name's sake. Amen.

E

V.

SAFE IN THE FATHER'S CARE.

Thus hath the Lord spoken unto me, Like as the lion and the young lion roaring on his prey, when a multitude of shepherds is called forth against him, he will not be afraid of their voice, nor abase himself for the noise of them : so shall the Lord of Hosts come down to fight for Mount Zion, and for the hill thereof. As birds flying, so will the Lord of Hosts defend Jerusalem; defending also He will deliver it, and passing over, He will preserve it.— (Isaiah xxxi. 4, 5.)

THE kingdom of Israel in the days of Isaiah and later—the days to which this prophecy would refer—occupied a position between the two great kingdoms of Assyria and Egypt. It was, in fact, like corn between two millstones. But by some strange infatuation the people were always most afraid of Assyria, and most opposed to that state; and they were constantly desiring an alliance with Egypt, believing Egypt to be the stronger of the two, and hoping, that through the assistance of the Egyptians, the Assyrians might be kept in check. You will see again and again that, contrary to the bidding of God's servants, the prophets, they tried to enter into league with the Egyptians, when they ought, according to the divine direction, to have submitted to the sway of the Assyrians. Again and again were they rebuked for this, and never more pointedly than in the language with which this chapter opens. They are told that woe shall be unto them because they stay themselves upon Egypt, and they are reminded that the Egyptians are men and not God; and their horses are flesh and not spirit. The prophet tells them of the right place for their confidence. Where strength is to be found there will he have them place their faith. The infinite Jehovah was greater than the Assyrians or the Egyptians, for He is Lord of all. And Isaiah would have his people confide in the Lord and put their trust in Him. To this end he presents to them in the verses before us prophecies of the divine protection in which God is represented under two figures.

And here let me say how condescending it is of God that
He should represent Himself to us by metaphors at all, for
nothing that exists can be a true picture, nothing that exists
through His creation can be a true picture of Himself, the
self-existent one. The whole sea is too small a mirror for the
Almighty to mirror His face in it: the whole universe is too
narrow to express the attributes of God. But let it be a matter
of astonishment to us that the Lord selects even animals to be
the types of Himself—wild beasts and little birds. This is
frequently done throughout Scripture, and is done in our text.
First, the Lord is likened to a lion, and in the next verse He is
likened to birds. To a lion—this shall be our first point—for
strength: to birds flying—for solicitude for His people's good.

I.

First, then, the Lord for the defence of His people is
represented as a lion—illustrative of his power.. We will read
the verse again. " Like as the lion and the young lion roaring
on his prey, when a multitude of shepherds is called forth
against him, he will not be afraid of their voice, nor abase
himself for the noise of them: so shall the Lord of Hosts come
down to fight for Mount Zion, and for the hill thereof."

Note, then, for strength the Lord here on His people's
behalf compares Himself to a lion. A lion—a beast of such
matchless strength and courage that he is set down as the king
of beasts, the emperor of the forest. He seems to be formed
and fashioned by creative wisdom on purpose for strength.
Those that examine his form mark the development of his
muscles, see how mighty is his spring and how quick he is to
devour and how terrible are his jaw teeth to break the bones
of his prey. There is none that can match him. Among the
wild beasts he still wears the crown. The king of the creatures
that God hath made in the forest is the lion. But oh, brethren,
what is the lion when compared with the great King of kings?
What is a lion? Why, the mere insect of an hour is greater
in comparison with a man than a lion is in comparison with
God. All power belongeth unto Him. When we speak of the
arm of God we mean Omnipotence; when we talk of His power
we mean that He is Almighty. None of us can have any con-
ception of the power that dwelleth in the Lord of Hosts.

Now all that power is pledged for the preservation of those
that trust in Him. There is not a grain of strength in Jehovah

that is not promised, engaged and certified for the defence of all His saints. When next you doubt, remember that you doubt Omnipotence. When next you tremble lest He should not be able to fulfil His promises, remember that you mistrust the Almighty one Himself. If there were a limit to the power of Jehovah, there might be a limit to our faith, for it were fair to measure our faith by the resources of God; but since there is no shore to the sea of His strength, no summit to the mountain of His might, for us to be dispirited, downcast, and distrustful is to forget the mighty God who feeds the strength of every saint. For the defence of everyone of His chosen and of His whole Church collectively God manifests Himself as the strong one, "the Lord strong and mighty, the Lord mighty in battle, the Lord Who only doeth wondrous things Whose name be blessed for ever and ever."

The text having given us the figure of a lion, then passes on to speak of a young lion. Very frequently, when the idea of majesty and strength is to be conveyed to us strongly, not only is the lion brought in, but the young lion; by which is meant the lion in the prime of his strength, in the freshness of his youthful vigour—not the old lion who has seen many fights, passed through many years, and is beginning to grow decrepit. But the young lion leaps and springs with all the agility of youth, and tears and rends his prey with all the fervour of new-discovered strength. Now the Lord God, on behalf of His people, is not only the lion—strong—but the young lion for ever strong—the young lion full of strength, in the freshness of his vigour—the young lion delighting to use his strength, in whom there is no failing, from whom his strength has in no measure departed.

How I like to think of this! We are very apt to think that in the days of the patriarchs faith in God could do wonders, and in the days of David it might slay giants, but now—now we have fallen upon degenerate times, and as the fable is that men were once greater in stature than they are now, and we are dwarfs compared with our sires, so it is thought that the power of faith is much weaker now and its accomplishments must necessarily deteriorate, and hence it looks as if the security of God's people was not as great as it used to be. He could deliver then; will He deliver now? He could spread a table in the wilderness then, and He could divide a Red Sea to swallow up His people's enemies; but now can we expect anything of the sort? Have not we come, as it were, to the end of the feast when the great Master bringeth forth that which is worse, having already set forth the best wine? Beloved, it is not so. It is unrighteous of us to think it is so. If there be any failure anywhere, if we be straitened in any place, let us rest assured of this, that we are not straitened of God. If faith doeth fewer wonders to-day than in the centuries gone by, it is because faith herself is weaker; but if she could deal with God as Abraham dealt with Him, if she could lean upon Him as David leant upon Him, she would find Him the same God, able to do the same wonders, yes, and ready to do them and delighting to do them on behalf of His people.

Grow old! Nay, never can this be said of our God. He is no older now than He was myriads of ages ago. Time makes no difference to Him. The ages yet to come are present with Him as are the ages past. He is for ever the same. It has been said of the Lord Jesus Christ, "Thou hast the dew of Thy youth." He is still young. Though he is described in one place in Scripture as having a head and hair like wool, as white as snow to show that He is the Ancient of days, yet in another place it is said of Him, "Thy locks are bushy and black as a raven's," to show that He is still in all the strength and vigour which He ever possessed. Oh, let us not think that God has changed. From this fountain there has been no diminution; it brims as it did of old. Is it not said, "I am God! I change not. Therefore ye sons of Jacob are not consumed"? Is He not "the Father of lights with whom is no variableness, neither shadow of turning"? Beloved, it should be our delight to think that our Protector is not only strong but as strong as ever He was—not only the lion but the young lion for the defence of His people.

II.

Now, pass on to a very important part of the metaphor. The Lord on behalf of His people is like as the lion, and the young lion, roaring on his prey. Now, there is no condition in which the lion is more terrible. We know that any creature when it is feeding becomes fierce, if we attempt to disturb it. Try to take a bone out of a dog's mouth, and you will soon see that what strength it has will expend its fury, for it is soon awakened then. But a lion, when it has slain its prey, and begins to devour it, and the shepherds come to take the sheep away or snatch the lamb from him, is all awake. If it be possible, he will certainly defend himself, and that which he has gotten with so much trouble ; for the whole lion is there ! He is all awake, aroused and furious for the war. And such is God for the defence of His people. " He that toucheth you toucheth the apple of Mine eye "; that is to say, to touch a saint is to touch God in His tenderest place.

Now, there are many things which provoke God. All sin does so ; but this is a peculiarly God-provoking sin at any time to touch His people—molest His servants ? He may bear long with you, but He remembers it. He may not for the moment avenge them ; but there is an answer to that question, " Shall not God avenge His own elect ? I tell you that He will avenge them speedily, though He bear long with them." I like to think of this—this picture of God over His people protecting them, being as fully awake and aroused as the young lion is when he bestirs himself to protect the prey that the shepherds would take away from him. It is the picture of intensity of purpose. He means to have the prey, and it shall not be taken from him. All his strength shall be put forth to prevent it. The same intensity of purpose we see in our God. He determined to save His people before the Day-Star began to shine, and from that purpose He has never turned. Sooner than turn aside from His purpose, He gave His Son to die, sent His Spirit to indwell in the hearts of His people, and nothing shall turn Him aside from that purpose now. Behold, how Satan comes out against Him ! See how the powers of darkness rise with all their force ! See how they come forth to take the prey from the mighty God, to deliver out of God's hand into a dire destruction ! But shall they conquer Him ? Ah ! no. For the whole of God is set for the defence of His Church. It is not one attribute that is there; they are all there. As I said of the young lion over his prey, he is all a lion ; every nerve and muscle and bone of his body seems to burn with indignation against his foes, so every attribute of God —all His power, His wisdom, His justice, His holiness—all these are intensely aroused and all set with intense purpose for the defence and the deliverance of His people.

How safe, then, are those that trust in God ! You have not only God to defend you, but that same God most fixed and settled as to His mind's eternal will—that God concentrating all His majestic attributes upon this one point, that He will save His people. He would sooner that the world should crash and the solid wheel of nature should be snapped than that this which is His innermost decree, the secret purpose of His inmost soul, should fail—even the salvation of His people. O, my Lord, if I have ever doubted Thee, let this figure chase the doubts from my mind. Hast Thou brought me into the bond of the covenant and sprinkled me with the blood of Thy dear Son, and shall I not depend upon Thee? And now that I see that Thou hast bestirred Thyself and shown Thyself strong on behalf of Thy people, aroused Thy whole nature to the fulness of its majestic potency for the deliverance and salvation of Thy redeemed, shall not my spirit be quiet and still and calm? "The Lord of Hosts is with us: the God of Jacob is our refuge." "If God be for us, who can be against us?"

Still, let us pursue the figure. This lion is represented as being surrounded by a multitude of shepherds who have been called forth against him. The cry has gone amongst the shepherds, "A lion! A lion has seized a lamb! Come forth, ye shepherds! Take the prey out of the monster's fangs!" You see them come—some timidly, advancing slowly, some more bravely, each one with his crook in his hand or such instruments as they can gather. They find out the thicket where the young lion is feeding himself, and they come as near as they can and create a great din and make a noise that they may frighten him. But observe how it is put. "He will not be afraid of their voice." He listens, looks around, sees who it is, lifts himself up, and, perceiving that they are nothing but a company of feeble men, he just lies down on his prey again, and goes on with his repast. "He will not be afraid of their voice." It seems to me to be a grand picture of the sublime indifference of God to His adversaries. "Why do the heathen rage and the people imagine a vain thing? The people set themselves and the rulers take counsel together: 'Let us break his bands asunder and cast his cords from us. He that sitteth in the heavens doth laugh. The Lord doth have them in derision.'" He is not stirred by them. What a grand passage that is in the song of Miriam where the enemy said, "I will pursue; I will overtake; I will divide the spoil; My lust shall be satisfied upon them." Hear the rage of that boast, and what follows? "Thou didst blow with Thy wind: the sea covered them. They sank as lead in the mighty waters!" Oh, how placid it is! How calm is God! His enemies are in a rage: they stir themselves like these many shepherds—all excited—and they come against the lion, and

make strange noises to alarm him. But there the mighty
monarch of the forest lies still, and turns his royal eyes upon
them, and lets them menace as they will.

III.

So for the defence of His Church this day and every day,
in past times and in all times to come, the Lord of Hosts is
not afraid of all His enemies, neither doth He disturb Himself on account of His adversaries. You see sometimes in
history very grand commotions. It seemed as if the whole
world were stirred to put down the Gospel about the days of
Luther, and the trembling children of God were not a little
afraid. But how very quietly the Lord went on! He only
enabled His servants to preach the Gospel, to translate the
Scriptures, to teach children the Psalms—simple, homely
means, and yet by such means as these He checked all the
power of Rome and all the cunning of the College of the
Jesuits. And this day sometimes, as we look abroad, our
hearts sink, and we say, " Alas for God's Church! What
will become of His truth in the land? Surely we shall see
back the days of the Martyrs! " and all that kind of thing.
" In quietness shall be thy strength." " Stand still and see
the salvation of God." He in whom we trust is not afraid.
Oh, if it were possible to think of God, if our minds could
conceive Him! How He must scorn the machinations of
men! They meet together in their council chamber ; they are
devising a plan by which they shall establish Antichrist as
on a rock, and God looks and He sees the rock is nothing
but sand, and that the building itself is all honeycombed,
and if a fox pass by it it shall fall. And then they meet
together and say, " There is no God," and in their wisdom
they concoct methods by which " the fools that believe in
God " shall be put to nought, and God's cause shall be
stamped out like a spark beneath a man's foot!

Oh, how contemptible it must seem to the Most High!
What miserable worms that they should come together and
think that they can in any way affect His kingdom! Let ten
thousand drops of spray conspire to move a rock in mid-ocean
from its base! Let a company of ants unite to shake a con-
tinent and move it from the place where God has planted it !
Their schemes and devices would be infinitely more rational
than the attempts of men to stay the course of God.

When He makes bare His arm,
What shall His cause withstand?
When He His people's cause defends,
Who, then, who shall stay His hand?

He looks upon His adversaries with scorn and contempt. Brethren, stay yourselves upon Him then. Be of good cheer, for the Lord is confident ; and let your hearts glory in the strength of Him who has espoused your cause.

To complete our interpretation of this, it is necessary to notice that He says, " He will not be afraid of their voice, nor abase Himself for the noise of them." A cur at the sight of so many shepherds come out armed would turn tail and hide himself ; but not so the lion. He does not abase himself ; he does not crouch and whine, as though he asked his life of them ; neither doth he turn away and look into the thicket to find a shelter where he may conceal himself, but he goes on quietly with his work and bids them do their worst. God will not alter His purpose to please the devil nor shape His plans because of the power that is brought to bear to stop them. All that has ever been done in this world has not affected the divine purpose—nay, not a solitary atom. Up to this moment He hath done as He will amongst the armies of heaven and the inhabitants of this lower world. The most violent antagonists of the divine dominion have still been subservient to His supremacy. He has yoked the tempest that came forth against His Church. He has yoked it, I say, to her calm, and He hath ridden upon the wings of the wind and made the clouds His chariot. It shall always be so. The powers of evil shall be servants to the dominion of the Most High. He will not abase Himself to them.

Now ye, His children—children of the living God, children of the light and of the sun, abase not yourselves; walk not in the midst of God's adversaries with bowed head. Be ye like Mordecai, who scorned to bow to men. Know ye that ye yourselves are of the seed royal, and a royal mien becomes you who are the descendants of the King of kings. Tremble not when they tell you that science has discovered the unsuitableness of revelation ; fear not when they say that some great one of the earth has disturbed the very keystone of the Christian arch. Are ye fools and slow of heart to think this? Do ye yourselves degrade your own pedigree by doubting your Father and distrusting the power of the eternal King? Nay, rather go on in confidence, in strong reliance upon the almighty

God, and you shall find that He will surely defend His own, achieve His purposes, and win His victory, and at the last it shall be seen that the Lord reigneth, even the Lord God omnipotent reigneth.

Now, the second metaphor has in it solicitude. Somehow or other strength does not seem to comfort us when it is alone. That God is strong for His people is a very precious truth, but we are so tender and trembling that we want to see united with the power some tender attribute, and therefore we have a tenderer figure here. " As birds flying, so will the Lord of hosts defend Jerusalem." I suppose this alludes to birds flying for the defence of their young, and if so (and I think it is so) it means this : First, the bird when it has little ones in its nest is never long from the nest. It flies away for food for the young, but it never flew so fast before as it does then. Its little heart never forgets the nest, and if necessity takes it away for a few minutes it is quickly back, and long, weary hours will the little birds sit there over their young charges, lending to the little ones the warmth of their very life. But when they do go abroad they fly swiftly. Now, it is just so with God. If we could conceive it necessary for Him to leave His people for a while to attend to other concerns, yet His heart would be with them, and He would fly back to them. The bird is thinking of the worm, but only thinking of the worm for its little ones, and as soon as ever it has got it, it flies back again to the nest with eager wings. So if you have to conceive of God that He has to think of the management of the world and the arrangements of providence, yet He only thinks of those things for the good of His people; His heart is still with His chosen and He comes back to them. Only the figure falls very short, for the Lord never has to leave His people. He can think of all other things, and yet think of them as if there were none others in the world but them. I have often revelled in that thought that the Lord can think of one of His people as much as if there were no other being in existence but that one individual. If you were the only being God had made, how He would think of you and what care He would have over you ! He has just as much thought and just as much care for you as if you were the only one, though He has no need to neglect anything because His mighty mind comprehends all. Neither has He ever to leave His people. You know that precious word, " I, the Lord, do keep it. I will watch it—keep it every moment lest any hurt it. I will keep it night and day." The Lord is ever with His people. " I am ever with you," is God's word to His children. " I will never leave thee nor forsake thee." But the argument is drawn from the bird, who, if it leaves for a moment, comes flying back. So the Lord's thoughts and cares are ever towards His children.

But the little birds fly very swiftly in case their young should be in danger. That, perhaps, is more the point of the picture. If they discover by some cry from their little ones that some robber is about to injure the nest, how quickly they come back ! Only let the sound reach their ears and back they are at once for the defence of those they so dearly love. Now, the Lord comes quickly for the defence of His people. You remember that delightful psalm where David says that he was sunken in many waters and he cried unto the Lord; the Lord came, and David says, " He did ride upon a cherub and did fly ! Yea, He rode upon the wings of the wind." It was the fastest that could be found, and therefore God used it. He sometimes appears to us to tarry, but He never does. He is always swift for the defence of His children. We cry, " Make no tarrying, O our God," and when we come to see the story in its true light, we shall find that He did make no tarrying, but came quickly, yea, came at once to defend His children.

IV.

Birds, too, not only fly to come to succour their little ones, but they fight on the wing and fight very bravely too. I was reading the other day a story of a man who went to an eagle's nest to take its young. The young birds began to cry as soon as he touched them, and he was at once assailed by the mother bird. It darted at his eyes and head, and he almost lost his life. In fact, though he escaped, he was a long time laid up in consequence of the serious wounds he received. He managed to use his gun and kill the bird, otherwise his own life would certainly have been taken. And it is not so only with eagles. Naturalists tell us that the smallest birds will seem to gather unusual courage and marvellous strength for the defence of their little ones. Birds that would ordinarily fly at the approach, the mere sound of human footsteps, have been known to attack and defend until their little ones have been able to escape. Now, God will thus fight for His people : He will not suffer anyone to harm us. He will defend us against Satan ; He will guard us against persecutors ; He will avenge us against slanderers; He will put forth all His strength in order that His children may be secured. Think of the little birds in the nest; there is the mother bird flying round and round the nest, watching to see if there is an enemy near, and if an enemy comes then that same bird is flying at the foe right and left. Even so God is watching over His people lest any should hurt them; and when a foe comes near them, then He flies on wings of love and darts at them, showing Himself strong for the defence of His own people. As birds fly, so will the Lord defend Jerusalem. These birds, whether big or little, however, expose themselves to danger sooner than their young should be injured. They seem ready to throw away their life for them, to preserve the lives of their offspring. And God, though He cannot expose Himself to danger, yet, yet—I must say so—He makes a sacrifice of Himself for His people. Did He not do so in the person of the only begotten? Did *He* not come and lay down His life for His people that they might be preserved? As the bird flies into the danger to save its young, so doth Jesus fly into the jaws of death that He might save His people.

And birds use many arts for the defence of their young. Some will feign to be wounded. You have, perhaps, walked in the morning and seen a lapwing appear to be wounded, and you have thought, " I can catch that bird." You have followed it, and it seemed to fall right in your path where you might easily take it. It was not hurt at all; it was only decoying you away from the nest of its young. Many such arts have they. Love makes them wise for the defence of their little ones. And the Lord has infinite plans of wisdom, deep designs of providence, marvellous touches of supreme love and wisdom by which He will surely deliver His people out of the snare of the fowler and bring them safely to their desired rest. Oh, let us feel quite safe. Little birds are safe enough with their mother. To the best of her power will she protect them. And we are safe enough with our God. Let us not fear and tremble : quietly and patiently wait—always wholly, fully, believing in Him.

Now notice the last two sentences of our text, for they are very well worthy of our observation. " Defending also, He will deliver it, and, passing over, He will preserve it." Now it is a precious thought that " defending also, He will deliver it." There is a defence sometimes which does not end in deliverance. Valiant warriors have defended cities, but after all have fallen a prey to the besiegers; but God will defend His Church and He will defend it till He has delivered it from the last attack. God will defend His people, and He will hold His shield over them till no more swords shall be forged against them, and no more arrows shall fly to their hurt. God does not begin and stop short.

> The work that wisdom undertakes
> Eternal mercy ne'er forsakes.

"Defending also, He will deliver it." And then that last sentence, "passing over, He will preserve it." Why, it takes me back to the days of Egypt; for God preserved His people there by passing over. It was the passover that preserved Israel. Forth into the black night went the angel of vengeance with his unsheathed sword, but the blood-mark was on the lintel and on the two side-posts of the house of Israel; and the angel sped past quietly and disturbed not the household. Into every house untouched with blood he entered and left the slain as a mark of his having been there. But Israel was preserved. Glory be to God, in that last day when the destroying angel shall come abroad, passing over, He will preserve His people. They shall not be hurt—nay, not a hair of their heads. The earth shall reel; the stars shall fall like withered fig-leaves from the bough; all nature at the sight of the great Judge shall prepare to flee away; but in that moment the people of God shall be secure in the bosom of Jehovah; they shall enter into the chamber and shall shut to the door till the tempest is overpast. "Passing over, He will deliver them."

And until then, that great and last passover, it shall always be so. Nothing shall hurt us. God will protect us. Oh, come and cower down beneath the eternal wings. As I have seen at night-fall all the little chicks gather together at the mother's cluck and there, under the feathers, hide their little heads and rest; oh, come ye children, ye people of God, come and shelter beneath the bosom of your Lord. Is it not written, "He shall cover thee with His feathers and under His wings shalt thou trust. His truth shall be thy shield and buckler." Come, then, and cower down there for the night. And what day shall tempt you to come out? Nay, stay there till the day break and the shadows flee away. Rest ever there till the last night's dew has fallen and the last kite, the last hawk, has been seen in the sky, and disappeared for ever. Stay there and trust ye in the Lord for ever, for in the Lord Jehovah there is everlasting strength.

I sorrow deeply that any of you now present should be unable to trust in the Lord; but I pray you may. It is a blessed life, the life of simple faith in God. The way to God is through Christ's wounds. There is one door to heaven and that is in the side of Christ. Go and rest in the atoning sacrifice and then trust in the ever-blessed Father of your spirits and be not afraid, but rather go forth and sing, " The Lord is my strength and my song! He also is become my salvation!" And let this spirit be upon you evermore. Amen.

VI.

SALVATION AT THE CROSS.

And the land shall mourn, every family apart; the family of
the house of David apart, and their wives apart; the family of the
house of Nathan apart, and their wives apart; the family of the
house of Levi apart, and their wives apart; the family of Shimei
apart, and their wives apart; all the families that remain, every
family apart, and their wives apart.—(Zechariah xii. 12-14.)

ACCORDING to prophecy, we expect in the latter days the
conversion of the Jews to Christianity and their restoration to
their own land, but it will not be brought about in any manner
otherwise than the way by which the conversion of others is
brought about: it will be by a visitation of the Spirit of God.
He will come to them, and He will be poured out upon them,
according to the words of this prophecy: "I will pour upon
the house of David and upon the inhabitants of Jerusalem
the spirit of grace and of supplication." As the result of this
visitation of the Spirit they will turn their eyes to Christ, whom
they once rejected and crucified ; they will come to believe in
Him, and that faith will produce the same result in them as
it has done in others: it will lead them to mourn—to mourn
for their sin—not with the desperate remorse which sees no
mercy, but with that sweet evangelical penitence which is a
mourning for Christ and a mourning in connection with Christ
—a mourning which will soon turn into joy and melt into
intense delight and peace.

Now, I am not going to speak any more upon that matter.
We shall labour and pray for the conversion of the Jews, and
hope that this will be the result. But to-night we are going
to talk to ourselves, to the present congregation here.

And we shall begin by remarking that all true grace in
the soul always comes through the agency of the Holy Spirit.
There is no conversion that is worth having which is not
wrought by Him. Not the eloquence of the preacher, nor the
cogency of his reasoning will ever melt a soul so as to create
it anew. God must work, and God alone can work so as to
re-create a soul. Beloved, we have no hope for this congre-

gation, no hope in your prayers, no hope in the Gospel itself, apart from Him who alone can apply it to the hearts and consciences of men and make it the power of God unto salvation to them.

And the next remark is that wherever true grace comes it always leads the soul to Christ. If ever the Lord gives a man the eye of faith, that eye of faith looks to Him who was pierced. Any faith that rests short of the Cross is a faith that will land you short of Heaven. Unless the atoning sacrifice be perceived and rested in, unless, like the Jew of old, you come and lay your hand upon that sacrifice and accept it as yours, you may have a faith that believes the Bible and a great deal about God, and even have a faith which gives you a presumptuous confidence, but you have not the faith of God's elect. Brother, is Christ all in all to you? Sinner, do you look to Christ wholly and alone for your cleansing from sin? If not, may the Spirit of God come upon you and give you to look away from all else to the Saviour lifted upon Calvary, for, until you do, there is no hope for your soul.

And then, next, the context of the verses we have chosen leads us to say that every true and genuine look of faith to Christ is attended with more grief on account of sin. I am more and more afraid of that dry-eyed faith which I hear preached so continually. I have been alarmed when I have heard repentance spoken so lightly of by some. It is a mere change of mind, they say, and they quote the Greek word for it. Believe me, it is a change of mind, but it is no superficial change of mind. It is not such a change of mind as some suppose it to be. If you have never wept for sin, I weep for you ; and if you have a faith in Christ that never made you regret your transgressions and loathe yourself in God's sight because you committed them, then your faith is but a dream ; you have never looked on Him whom you pierced, or else you would mourn and be in bitterness as one that is in bitterness for his firstborn. Why, beloved, repentance for sin is not a thing that takes place just during the period of conviction; repentance is a perpetual grief; and the more advanced a Christian is, the more he repents of sin, and the more he laments that he should ever have fallen into it, and that he may fall into it again. If there be no tears in Heaven, and I suppose there will be none, yet, if I might make an exception, I would almost ask to be permitted to shed the sweet tear of penitence even there. Oh, beloved, it becomes such a blessed sweet bitterness to mourn for sin, that I would say with our poet—

> Lord, let me weep for nought but sin,
> And after none but Thee,
> And then I would, oh, that I might
> A constant weeper be.

Yes, true faith has a tear in her eye. The faith of God's elect sees Christ through the drops of penitence, and it is a blessed sight to look on Him who bleeds while our heart bleeds for Him.

Now, to none of these things am I about to call your special attention, but to one point only—it was needful to mention all these to come to it, viz., that in true sorrow for sin, that true sorrow which accompanies faith, there always will be a degree of separateness, a great degree of personality and individuality, and, consequently, of loneliness—every family apart and their wives apart; and my special prayer to-night is that God would give to this congregation that kind of mourning for sin which would come to families apart and to individuals apart.

I.

First, to families apart—let us speak about that. He begins with the family of the house of David apart. That was the royal family. In the day when grace visits households, it brings the same mourning into every house. A king must weep for sin as well as a peasant. The man after God's own heart and his family must be bowed down with the same grief for transgression as the poorest in all the tents of Judah. So, brethren, there are families here in this country that are royal, and I would God there were royal mourning, for there has been royal sin. God send it! And there are noble and princely houses in this land. It would be the best news that should ever be heard if amongst them there should come a mourning for sin, for in the high places of this land sin hath still her stronghold, and may God grant that repentance may come there. We have not any such here to-night, and therefore it is little needful to speak of it ; but I will liken those households amongst you that are rich and influential to the house of David. There are special sins that belong to rich families,

F

and I would that rich families would come together and confess apart their special sins.   There are sins of luxury, sins of
worldliness, sins that come from following the fashions of
the world.   There are sins that spring up out of the prosperity with which God surrounds us, sins that arise from a
lack of carrying out our stewardship when God's cause has
not been remembered in fair proportion, when the poor have
not been succoured, when the sick have not been tended.   Let
me put it to every family here that God has prospered—have
not you sins to remember before the Lord?   It would be a
blessed sign of grace if the father and mother should call the
household together and say, "Let us apart acknowledge our
transgression and cry unto the Lord that in His pity He would
save us."   For there are some of you that have not all your
children saved yet.   You have not your servants converted yet.
Let the family of the house of David be apart.   There is no
need that it should begin to make confession about the sins
of the poor and about the turbulence of the many.   Leave that
alone, and confess your own.   House of David, confess your
own sin ; keep to that, and be humbled for it before the Lord.

Then came the house of Nathan, and that had to be apart.
I suppose it is Nathan the prophet.   And in the prophet's house
there must be confession of sin, for the prophet is not sinless,
neither the prophet's family.   Alas ! how often have the ministers of God been the parents of godless children, and what
the father has built up on the Sabbath his sons have pulled
down in the week.   The name of Eli startles some of us.   It
had been better for us that some of our children should perish
at the birth than act as Eli's sons did at the tabernacle door ;
yet it may be so if in the prophet's house there be not the
confession of sin and prayer apart.   Let the minister call
together ; as the Lord speaks by him to the people, let him
take care that he speaks to the people also through his management of his own house, for if we rule not in our own house,
how shall we rule well in the house of God ?   And if we have
no concern for the salvation of our own children, how shall
we be as nursing fathers in the house of God ?   It would be
a happy sign for England if to-morrow all its ministers had
this mourning apart in the midst of our families, and I would
to God it might be so.

But, then, the text goes on to speak of the house of Levi ;
and I hope I do not strain metaphors when I say that this may
refer spiritually to all the families of Christian people, for we

have no priesthood now except the general priesthood of all the people of God. Christ hath made us priests and kings. So, then, I say, let every Christian man at the head of a family call his children and his servants together, and let there be prayer and supplication apart.

Now, I come home to many of you. You are working as Sunday school teachers, you are working as evangelists, you are going from house to house as tract distributors. Beloved brethren and sisters, never let even the tongue of scandal be able to say of you that you cared for other households, but not for your own. I remember well a man—his ease was a warning to me, and I hold it up as such to you. He was always ready to attend the open-air preacher and pitch the tunes ; he was always glad to walk into the country when the lay preacher went to a cottage meeting. There was scarcely a prayer-meeting at which he was not present. He was a man with a large family in poor circumstances. He ought often to have been at work with his boots and shoes when he was attending a prayer-meeting, and he ought oftener to have been praying with his boys at home than to have been out helping others to do good in the street ; for I saw his boys grow up one by one. I knew and I often had told him of it, that, as children, they frequented the public-house, as lads they were found in the theatre. He seemed everything that was devout and earnest, and I believe he was so, and about everybody's children he was careful except his own, and for the conversion of everybody else he prayed except for the conversion of his own children. To them he never spake—they said he never did ; with them certainly he never prayed ; and he was constantly out, so that, whatever good example he did give them, they could not see. And his sons grew up and died, one or two of them, in my presence through drunkenness ere they had completed the age of manhood—through drunkenness and vice—and none could say to that father a word of consolation, because he had kept the vineyard of others but his own vineyard he had not kept. It is right that you should take a class in the Sunday school, but not if your own children are neglected. It is right that you should go out and work for others, but not if your own household is uncared for. Therefore, I say to every Christian, call your children and your household together, and make a solemn approach unto the Most High with this prayer, " O God, save this household, for Thy mercy's sake."

II.

The prophet then mentions the house of Shimei, and as we know nothing about Shimei, though many have guessed a great deal, it may be sufficient to say, let his household stand for everybody. As Levi's may stand for the Christian, let Shimei's stand for those who make no profession. And there I could wish that where as yet there has been no family altar set up, where as yet there has been no profession of the faith of Christ, I could wish that the Spirit of God would move the parents of the household this very night to call the house together and to say, "Let us pray!" It were a good beginning if someone who stepped in here to-night, not accustomed to the house of prayer on the Sabbath, should say, "There is good sense in that! I am a father of a family, and where is my family going? I fear going down to hell! Where am I going myself? Certainly not to Heaven. This very night I will say to my wife, 'Wife, let us pray together; let us pray for the children.' I am afraid it will be poor praying, but everything must have a beginning." Oh, sir, what hope I should have of you if you had once got that length! I should trust that the Lord would never let you go back again, but that, having begun to pray, you would continue to pray till you had found peace and pardon. Why, there are some who might say, "This house of mine has been a drunkard's house. Forgive the sin! This house has heard the sound of profanity ; the oath has defiled this house. God forgive us! This house has been a Sabbath-breaker's house. This house has been the house of dishonesty. This house has been the house of quarrelling, of wrath, of envying and strife and bitterness! Lord, forgive us!" Oh that it might be said this night, "Salvation has come unto this house," if God should see here and there and in this city gatherings of families who have shut the doors and drawn down the blinds, and, now apart, are turning unto the living God! Thou blessed Spirit, grant it may be so, and Thou shalt have all the praise.

But now I must pass on, because the main point is the individuals apart. "The house of Levi apart and their wives apart." Wherever there is real repentance for sin there will be secret prayer, secret confession, secret crying unto God. I shall speak about that now. No man is really impressed with a sense of true religion till he does begin to feel that he must get apart. I have seen the huntsman with his gun intending to take a stag. He has got a herd before him; he is riding through. They know him, and are not much alarmed; but his object as he rides by them is to single out one. He must get that one apart and alone if he means to have it for himself; he must separate it. I often feel when I am preaching as if I were riding among a great herd of deer, and I want to single out one. I cannot tell him; I do not know him, but oh, the Lord does, and I have known many a time the man has been singled out and the gun of the Gospel has gone off and he has fallen. The Lord has saved that man and brought him down. It is a sure mark that God is at work when the man gets separate, when he feels himself to be alone. If you hear in a great crowd, no good will come of it, and when you come and pray with a number of persons and feel as if you were only a part of the company and not yourself praying, no good ever comes of that. National religion! Well, what is the national religion of England worth? If it were sold for a button with the shank off wouldn't it fetch a dearer price than it is worth? There is nothing in it: it is merely a name. You may call it " a Christian country " or anything else you like with almost as great truth. Personal religion is the only religion that is of any value, and until you get a man to feel, " I *must* have that thing for myself! I *must* be born again! I *must* have a new heart! I *must* have a right spirit! I *must* be washed in the precious blood of Christ! I *must* escape from the wrath to come!"—until he has got there there is nothing good in his soul. But the getting apart is one of the earlier signs of a work of grace. For, my dear hearer, have you not personal sins which you would not like to tell to anyone, but which must be confessed to God apart. I am sure if anybody here could tell to me or to any other living man all his actions he must be as shame-faced as well could be. While the soul has any modesty left, confession to a priest is impossible. It is only when it has a brazen forehead and is utterly shameless than it can empty out itself before its fellow man. I question if it is ever done even then, but before the Lord we lay bare our head. O God, thou knowest the sins of my youth. Thou knowest the transgressions which my father knew not of. Thou knowest where my heart has gone, and where my feet have gone, and what my hands have done, and what all the members of this flesh of mine have done. Thou knowest it all. And I say, dear friends, it is only apart that a man can tell what he really feels.

If anybody was listening, you could not say to the Lord,
" Lord, thou knowest how I feel! I would come to Thee, but
I cannot. I would melt before Thee, but my soul seems as if
it were made of steel that had been hardened in the vaults
of hell! My God, I would repent, but my heart is like a rock:
only Thou canst smite it and make the streams of penitence
gush forth. I want to come to Thee but Satan holds me back;
or perhaps it is myself, worse than Satan, and I am accusing
Satan when I ought to blame myself." But alone we can tell
to the Lord our fears, our doubts, our difficulties, the hardness
that we feel within. We could not do it if we detected somebody else's ear at the key-hole; we should have to stop at once.
Therefore, to offer acceptable mourning before the Lord, the
soul must get apart.

III.

And then, beloved, we should never forget that in our
coming before the Lord what we want is personal pardon and
personal cleansing. That is a good hymn we have in our book
which ends every verse with " even me, even me." My God,
my Father, if Thou wert to forgive all Thine erring children
and not me, of what avail were that to me? If peace and
pardon were scattered amongst all the thousands of this congregation, if I were left out, it would but make my case the
darker. To see the gleams of Thy love shining yonder and sit
myself in outer darkness—oh, that were to make my case worse
than before! Beloved hearer, you have personal sin; you want
personal pardon. You have gone personally away from your
Father, and you must, like the prodigal, go personally back;
you must have His arms about *your* neck and have His kiss upon
your lips and hear Him say, " I have blotted out *thy* sin."
Nothing short of this will ever give peace to your spirit. Do
you not feel it so? Well, then, get apart, and as if there were
not another sinner in the world go and confess your sin; as if
there was no other sinner that ever wanted a Saviour, go to the
Cross and take the whole Saviour to yourself; and as if no other
soul ever wanted the work of the Holy Spirit to work upon it,
go to the Holy Ghost and commit yourself to Him and say,
" Renew and sanctify me! Purify me, O blessed Spirit, by
Thine infinite power." May God send us very much of the
confession and the resulting comfort which alone can bring
peace to the soul.

I think I hear somebody say, " I understand that if I am to find peace and pardon as a sinner I must go alone and cry to God for it apart : when shall I do it ? To you I reply, " Now." I would not like to take the risk of saying, " Wait half an hour," for within that time the iron gate may have closed upon you. The only time I am ever bidden to speak of is " to-day." " To-day, if ye will hear His voice, harden not your hearts." You tell me that time does not suit you; you do not know when you could get apart and alone. If there be no other hour, the dead of night will serve your turn; God is awake. Rise before the break of day, if your labour calls you early away; rise betimes, spurn the soft couch, and cry to God in prayer. Man! if thou shouldst break any engagement, whatever it might be, it were worth while to do it to find mercy. But to-morrow is a holiday. A great many of you working people will have nothing to do to-morrow and are going to spend it in merriment, and I shall not condemn you for that; but if you have not found a Saviour, don't say to me, " I have no time for prayer." It were a blessed thing if you spent all Whit Monday in prayer, so long as you did but find Christ. Go to your chamber and say, " We will not leave this place till Christ reveals Himself to us! He has promised to be the Saviour of all that trust Him, and we will go and trust Him, and from His Cross we will never stir until the blood-drops fall upon our guilty souls, and we can rise and say we are forgiven." Oh, it were a blessed Pentecostal Monday if the Lord moved many to pray apart— pray right on till they found a Saviour. I knew one who once came to London and who was living in the country, irreligiously without thoughts of God. He came to London and heard a Gospel sermon. He was a gentleman who liked to hunt, and when he came home, one of his companions said, " Well, what's the best news you've heard in London?" " I have heard," said he, " that Jesus Christ came into the world to save sinners." The other said, " I think you've gone out of your mind!" It was a blessed going out of his mind. I could point him out to you. The Lord has kept him out of his mind ever since. He is here to-night. He has a very different sort of mind. He is now rejoicing and delighting to serve God, and a happier man there is not in this place than he, I believe. May God bring many to find true happiness and give up sham happiness, which the world tries to tempt us with. " Well, but," says somebody, " where's the place I could get to be alone?" Place? Anywhere. In your chamber where you rest. Any little place where you can shut yourselves in. Why, the very streets of London may serve you for loneliness; for sometimes one can walk along them and be as much alone as in the Desert of Arabia. Many a soul has found Christ in a hay-loft. I know one who found him in a saw-pit. He, having no other place to get to, went there. Behind the hedge, on the house-roof—anywhere where you can without disturbance tell out your soul to God. Anywhere. God does not care where it is. Sacred places this day there are none, save that all places are sacred where loving hearts look after their Lord. " But, oh," says one, " suppose the time and place are ready, in what manner shall I come? Could you lend me a book to pray with?" No, not I! Let the books to pray with be burned. A blessed day when every one of them was done with! Perhaps we might have a little real prayer if the books of prayer were all destroyed. Go to God and tell what is in your heart. Never mind the words. Any words will do if they spring from your soul. " But I have not any words," say you. Never mind words: go and weep before the Lord. Groan before Him and cry. Let your heart speak, and if it be language that no ear can understand, God knows heart-language. He is a Spirit, and He knows the language of spirits, and He will read the desire of your soul. There is no standing upon etiquette and fine manners and goodly periods and choice sentences. Say, " God, be merciful to me, a sinner! Save me, Lord, for Jesus' sake," and there will be more prayer in it than in all the collects and all the prayers that the most learned divines were ever able to compose. The fact of the case is this: you will soon have to die apart. At that bedside there will stand kind friends who must bid you adieu. They will have come with you up to the brink of Jordan, but through the cool, chill stream they cannot go. Your solitary spirit must go on its lonely way through the gate of iron. Oh, as you must live alone and die alone, may His Spirit help you! And the time is coming when you will have to be judged alone, for, though amidst the countless throng, you will have to stand before the judgment seat yet, to all intents and purposes, each man will have a separate judgment. Upon each man the eye of fire will rest ; for each man shall the books be opened, and upon each man will the sentence come, " Depart, accursed." As you will sink alone into the pit that is bottomless, and burn alone in yon Tophet, where the fire never shall be quenched, I pray thee—and God speaks through me to some of you to-night—I pray you turn and live ; and may His Spirit turn you—even His infinite and omnipotent Spirit—that you may seek the lonely place and with the lonely cry of a broken heart cry, "Lord, save me ! I believe in Jesus ! Save me for the sake of Thy dear Son ! Save me, and I will give Thee praise."

Some will say, "Well, you teach these people to be selfish —each one looking to himself." Yes, but no man can be unselfish till first of all his soul is saved. A man that is drowning—I need not talk to him about unselfishness. Fling him a rope, and when he can seize it and drag himself out of the waters, then he can help others, but not till then.

"But," saith one, "you may drive these people to be melancholy." Would God I could, if it led them to abiding and perpetual peace ! A man without God ought to be melancholy. Damocles, when he sits at table to feast, with a sword hanging by a single hair, ought to be unhappy. He must either be unhappy or mad ! But when the sword is taken away, when repentance hath cried to God, and mercy hath forgiven sin—then will be the time to have peace and joy ; not till then. God make you miserable until you have found a Saviour. Then you shall know a joy and a peace which only Heaven can equal. God grant you to know it to-night ! May you not give sleep to your eyes nor slumber to your eyelids till you have nestled in your Saviour's bosom where the spear-print is still fresh—memorial of His dying love. Come, nestle there, and trust Him, and you shall be saved.

God bless you, for Christ's sake. Amen.

VII.

GIVING GOD HIS DUE.

I will offer to Thee the sacrifice of thanksgiving, and will call upon the name of the Lord.—(Psalm cxvi. 17.)

BRETHREN, this ought to be the result of every Christian's experience of divine grace. "O Lord, truly I am Thy servant and the son of Thine handmaid ; Thou hast loosed my bonds ; I will offer to Thee the sacrifice of thanksgiving." Being delivered from spiritual bondage, and made servants of the living God, we must and will praise the Lord as long as we have any being. Thanksgiving should always run parallel with prayer in connection with the Church of God. What is true of the individual is true of individuals collected as a corporate body. There is not a true Church of God on earth, but what has abundant cause to say, "I will offer the sacrifice of thanksgiving "; and we make a great mistake if, when we hold our days of prayer and cry unto God, we do not at the same time make them days of praise, and bless His holy name for what we have received. David seems to me in this verse to stand out in contrast with many, for there are some who will say, "I will continue to pray." "Yes," says David, "but I will offer the sacrifice of thanksgiving." Others will say, "We will meet together and sorrow over the sad estate of Zion; we will speak with one another about the defections of the faithful, the lack of piety, godliness, the superficiality of piety, the heresy of much of the doctrine that is preached, and the worldliness of much of the living that is lived." "Yes," David would say, "and I will come with you, too, and make confession and humble myself before God, but I will also offer the sacrifice of thanksgiving."

There is a tendency in the Church of God to play very much upon the discordant strings of the heart rather than those which still remain in tune. David would not forget how much there is that is out of joint. He would be among the first to humble himself before the Lord, among the first to join with Jeremiah and say, "Oh, that my head were

waters, and mine eyes a fountain of tears, that I might weep
day and night for the slain of the daughter of my people";
but still he resolves upon it, he declares it against all comers—
" I will offer to Thee the sacrifice of thanksgiving."

Now, I want you, dear brethren, if at any time you have
been inclined to deal out the word of discouragement, or even
the more bitter word of censure, all round, upon this Church
and that Church and the other, and upon this people of God
and the other people of God—instead of that, to come to the
resolution of the Psalmist which now lies before us and say,
" With all the Church's faults and with all our own, with all
that there is to deplore and all that there is to confess, yet
from this we will not start aside : we will offer the sacrifice
of thanksgiving."

I make that my resolve to-night ; and I do it for four
reasons. First, because I believe it is due to God ; secondly,
because I believe it is good for myself; thirdly, because I
believe it is encouraging to my fellow-workers; and fourthly,
because I think it is one of the helps towards the accomplish-
ment of the purpose we are aiming at.

I.

First, then, dear friends, I will offer the sacrifice of
thanksgiving because it is due to God. Whatever happens, let
not God be robbed of His praise. Suppose it be true that
the ministers are not faithful. Shall not God have glory?
Suppose it be true that many of the members of Christian
Churches are not what they profess to be. Shall we leave off
glorifying God because of that? Why, if He is robbed of
His glory by ministers or people, the more reason why those
who do love Him should sedulously cultivate His praise and
earnestly offer to Him the sacrifice of thanksgiving, for, notwithstanding all the gloomy views that may be taken of religion in the world, we have this to recollect—we ought to
praise God that there ever was a Gospel at all. He might have
left the world not only in heathenism, but under the ban of
everlasting perdition ; He might have left us without a Gospel
to preach, without a way of escape from His wrath, with
nothing before us, as the sons of sinful Adam, but to go back
" to the vile dust from whence we sprang," and then to descend
with the serpent into the place where he bears the wrath of
God for ever. I will rejoice and bless God while I have any

being that there is a Gospel, that there is an incarnate God, that there is an atoning sacrifice, that there is an ever-living Saviour. If I have nothing else to rejoice in, I will bless Him that ever these words were possible: " Jesus Christ came into the world to save sinners," and that ever it could be within the compass of fact that such a thing should be true, that we should be here to hear it, and that our lips should be privileged to speak it. I will offer to Him the sacrifice of thanksgiving.

And I will thank Him that, notwithstanding all the sins and infirmities of His Church, God has borne with us. Christ has not sued out our divorce yet. We sometimes speak against the Church, and very well we may, including ourselves in it. There are many faults and many failings, but for all that the Church of God on earth is Christ's bride, and if *He* can put up with her, I think we ought to do so too. If He still loves her, if still, for all her faults, it is through her that His spiritual children are born into the world ; if He saith He hateth putting away, it is not for us to put her away, and, as some do, talk about independent action altogether from the Church being that which God is most likely to bless. I think that is most likely to bring spurious results. But that which is done in connection with the visible Church in due order, and after the Lord's manner, honours the Church, and God would have the spouse of Christ honoured as well as Christ the King.

Beloved, I thank God, and I will, as long as I live, that He bears with His Church. The Spirit of God has not gone from her. Still there are the living in Zion ; still her prayers go up ; still her praises are received. There is a Church of God in the world. Yes, blessed be His name for that !

And I thank God, beloved, that the Gospel is preserved among us. I believe that in many pulpits it is perverted, philosophised upon, till the very soul of it has gone. We know that in some of the Churches ritualism on the one side has stamped out the Gospel, and rationalism, on the other, has all but buried it ; but for all that, the Gospel was never more truly preached than it is now. If anybody wants to hear the Gospel they can hear it in this land, and hear it distinctly and plainly, too ; for many run to and fro, and the knowledge of God is increased in the land. And I will offer to God the sacrifice of thanksgiving for this.

And I will thank Him that, notwithstanding all the dullness of the times, there is probably more Gospel abroad in the world than ever there was. Why, in the days of the apostles, there was not one Bible probably in the world to tens of thousands that are existing at this present moment. The invention of printing was a great blessing to the Church. You know that in our own English history it would have taken a man almost a year's labour to have bought a Bible, and now one can have it almost as a gift ; and there is scarcely a language under heaven but what the Bible is translated into, and the copies fall as thick as leaves in Vallambrosa all over the lands. Oh, blessed be God, I will offer the sacrifice of thanksgiving whatever anybody else may do.

And I thank Him, too, that we have got over the dark times of the Church. Oh, brethren, if once we were to come under a tyrant's power again, and it was death to believe in Jesus, and imprisonment to speak a word in Christ's name, we should begin to sigh and cry for these times ; but to-night I am not standing by a burn in Scotland between the hills in some dark glen reading my Bible by a lightning flash, or talking to armed Covenanters who are ready to guard their lives with swords. We are in the land where whoever wills to talk of Jesus may do it. There is none to hinder us ; none to make us afraid. " I will offer the sacrifice of thanksgiving, and will call upon the name of the Lord."

And, more than this, we have seen in this Church, and our brethren in their measure have seen in other Churches, that the Lord is still at work. The Gospel preached to-day saves souls as it did in days gone by. What if we do not see three thousand impressed by one sermon, yet he who speaks to you now can count those converted under his ministry not by thousands only, but by tens of thousands ; for to my own personal knowledge, either by conversing with them or by letters from them, many more than could be compassed in twenty thousand have I known to have been brought to Jesus Christ. And I know that under our own college, the men trained in our own Churches have been privileged to bring into the Church of God many more than ten thousand more souls whom God has blessed them with. The kingdom does grow. It is not as we like, but still, God be thanked that it grows at all. It might have gone back. " I will offer the sacrifice of thanksgiving and call upon the name of the Lord."

And, once more, we will do this because He is ready to do a great deal more. God is ready to convert millions instead of thousands, and He has given us a promise of this that we so much delight to sing—

> And a new song is in my mouth,
> To long-loved music set;
> Glory to Thee for all the grace
> I have not tasted yet.

Glory be to God for what He is going to do! Clap your hands, oh, saints of the living God, for He is about to win the nations unto Jesus. Ethiopia and the land of Sinde and the dwellers in Arabian deserts—they shall come and bow before the Lord. The joy of the latter days shall be so great that we may well anticipate that joy and begin to rejoice in it now. As the husbandman rejoices in an expected harvest, so let us lift up the shout of joy because the harvest is certain, and if it tarrieth, it is that it may be the greater when it comes. I will offer the sacrifice of thanksgiving, let others do what they will. Now, that is because it is God's due.

II.

The second head was because it was good for ourselves. And it is clear, bcause it is always good for ourselves to be just—good for our souls to perform a duty well. It is just to praise God; and it is one of the obligations of the saints to praise God's name. So it is good for ourselves besides. If we do not praise God we shall catch ourselves getting sour and morose. A man that does not praise God is not much liked, and then he goes off into a nasty sour, crab-apple disposition, from which the Lord save us! There is a person that cannot look at any work that is done except like a jackdaw or a monkey to pull it to pieces. There is a revival. "Oh, yes, that is mere excitement." There is a Church with a large increase. "Yes, there are a great many Churches, and they do gather in a great deal, odds and ends, and all that sort of thing; but they are not strict enough in their discipline." There is a young man raised up to make a stir in a provincial town. "Ah, yes, they have gone up like a rocket, and come down like a stick." That is a style to which one can be easily educated. I do not think anybody ought to pay very heavy fees to be a nasty critic; one can grow into that with a little watering very speedily.

Now, to keep our souls sweet, let us offer the sacrifice of thanksgiving just to keep this sour stuff, this horrible leaven, from making us as some are—by making us a lump of bitterness. Let us praise and bless the Lord. I have felt sometimes like the Quaker, who, when he heard a man swear, said to him, "Swear on, friend ; get rid of all that nasty stuff thou hast in thy soul, for thou canst never go to heaven while thou hast that in thee. Get it out as soon as ever you can." And the best way of curing ourselves of the spleen is to offer the sacrifice of thanksgiving. Thanksgiving will sometimes cure impatience, too. Sometimes in our zeal we really wish that we could get up to God's throne and manage things better. That is the short and long of what we are thinking of. We are not satisfied with the things as they go on. We want to push the Church before us, and drag the world behind us, and do in a day what ordinarily takes a century to accomplish—a very proper thing when it is not carried too far. But when we thank and bless the Lord, it kills our impatience, it prevents our falling into unpractical speculations, it enables us in patience to possess our soul and to go plodding on with God's work, leaving the results with God, who knows better the times and the seasons than we dare pretend to do. But, brethren, if you have got into a bad consumptive state, and your soul is dreary and heavy, and you are reading all the books that foretell that Popery is going to cover the land, and you go to bed by daylight and think the sun is set, get somebody, get especially the divine power, to help you to sing, to help you to praise God. Oh, that you could get the good air into your lungs by prayer, and then breathe it out again in a mighty burst of praise! Nothing is so good for a man as to praise God. The man that prays but never praises has not only the spirit of a beggar, but a beggarly spirit. If we are always asking something from God and never thanking Him for what we get, the Lord might well discharge us and say, " I will hear you no more; you are always begging, and you never thank Me; and if you are not grateful for what I give you neither will I give you more."

III.

Well, now, thirdly ; I will offer the sacrifice of thanksgiving because it is encouraging to my fellow workers. You know a very great deal in a Church will depend upon the leader. Christian ministers are but men; but still, when God sends them and they are what they should be, they very much affect the entire Church, and if they get into a dull desponding spirit, the workers, the most of them, feel the effect of it.   If you have a frost in the pulpit, you will not, as a rule, have too much warmth down below.   If the pastor's spirit is depressed, and he does not believe that God is doing good, why, the people begin to catch the infection and feel the same.   Hence it is important, my friends, deacons and elders round here, to keep up a cheerful spirit.   You, my brethren in the Sunday schools, keep up that lively cheerful tone of thanksgiving to God, or else the teachers may get discouraged when they see that the superintendent gets dispirited ; for there is always a party in the Church that are naturally desponding.   They cannot help it. They were born in December, and they will never have a birthday in June.   They are of that kind of spirit that they flourish best in the midst of a thaw and in wet times.   They always look at the dark side of matters.   For their sake let us look at the bright side.   Then there are always some workers who are working under some very great discouragement; and if we do not thank God for what He does, then they say, how can we expect any good result to come of our labours.   They think a great deal better of us, too often, than we deserve. Why, there is nothing in the world, after all, among Christians that will have a greater effect upon them than the courage of real believers.   When things are going heavily the bright eye and the cheerful ken of some one fellow worker will often inspirit all the rest.

When Paul was in the storm everybody's heart sank, except Paul's, and because he was courageous he had an influence over all that were in the vessel.   I have known a dear young brother, and I did know one dear aged brother, whose word and whose presence always cheered us.   I was reading last week a story of a ship, one of our ships of war, which had been in desperate combat with the enemy.   Into our ship was poured a tremendous broadside; the deck was strewn with dead sailors, blood was flowing on all sides, and the captain was just about to issue orders to strike the flag.   There seemed no hope but that the vessel would be blown into atoms unless the battle was stopped.   Now, there were on board the vessel some chickens.   One of the shots had broken the hencoop, and just at that moment a small bantam cock came and stood on the side of the vessel and gave a tremendous crow. As soon as ever he did that every man that was alive on board deck gave a loud cheer; the gunners rushed to their guns and

sent back a tremendous broadside; and, instead of striking their
flag, they captured the foe. It was no doubt a true British cock
that did that. And I like to see some of that true British pluck
in Christian men, so that when others are all desponding and
despairing they can step forward and say, " I will offer the
sacrifice of thanksgiving." Come, brethren, you may go away
from your guns if you like, and you may cry, and you may
weep, and you may say, " This cannot be done and it shall
not." I see enough blue in the sky to betoken a good fair day
ere the sun goes down; I see enough brightness in the promise;
I see enough in the gloomy hills of darkness, as my soul gazes
upon it, to believe that the promises do travel towards a glorious
day of grace; and therefore will I offer the sacrifice of thanksgiving and call upon the name of the Lord.

IV.

We will do this and offer the sacrifice of thanksgiving,
because it is one of the best ways of promoting the great end
we aim at.

Do this Godward. We aim at God's glory. It is well to
offer thanksgiving, for it is to glorify Him. " Who so
offereth praise glorifieth Me," saith the Lord. And to do this
in dark times is to glorify Him doubly. Therefore let us be of
a large and joyful spirit and praise His name; because we are
striking the very centre of the target when we are glorifying
God. And this is the object even of the salvation of sinners.
For sinners to be saved is not our object ultimately. The
ultimate object is God's glory through the salvation of sinners
Let us get that then; and we shall do so if we offer the sacrifice
of praise.

But secondly, we promote our object in the saints, for when
the saints are encouraged and led to thank God they are better
for service; they are more able to do it; they will do it in a
better way; they will do it with more faith; and the more of
faith the more of result is there sure to be; for the rule of the
kingdom is, " According to thy faith so be it done unto thee."
If you want your men in good trim, O commander, say not a
solitary word that shall lower their spirit, but rather show them
how to magnify the name of the Lord.

And again. This answers our end sinner-ward. O sinner,
if you see us thanking the name of the Lord we may remind
you that you have much to thank Him for. What if you are

G

not saved? Yet you are not yet shut up in hell. What if you are not forgiven? Yet you are where forgiveness is to be had. What if you cannot say yet, " I am in the family of the Lord "? Yet still there is space for you to arise and go unto your Father and confess your sin to Him. Oh, you ought to offer the sacrifice of thanksgiving that you are on praying ground still, and are yet where the Gospel is preached to you. I see much reason why even you should thank God for what you have.

And then I feel persuaded that the unconverted are more likely to be converted—we speak after the manner of men— by thankful Christians than by any others. I dare say there are some persons whose hearts will be won to Christ by preachers of a very sorrowful, heavy countenance and disposition. I suppose that when religion is painted as a dark and black thing there may be some hearts that are attracted by it, but I believe there are more flies caught with honey than with vinegar, and that there are more people led to think about their souls by grateful Christians than by the murmuring of believers.

I am inclined to believe that in the minds of a great many it is a very important question, whether religion does make men happy; and when they see it does, and they see us thankful and happy, then they say, " We will find out the secret that makes these people happy; we will go with them that we may share in their blessedness."

And I think this leads the sinner to think all the better of God. I should not like to keep a servant that was always very miserable, so that everybody said, " Ah, that woman has got a bad master at home, you may depend upon it." I should not like my horse, when he stood in the street, to be of such a sort that those around him should say, " Whose horse is that?" " Why, it is the minister's of the Tabernacle." " Is that how he keeps his horse? Why, you can see his ribs. What a master he must be to keep such a horse as that." The world looks at professors. " This is one of your Christians, is it? Christians! Why, he is enough to make a tempest in the house —the very sight of his face, and if all the world were happy and he were to step in you would suppose that every wedding

had changed into a funeral." I think the world would say,
" Oh, they serve a bad master, you may depend upon it. The
God they profess to believe in gives them a very few consolations." I think they say, " We are happy, you know; we can
be happy." But they forget the future and only think of the
present, and they think their position to be much superior to
that of the mournful Christian. Don't let them say that,
beloved, but, on the contrary, let us say to-night, " I will offer
the sacrifice of thanksgiving."

That my soul is resolved to do.

VIII.

THE CHRISTIAN'S BADGE.

For the Lord's portion is His people; Jacob is the lot of His inheritance.—(Deuteronomy xxxii. 9.)

MOSES, I have no doubt, had in his mind's eye the division of the land of Canaan among the tribes. After they had crossed the Jordan and had entered into the promised land, the land was marked off, so much for Reuben, so much for Simeon, so much for Judah, so much for Ephraim, and so much for Manasseh, so that each one of the tribes had his own peculiar portion. Moses represents the whole world as lying, as it were, like a map before the eye of the eternal God, and the Lord strikes out for Himself a portion which is to be the lot of His inheritance. That portion was in Israel's day the nation of Israel. The Lord's portion of ancient Israel—the nation—typified the spiritual seed of God, the children of Abraham who are descendants of the Father of the faithful. These, the chosen of God, the called of God, the regenerated, sanctified believing people of God—these are God's portion.

Now, in certain respects the whole of Canaan belonged to every Israelite. As soon as ever he crossed the border, he was in his own·native country. But yet there was a special sense in which a part of the promised land belonged to each tribe. The man of the tribe of Simeon said, wherever he might be in Canaan, " I am in my own land," but when he reached the peculiar possession of his tribe, then he said, " This land especially belongs to me." So the whole world belongs to God; the earth is the Lord's and the fulness thereof, the world and they that dwell therein; but yet there are peculiar people in the world whom God calls specially His own, and of whom He says by the mouth of an ancient prophet, " They shall be Mine, saith the Lord, in that day when I make up My jewels." All things are God's, but His people are especially His. Just as a man may possess large estates, broad acres and abundance of gold and silver and cattle and herds and crops, but he possesses his own children in a different sense from that. He says, " All these things are mine, but still my children are peculiarly my own." And so we are to understand the text. " The Lord's portion is His people; Jacob is the lot of His inheritance." Out of all the world besides, God condescends to call His people His own possession.

We will dwell a few minutes upon the fact, then upon the privilege which it brings us, and then upon the duty which it binds upon us.

I.

Now, first, upon the fact. We must make this fact of God's people being His portion run parallel with the figure— the figure of Canaan being divided into portions. So we notice, first, that the portion of any one tribe was peculiarly its own. Judah said, " This land is mine." Simeon said, " This land is mine." So also God saith of His people, " They are peculiarly Mine." I have already mentioned this fact in the outset, but I want you to realise it. It is not so much a thing to preach about as to think over, to mark, learn, and inwardly digest. You, O believer in Jesus, are peculiarly God's portion. There is about His possession of you a speciality. Will you think of this ? You are in yourself an inconsiderable member of a vast community; you are unworthy in your own esteem; if you judge rightly, you are as nothing and less than nothing; and yet you are not so to God. To Him you are a precious thing. " Since thou wast precious in My sight," saith He, " thou hast been honourable." God has an esteem for you. Though the multitudes of men would pass you by and forget you, and though some of the great ones of the earth would look down upon you, yet the Lord hath remembered the low estate of His handmaiden and looked upon you, my sister, with an eye of love. And you, my brother, though you feel you were but as a beggar upon a dunghill, He has taken you to be His, and in so doing He has set you among princes, even the princes of His people. One sits down and rolls this under his tongue as a sweet morsel :—" The Lord hath regard for me; He views me with a careful eye. He watches over me. He hath designs and purposes of love towards me. He will watch over me till life's latest hour and will bring me to Him-self, because I am His. He has given Himself to me to be my Father and my God, but He has also taken me to be a part and parcel of what He calls His own inheritance." I cannot dilate upon that thought, for time would fail me, but I do want you to get it, that you may have the sweet enjoyment of it, for ye are Christ's and Christ is God's. "Ye are a chosen generation, a peculiar people." You belong especially to the Lord, as many of you as have believed in Christ Jesus unto eternal life.

Note, next, in this fact, that each tribe had to conquer the inheritance which belonged to itself. There was the land marked out upon the map, but they had to go up and take it, for it was possessed by the Hivites and the Perizzites, and these must be driven out. Even so the Lord's portion is His people, but He has had to conquer us; for when He began with us what were we but a prey to divers lusts and evil powers? Satan ruled us, indwelling sin had dominion over us; the world rode rough-shod over us. We were evil. There was none of us that did good, no, not one. But, blessed be the name of the Lord, He has conquered us. It was a hard fight in the case of some of us, for we were exceeding strong against the God of grace. Why, there are those here to whom earnest sermons were only like paper pellets against a granite wall. A mother's tears fell on them and never melted them, and yet they are mighty things. For them a father's exhortations were in vain; for them a shipwreck and a battle and a fever and a lying upon the borders of the grave—all these were fruitless. They remained still incorrigible. Their sins were like those Canaanites that had chariots of iron, and it did seem as if the land could never be conquered for God. But He has done it, glory be to His name! He has subdued our wills. He has brought us to the foot of the Cross. He has made us love what once we hated, and prize beyond all worth what once we despised. The Lord's portion is His people, and therefore by His mighty reigning grace He overcomes them and puts them under dominion beneath the feet of His mercy. Give glory unto the conqueror, my brethren. Bow down willingly. Held in the silken fetters of love, bow before the Prince of Peace, and hail Him as your King.

And then the tribes, after they had conquered the land, had another task to do, namely, to extirpate the old inhabitants. For they were not merely to bring them under subjection, so that Judah or Reuben might possess his land, but they were to slay them utterly, for their sins had been great, and God had doomed them to die and the Israelites were to be their executioners. Now, this is what God has to do in each one of His people, viz., to exterminate our sins. O brethren, what a battle that would be for us! Why, our sins, when we attack them single-handed, soon overcome us. Why, the very weakest sin that is in any one of us would be our downfall if we were let alone; and as for our stronger passions, if opportunity and temptation should come together and then our evil desires should leap up at the same time, who among us could stand in such a conflict? And yet, as surely as God has undertaken the work of our salvation, He means to take up root and branch all our sins. Can you realise it? O my brethren, who are daily fighting with inward sin, can you realise it, that the day will come when you will have no tendencies to sin, when all your powers will go towards righteousness and to righteousness only? Can you grasp it? " Oh," say you, " it is a heavenly thought." Yes, and in Heaven it will be realised, and you will have more and more of Heaven here below in proportion as it is realised here. Holiness is the royal road to happiness. The death of sin is the life of joy. At the root of every sin there is the bitterness of sorrow. Sin is the root of bitterness. When God shall tear up every one of these roots of bitterness, it will be a blessed thing for us, but this He will do. The quick-tempered brother shall no longer be liable to bursts of passion; the sluggish-minded shall no longer be tempted to indolence; the man of imperious pride shall bow as humbly as the seraph who veils himself with his wings; there shall be in us every propensity to good and no inclination to evil.

> O sacred hour, O blest abode!
> I shall be near and like my God,
> And flesh and sense no more assail
> The solid pleasures of my soul.

I shall be for ever free from that which brings me sorrow, and shall possess that which brings me joy. The Lord's portion is His people, and He will not leave a Canaanite in the land. He will cut them up altogether.

II.

Run on the parallel with the fact, and you get another thought. After the people had conquered their own portions, they had to cultivate them, and they did cultivate them well till the very tops of the hills were covered with vines, and the valleys laughed with joyous harvests. Now the Lord will cultivate His Church. We are as yet poor, barren soil; but the Lord knows how to plough us, and to till us, till we shall yet bring forth a hundred-fold to His glory. We hear sometimes of high culture. I would not be envious of the highest mental culture which the university would yield ; but I envy above all things the spiritual culture of the Holy Ghost. " Ye shall be sown and ploughed," saith the Lord, and blessed be they that can come under the divine tillage ! " He will make her wilderness like Eden, and her desert like the garden of the Lord." Rest assured that any portion God undertakes to till, He will be first in it. None shall be such a husbandman as our Father. He is the Husbandman, and He will get better harvests out of us than by any other means could be produced. We are in good hands. Sorry soil we are, but yet He will produce unto Himself harvests that shall be for His eternal honour. Let us have good hope and confidence since this is the fact.

And the people had not only to till the soil, but they had to protect it, for around them were many robber tribes that assailed them, and, therefore, they had, while they cultivated the ground, often to beat their ploughshares into swords and their pruning hooks into spears. And God will do that for us. The everlasting arm will well protect that which it has so dearly won. Jesus, who bought us with His blood, will not lose us. The Holy Spirit, who redeemed us by His power and brought us unto Himself, will not suffer the adversary to overcome Him. He will preserve our souls, and present them unblemished and complete at the last. " The Lord's portion is His people," and as the tribes held their heritage, so will God beyond the mighty, and in the teeth of all our adversaries keep every one of His people—every inch of His inheritance—to the end.

One other thought only upon this, and that is, the tribes, having had to fight for their country and till it and defend it, expected to enjoy it. They expected to sit every man under his own vine and fig tree. They expected to drink of the rivers that flowed with milk and honey ; and they did so. And God expects from His people to obtain joy. Can God receive joy? Well, perhaps, as abstract truth He cannot, for He is unspeakably and infinitely blessed apart from us, but yet He is pleased to reveal Himself as a Father. A father hath joy in his children, and God hath joy in His children. And, indeed, it lies in the very marrow of the metaphor now before us. A man hath joy in his portion ; so hath the Lord joy in His people. And you know that memorable passage ; I scarcely ever dare to quote it without deep emotion, so wonderful a passage is it : " He shall rest in His love "— as if God found rest in loving His people—" He will joy over thee with singing." It is a wonderful passage. Have we not before told you that when God created the world the angels sang for joy. God did not sing : He said, " It is very good." He spoke, and expressed His approbation, but I hear of no song. But now, in the new creation, when He sees His dear ones chosen before all worlds, for whom the only-begotten poured out His life-blood—when the Spirit of God sees His workmanship, it is written, " He shall joy over thee with singing." God singing ! Can you catch the thought ? This is sweeter than the angels' song or than the song of all the beatified that surround the crystal throne. It is Jehovah Himself that sings—like a husband rejoicing over his bride, or a mother singing over her child. For God hath joy in His people ; Christ findeth satisfaction in the fruit of His agonies, and the Holy Spirit takes delight to view the soul that He Himself hath formed anew. This is unspeakably precious, but it is true ; the Lord finds delight in His people and enjoys them, for " the Lord's portion is His people." And I believe, brethren, that the fruit that God looks for from us is our love. You do not expect your children to do anything for you, but you do expect them to love you, and you expect their gratitude. When their eyes sparkle, and their little lips almost incoherently tell you how thankful they are to you for your kindness, you rejoice in that. And praise is pleasant to God. He delights in the love of His people and in their thanksgiving. And, moreover, fellowship with God is sweet to Him. For it is said of Jesus, " His delights were with the sons of men," and all through the Song of Solomon the spouse represents Himself as ravished with the love of His beloved. Christ always speaks there of His Church as being able to communicate joy to Him by the sight of her fair face, and the words of her lips. He says, " Let Me see thy face ! Let Me hear thy voice ; for sweet is thy face, and thy countenance is comely "—sweet to Him and comely to Him. Oh, dear children of God, rob not God of His fruit that comes of His portion. Give Him your love ; give Him your fellowship ; walk with Him as Enoch did ; for this is Christ's joy—that you should have joy in Him.

But now a few words only about the privilege which all this implies. "The Lord's portion is His people." This implies great honour ; for to be God's above other men is to have special honour upon one. Better than to be a Knight of the Golden Fleece, or of the Order of the Garter, is it to be one in whom God takes delight. This is the highest honour, before which imperial dignities must lose their lustre—the dignity of belonging to the King of kings. It brings honour. It brings, brethren, with it security, for if we be the Lord's portion, He will preserve us. One of the crests of our nobility has upon it, "I will maintain it" ; and rest assured, God has said of His Church, "I will maintain it" ; "I give unto My sheep eternal life, and they shall never perish, neither shall any pluck them out of My hand." If I belonged to an angel, I might be lost, but if I belong to God, God will not lose His own. There is the privilege of honour and security. And there is the privilege of His presence. The tribes dwelt in their portion, so will God dwell in His Church. "The Lord's portion is His people." That explains the question which an apostle asked of his Master, "Lord, how is it that Thou wilt manifest Thyself to us, and not unto the world?" A man in his own garden takes his ease; a prince in his own province feels at home. And God has made His Church to be His peculiar dwelling-place where He shines forth in all the majesty of His love. Brethren, if this be our privilege, let us enjoy it. What a shame it is that many of us are worth thousands a year, and live like beggars—I mean, that we might have God's presence, but, through our carelessness, we live at a distance from Him and are unhappy. Enoch's God is my God, and if I seek grace enough, I may live Enoch's life. You may, my dear brother, enjoy the presence of God in unbroken continuity, evermore abiding in Him, and as Christ Himself did, if you will but seek it with all your heart. God grant you may so seek it as to find it. For this privilege gives us another privilege, namely, that of delight. Where God is, there is sure to be happiness.

> My God, the spring of all my joys,
> The life of my delights.

We can truly call Him by that name—

> 'Midst darkest shades, if He appear,
> Our Eden is begun.

We only want God's presence, and we have got all the happiness our soul asks for. Take our God away, and the bursting barn is famine and the overflowing wine vats yield no joy. Friends cannot make us otherwise than friendless if God desert us, and all the helps of the creature leave us helpless if the Creator turn aside. All our fresh springs are in God ; and, since He dwells in His portion, we are a happy and a blessed people.

Truly the privilege, if we had time to think upon it, has much in it that would comfort us, especially in one aspect of it, for it opens up to us a glorious future. If we are God's portion, then depend upon it, He means to do something great with us. It is the honour of a king to make his country famous and illustrious ; it will be to the honour of God to make His Church something far nobler than she is to-day. He will come by-and-bye, and He will take us away from this land of our banishment to our own country. We dwell here as in tents, sojourners as all our fathers were. Wait awhile, for the hour cometh when He will translate us to the city that hath foundations, whose builder and whose maker is God. Farewell, ye scenes of earth with your attempts at joy ; we go unto the land where joy for ever blooms and bliss never fades ; for the Lord's portion is His people, and He won't let us lie out in the field for ever. When the wheat is ready, He will gather it into the garner. We are His gems to-day, but we still lie in the mire. He has brought some of us up from the mine and polished us somewhat, but He will take us from the lapidary's wheel with all its cuttings ; He will set us in His royal crown, and we shall be unto Him a joy and a glory for ever and for ever. Thus, you see, there is a great deal of comfort to be drawn from the privilege which the text implies.

III.

Now, brethren, I hasten on, because the sands of time drop so hastily, to notice the duty which is wrapped up in all this. " The Lord's portion is His people." What, then ? Why, let us own the blessed claim. Let each Christian here say—

> 'Tis done ! The great transaction's done !
> I am my Lord's, and He is mine ;
> He drew me, and I followed on,
> Charmed to confess the Voice Divine.

Look back, some of you, to the years when first you gave yourself to God. I do remember well when I felt that I was bought with Christ's blood, how it seemed the most natural thing in all the world to say, " My God, I am Thine for ever —my body, my soul, my spirit, my time, my substance, my house, if Thou shalt give me one, and whatever of talent I may possess." I hope you meant it when you thus gave yourself wholly up to God. I ask you to repeat the dedication to-night. There have been some Christians who have written out a covenant with God—I think Dr. Doddridge did this, and then signed it with his blood. But such things are very apt to bring the soul into bondage. They are not prescribed in Scripture, and we had better not do anything of our own head : we had better leave such things alone. Yet still, as a matter of fact, I hope we should be prepared to sign it with our blood. If I saw before me a deed engrossed in which I was proclaimed to be God's chattel—all that I am and all I have to be God's for Him—to do what He liked with me, I would sign it and bless the God of grace that permitted me to give myself over to Him. And yet, dear brethren, though I know you would sign it, too, there are times when it comes to suffering for Christ, and are you not a little put to it? And perhaps you have long and severe pains, and then you begin to start back from the surrender, and can hardly feel resigned to the divine will. Come, let us now again go to our God and say, " Whereas we have sometimes drawn back as though we would no longer be Thine, we do to-night desire to confess that we are Thy portion ; that we are not our own ; that we are bought with a price ; we would renew our vow in Thy presence ! O Lord, I am Thy servant ; I am Thy servant and the son of Thine handmaid. Thou hast loosed my bonds."

And, next, let us recollect that every man's portion is separated from everybody else's. Judah's portion was separated from Simeon's, and Simeon's from Ephraim's. Now, if we are God's, let us maintain the separated life. I do not know any practical truth that wants preaching more to-day than this —that God's saints must be separated from the world. Now, nonconformity—you may say what you will of that, but one thing is certain, that nonconformity to the world is the badge of the Christian. " Be not conformed to this world, but be ye transformed." I wish that all Nonconformists were more non-conforming to the world. And oh, that all professors of religion were more distinct from the rest of the world ! Whenever you make the lines of demarcation between the Church and the world to be indistinct, you do both the Church and the world a serious damage. The Flood was probably brought upon this world because the sons of God saw the daughters of men that they were fair, and so there was a blending of the two, and the distinction ceased. Then God swept the whole population away. "Ye are the salt of the earth." "Ye are the light of the world." "What communion hath light with darkness?" "What concord hath Christ with Belial?" How can you eat at the table of the Lord and then eat at the table of the devil? How can you be Christians and yet be world-lings? "Ye cannot serve God and Mammon." There must be the separation, for "no man can serve two masters: either he will love the one and hate the other, or else he will despise the one and cleave to the other." "Ye cannot," says Christ, "serve God and Mammon. Come ye out from among them. Be ye separate. Touch not the unclean thing, and I will be a father unto you ; and ye shall be My sons and daughters, saith the Lord God Almighty."

So with that I shall conclude. If ye be indeed God's portion, I exhort you, my dear brethren and sisters, to render yourselves up more and more to God from this day; serve Him with all your might; serve the Lord with gladness; lay yourselves out for His service; watch for opportunities of bringing Him glory ; and never be content with what you have done. Be seeking still to do more and more for that God of grace who says that you are His portion and the lot of His inheritance.

IV.

This sermon, I fear me, has not been addressed to all of you. There are those in this house to-night to whom there is no voice in the text, because whatever people you may be, you are not His people, and whose ever heritage you may be, you to remember that truth? You are prayerless, Christless, graceless. You have never believed in Jesus Christ, and though you sit with God's people and belong to a godly family, yet when the Lord cometh, if you are then as you are now, He will say to you, "I never knew you: you are none of Mine. You loved the world and belonged to it. You loved sin; you shall have its wages. You neglected the great salvation ; how shall you escape?" Do I hear you say, "But may there not be a change in me? May I not become one of

His people?" Oh, happy enquiry! Only ask it sincerely, and I will answer you thus: "Let the wicked forsake his way, and the unrighteous man his thoughts, and let him return unto the Lord, for He will have mercy upon him, and to our God, for He will abundantly pardon." "Whosoever believeth on the Son of God hath everlasting life." And if, as a guilty sinner, you shall come to Jesus and take Him to be your only hope and trust, you are saved ; your sins, which are many, are, in a moment, forgiven you, and you are the Lord's. But living and dying without faith in God, your baptism will not save you; your confirmation will not save you ; your attention to sacraments will not save you. "Ye must be born again."

May God bring us to a saving faith in a precious Saviour, and may our names be written in the Lamb's book of life. And when He calls for His chosen, may we be able to answer to our names ; in that day when the sheep pass under the hand of Him that telleth them may every one of you be there, and God shall have the glory. Amen and amen.

IX.

FROM GLOOM TO GLORY.

Man that is born of a woman is of few days and full of trouble.
—(Job xiv. 1.)

"A VERY mournful text," says one: "we would prefer to have something cheerful." Well, certainly, the bell has a very solemn sound, but it was cast in Heaven's own foundry, and there is a reason for it. God has hung it in the belfry of inspiration, and He meant it to be rung. It is sometimes of very great service to us to have to think of solemn things. But, then, I would remind you that the bell that tolls the funeral knell needs but to be sounded in another way, and it can give forth the most delightful sounds. And so, truths which are even terrible and dreadful under some aspects may be bright and comforting under others. The trumpet may have a different sound to one person from what it will have to another. They used to sound trumpets when the judges came into an assize town, and if the prisoners heard those trumpets, they would either be sweet or sad to them, according to their character. He who knew he was to be tried for murder and was guilty of that crime, would hear in the sound of the trumpets the most mournful tidings, but he who had a clear conscience would be glad to think that he was about to receive an acquittal at the hand of righteousness. I should not wonder but what these words, "Man that is born of a woman is of few days and full of trouble," while they may sound mournfully to many hearts, will also have a ring of the joy note in your ears, so that out of this eater shall come forth meat, and honey shall be found even in this lion-like text.

The statement here made is one of the most sweeping character. It says, "Man that is born of a woman is of few days, and full of trouble." That is to say, every man, for there was but one man who would not come under this description—the father of us all. But as for the rest, we are all born of a woman, and therefore all of them have few days and full of trouble. It is applicable to kings upon their thrones quite as much as to the prisoners who are in the dungeon. It is certainly as true of the stalwart guardsman as of the poor, pining, consumptive girl. Each one that is of woman born must speedily to the dust return, and meanwhile must find the way to the grave to be rough with sorrows.

The text is sweeping, and at the same time by using the term, " Man that is born of a woman," it uplifts the veil a little why it is so. Who can bring a clean thing out of an unclean! Who shall bring strength out of weakness? Who shall bring immortality out of mortality? Who shall produce men of iron when they have to be born from women of clay? It is because of our first birth and the sin—the transgression that comes in with it—that therefore we are of few days. We say, " short and sweet," but here we have brief and bitter. The sin that we inherit causes us also to inherit the fewness of the days and the fulness of the trouble. And this statement is true in all ages since it was uttered. I suppose that even to the antediluvian men life seemed to be of few days. Though to us their age seems extremely long, yet it may not have been so to them, for we well know that our days grow shorter as we grow older. A period of time which seems immense to the child, and tolerably long to a young man, becomes short to a man of middle life, and to the aged man appears to be as nothing at all. The astounding rapidity with which life flies often staggers me. I remember when a day, a week, a month seemed something, but now Sabbaths fly round and one seems no sooner to have left the pulpit than to have to be ready to go into it again. Time flies the more rapidly as life advances. But in all the periods of time since men have been upon the earth this is indeed true, and we must none of us expect to escape from the general rule. This is true to you young people; you will be " of few days and full of trouble." Take not the word from my lips ; take it from the Holy Spirit Himself. This is true to you strong men who are now in the vigour of life ; you will be " of few days and full of trouble." You of grey heads, whose strength has survived these many years, who lean upon your staff—*you* will be of few days ; and, as you have had trouble, you must expect it to the last. You are not out of gun-shot of Satan yet, not beyond the temptations of the corrupt nature yet, not beyond the trials of life yet. He that has come into the safe harvest of competence, and dreams of spending a long period of time in retirement, may still remember that trouble will follow him, even in his rural retreat, and that he may not reckon upon many days, for he is of few days, God hath said, and of few days he shall be. Let each man quietly turn over this word of God in the stillness of his own soul, " I, like my brother, am of few days and full of trouble."

Now, take the first statement, and then the second, and then blend the two.

I.

Take the first statement: " Man that is born of a woman is of few days." It does not say " of few *years*." It is as if his years were almost too few even to be thought of, and as if man ought never to live by the year. I do not remember a passage of Scripture which says, " Teach us to number our years " ; neither do I recollect a prayer in which we are to ask for yearly bread ; but I remember that we are to ask to be taught to number our days and to say, " Give us day by day our daily bread." Now, our days do seem to be many. There are three hundred and sixty-five days in each year, and then we look for a considerable number of years, and according to our thoughtless calculation it would appear as if our days were, after all, rather considerable. But the text says, " No! Man that is born of a woman is of few days." And this is true, if you compare man's life, first of all with the life of God. It seems scarcely to be spoken of—fitter for contemplation than for speech. When as yet this universe was not, there was God. Long ages before He began to create sun, or moon, or stars, there was God. And when all things that now are shall pass away like a vestment worn out to be put aside, there shall still be God—no older, for there can be no age with Him ; no further advanced in years, for He hath no years. It is *now* with Him—no past, no future.

> He fills His own eternal vow,
> And sees our ages pass.

" Of few days," indeed ! Why, we are but of yesterday. Fly back a moment to the time when Christ was hanging on the cross. Where were you then? Think of the times of Solomon and David. Where were you? A thing unthought of. And in that day when Jehovah walked the glades of Eden and

H

communed with our unfallen parents, where were we! We are infants; we are not worthy to be mentioned. We are " of few days."

Why, we are even of few days as compared with the world in which we live, and yet that is but a novel thing. It was but yesterday this world flew like a spark from off the anvil of eternal omnipotence; yet to us it seems ages indeed. Yon mountains, with their snows, seem hoary with age, and yonder deep, which has swallowed so many of the navies that mortal ambition has built—how old it seems compared with us ; yet those things are mere novelties. Then what are we? We seem only to have sprung up like grass in the summer, and like grass we already feel the mower's scythe. We are " of few days."

We are of few days as compared with what our days might have been ; for, had not our first parents sinned, I know not that we should have lived here for ever, but certainly we should not have died. There is, according to some teaching, no absolutely physical reason why the human body should not continue to live on. At any rate, if there be reasons now why the body should at such and such a period begin to decay, then probably there were no such reasons in the con-formation of the first man. Perhaps that tree of life in the garden might have furnished Adam with food for perpetual youth, so that he would have renewed his strength like the eagles, and we too, his children, might have lived in perpetual happiness here. Well, the dream is gone: it shall not be realised. Still, compared with what they might have been, sin has made our days few.

Compared again—and this is a far sweeter thought—com-pared with what they shall be, our days are few, for, O, beloved, when this life's toil and trouble shall all be over our immortal spirits—what shall be their duration? We shall receive a life coeval with the life of God, and no more be capable of death than God Himself. As many as have be-lieved in Christ Jesus shall enter into a felicity that shall know no bounds. Ay ! and this corruptible shall put on incorrup-tion, and this mortal shall put on immortality. And even that of us which to-day draweth down to the worm and to the dust—the rottenness—shall rise in power and glory and be spiritually fashioned in the glorious image of the second Adam. Blessed be God, the life on earth is nothing compared with the life to come. A mere handful of days we have here; but there, with the Ancient of Days, we shall dwell for ever and ever.

Now, this being the truth, what then? Let us ring the bell a minute and listen to it.

First, then, if our days are few, how earnest ought each one of us to be that he should find reconciliation with God and eternal salvation, and find it at once! I have spoken to some of you many hundreds of times about your souls and you have never quarrelled with any statements of truth that I have made. I almost wish you had. You have said, "Yes, that is important. Yes, we are sinful. Yes, we do need a Saviour." But while you have said you were sinful, you have not repented nor confessed your sin to God. Though you know you need a Saviour, yet you have not found Him. When do you mean to attend to these things? "By-and-bye," say you? "Man that is born of a woman is of few days." You have had a few days already ; perhaps you have had all you will ever have. If you could see the sand-glass of your lives, some of you—if I could see mine—there may be far fewer sermons to be uttered below than we had dreamed. The thread that we think to be so long may almost be at an end. Dear heart, do you intend to die impenitent? Do you mean to pass into another world without a Saviour? Can you be so mad as that? No, I know that is the last thing in your thoughts. You are intending and you are resolving well. And you resolved ten years ago, did you not? Do you remember that impressive sermon? How you trembled! Perhaps it was twenty years ago. You recollect that sickness, that cholera in the City, and how you resolved and re-resolved? And yet you are just the same as you were then. Are not the probabilities very strong that you will continue the same as you now are, and that you will open your eyes where it will be too late to open them—like the rich man of whom it is said, " In hell he lift up his eyes "? It were far better to lift them up here than to lift them up there, where you will see no hope, no Saviour on a throne of mercy. God grant to us to snatch the present day. The most important of all interests cannot be postponed until to-morrow. He who was slain with a dagger had a warning, as you know ; but he said he would attend to it by-and-bye, and he went to the Senate house and fell beneath the daggers of his foes. You have a warning

H 2

to-night ; this very text has spoken it to you. Perhaps to-morrow you will have to rue, and rue for ever, that you postponed the thoughts of the things of eternity.

II.

Another lesson comes from this, and it is for those who are already saved—the people of God. Dear brothers and sisters, our one desire is to glorify God. Now, we shall glorify Him for ever and ever; but there is a particular form of service which only belongs to this life. Are you not anxious —very anxious—that you should honour Christ here and do as much as you can? Well, you have few days—but few days. Oh, one could almost wish to live to be as old as Methuselah for the sake of winning men's souls and bringing sinners to Christ. But it cannot be. Oh, how we ought to work for Jesus, seeing He is such a Master, and deserves to have so much from His servants. And yet there is so short a space to do it in. If we are painting for eternity, oh, let us move our hands with skill and with rapidity as hearing the chariot wheels of eternity behind us. Can we afford to waste hours or even minutes? I have heard of a Puritan who used to rise and study at five in the morning. But one day he heard a smith's hammer while he was getting up, and he said, "Shall a smith work harder than a minister of God? Shall he give to his hard service more time than I give to my Lord and Master?" And he would thus chide himself, though he was one of the most industrious of men. Remember, dear friends, that you are born of woman, and that you have but few days—few days in which to bring sons and daughters to the Saviour, few days in which to save that Sabbath school class, few days, oh, preacher, in which to make this place ring with salvation, few days in which to be a shepherd to the people of God—a few days in which to call sinners and to warn backsliders. Let us live, while we live, brethren, to the utmost power and capacity of our manhood, for we are of few days.

Now, let us ring that bell again, and hear whether there is not sweet music in it.

Well, then, if we are "of few days," our troubles will the sooner be over. If we are of few days, we have but a short time in which to bear the labour and the suffering, the weakness and the want which are often our lot and our portion.

"Of few days," then the sooner we shall be in Heaven. So much the nearer are yon gates of pearl ; so much the sooner yon streets of gold to be trodden by our feet ; so much the sooner shall the crown encircle these brows. It seems to me that the bell rings out a marriage peal, the very bridal of our souls with Christ in the new Jerusalem. Man that is born of a woman, banished from his Saviour, is banished but for a few days. Man that is born of a woman, being twice-born through the Holy Spirit, is but a little while in the furnace ; he shall be for ever in the paradise of God. Who wishes to lengthen out a life which detains us from a face-to-face view of Christ ? There are reasons for wishing it long—reasons of self-denying service, but, oh—

> Our heart is with Him on His throne,
> And ill can brook delay ;
> Each moment listening for the voice,
> "Make haste and come away."

As the bride desireth the marriage day, our soul desireth the bridegroom, even Jesus. As the child longeth for the home-bringing when the school days are done, and the rest-hours of home are come, so our hearts, when in a right mind, long for the coming of the Lord. Glory be to His name, for it is true, "Man is of few days."

And one other thought comes over my mind here, and it is this: Ought not this to make us feel the more deeply in-debted to the matchless love of God that, though we are of few days, the love which deals with us is not ? It never had a beginning ; it never will have an end. From everlasting to everlasting God loved His people. Oh that everlasting love should be set upon a mortal man ! Oh that the long ages ere this world was made should yet be witness to our names ! Think of it. Ere suns began to shine, or the day-star knew its place, we were even then dear to the heart of God. Christ loved us then ; for has He not said, "As the Father hath loved Me, so have I loved you," and that is without beginning, without end, without measure, without limit, without bounds, without change. Oh, then to think that we should be objects of such love as that makes the few days of this mortal life glow with glory as the bush in Horeb glowed with the presence of Deity.

Now, let us take the second half of our text, and that briefly. "Man that is born of a woman is of few days and

full of trouble." "Full of trouble." Is not that a doleful
sound? And alas! the fact is as dolorous as the sound; for
if you turn over the experience of good men and all men you
shall find that there is no lack of trouble. The roll of trouble
is like Ezekiel's roll, written within and without full of lamentations and mourning and woe. Sometimes we have troubles
of the country, and wars and rumours of war, or poverty and
famine, or sin and wickedness in our streets. Then we have
the troubles of the Church, the heresy, the schism, the divi-
sions among brethren, the heart-burnings against each other,
the coldness towards God, the lukewarmness to Christ. And
then we meet with troubles outside in the world, the battling
for existence with some, the trouble of getting the trouble of
spending, the trouble of keeping, the trouble of losing,
troubles on all sides, in the shop and in the field, troubles
that come to us in the bed-chamber, that walk arm-in-arm
with us in the streets and follow us to the retirement of the
woods. There is no place free from them. A good old Puritan
divides the troubles thus: " There are troubles in doing
our duty, troubles for doing our duty, troubles in not doing
what is our duty, and troubles in doing what is not our duty."

And truly every man has met with these—troubles in doing
our duty, striving against flesh and blood, fighting against
inward temptations and Satan and defying the world;
troubles for doing our duty, coldness and ill-treatment, crosses
and losses that come necessarily to those who walk uprightly.
And then troubles for not doing our duty, which are far
sharper and which come upon God's servants for omissions
and commissions, for the Master's will, known and not obeyed,
for the Master's will not known and not obeyed—many stripes
and few stripes, but still stripes all the journey through. And
then troubles for doing what is not our duty, viz., running
into this or that which is aside from the straight path of the
upright. How many troubles do we bring upon ourselves in
that way? There are troubles within and troubles without,
troubles that come to you while you are active, troubles that
besiege you while you lie passive upon the bed of pain—the
troubles of our childhood, which I believe are not quite so light
as some think them to be. There is a fiction that children have
the happiest days: I know I had not. I do not know how
many are able to bear witness to the same. There are troubles
of youth, troubles of manhood, and troubles of old age. In

fact, "the Christian man," as John Bunyan says in his
quaint ballad—

> . . . is seldom long at ease,
> When one trouble's gone, another doth him seize.

Temptations of all sorts and sizes await the followers of the
Lamb of God. If others can be without trouble, they shall
not be, because they are God's people. God had one Son
without sin ; He never had a son without affliction, and He
never will have.

III.

What is the lesson from all this? If we are full of trouble,
let us reflect that there is plenty of weaning going on, and this
we ought to be glad of. We are so fond of the nest here that
we should never fly from it, only thorns are getting numerous,
and we shall fly soon. Here are knives that cut the ropes that
hold us. We shall begin to mount, for God's grace has made
us buoyant. Only let us get loose, and we will go away to
our own company in the skies. If we are getting settled on
our lees, let us thank God because we have abundance of
trouble. Then the joy is that we shall have abundance of
consolation, for it is a well-known rule of the kingdom that,
as our troubles abound, even so shall our consolations abound
by Jesus Christ. Who would not be glad to have the trouble
for the sake of the consolation ; for the precious Balm of
Gilead not only heals and takes away the pain, but it gives
positive pleasure. We always gain by our losses when we walk
with God. We get richer through being poorer, and healthier
through being sick. So, be willing to have rough winds, for
they shall bring us soft winds. When God intends to send
His servant a diamond more valuable than usual, He does it
up in a black envelope. At first it alarms us, and we think
it something terrible, but, when we open it, we find such a
sparkling love token that our fears disappear. Here is the
comfort of it : we have fuller opportunities of experiencing the
truth of the promises of God. Some promises would not be
worth a farthing to us if we were in circumstances that did not
require them to be fulfilled. Half the Bible would be useless
to us if we never had to meet a temptation. Doctor Affliction
is the best expositor of Scripture. I can recommend you Dr.
Gill and Dr. Adam Clarke and many others, but if you want

to understand the Word of God you must go to the school of trial. They say you can see the stars when you are down a well when you cannot see them up above, and many a starry promise shines out to a soul that is down in the deeps of affliction. Sympathetic ink does not show a bit till it is held to the fire, and often the promises are written in such ink: you must hold them to the fire of trial, and then the meaning appears, and you rejoice in it.

Once more—and I think this is a sweet note from such a harsh-sounding bell—if we are full of trouble, we are full of opportunities for understanding our suffering Lord ; we are full of occasions for knowing the heights and depths of His love that passeth knowledge. If I were to go to Heaven without ever having a trouble, why, how strangely ignorant must I be there ! I should hear the sacred ones speaking to one another of the sufferings of their Lord, and I should have to say, " What do they mean? I never had these sufferings." I hear them speaking of pain, and I say, " Pain! I never knew pain ! " I hear them talk about poverty and want and depression of spirit and about crying, " My God, My God, why hast Thou forsaken Me? " and I stand and look on in wonder and say, " What does it all mean? " But now the blessed scholars of the school of affliction, as they come to heaven, are entrapped by the angels and asked what it means, and they tell unto the principalities and powers in heavenly places the manifold wisdom of God. We have fellowship with Christ in His sufferings, and who does not wish to have full fellowship with Christ in them? Hence I feel very little sympathy with brethren who do not wish to die. I am ready to do what the Lord wills, but I would rather die, bearing on this forehead the death-seal, even as the Master did, that up there I may be amongst those risen from the dead, as He was, and have fellowship with Him who is the first-born from the dead. Certainly, those that are alive and remain shall have no preference, but I think that those who fall asleep will have a preference beyond them in that respect at any rate. Well then, let us rejoice and glory in tribulation also, and write down amongst the good things of God's gift in the covenant, amongst the things present and the things to come which are ours, our trials and the troubles of which our life is full.

Now, let us close by noticing the two together. I should like to hear these two bells ring together. If there is any roughness in one of them apart, ring them together, and you take it off. For instance, " Man that is born of a woman is of few days." Well, who wants to be of many days if they are full of trouble? Now, take it the other way: " Man that is full of trouble is of few days." Supposing it be thus, " Man is of few days and full of joy." What a clash! What a clash! A man says, " Then let me live." Full of joy! How it damps it all! Let a fight end as soon as you will, but a feast—let it continue. Must that lamp which shines so brightly go out soon and leave nothing but a smell of smoking flax? Ah! then the light itself is dimmed because it burns so short a time. But shortness of life becomes a blessing if it is full of trouble, and when life is short trouble itself seemeth to be congruous with it because it is so great a mercy that we are not to live for ever in the land of trouble. I like the two together. And then when I contrast them with the next life, man that is born of the Spirit is of eternal immortality and full of joy, the heart comes away from the gloomy text like a wedding guest at a banquet full of rejoicing, blessing the name of the Lord, and so do you too, brethren, every one of you, for Christ's sake. Amen.

X.

THE GLORY OF THE GRACE OF GOD.

The glory of His grace.—(Ephesians i. 6.)

GRACE! It is the subject of the Bible all through. You will tell me that the Bible speaks of the Fall of Man. Yes, and it does so that it may put a black foil for the bright jewel of grace. You will remind me that the Scripture speaks of the depravity of the human heart and of the corruptions of the various portions of our race. Most true again. I would say it treats of the disease that it might employ the remedy. Sin and depravity are brought to light in order that we may see what grace it is that forgives sin and overcomes the depravity of our nature.

This whole Book is a volume upon grace. You cannot find a single part of it that does not more or less bear upon that subject. It is true that it treats of the law, but the law is our schoolmaster to bring us to the school of grace, and while the commandment is exceeding broad and strict it only shows how great is the grace of God which forgives so many sins, and which, at the same time, works in us to will and to do according to God's good pleasure. Yes, the subject of the Bible is grace. Up in Heaven they sing of His grace, and here below on earth we have no sweeter song than that which tells us of the glory of the grace of God. I have a subject which cheers my own heart to speak upon; if there should be no eloquence and even little fluency, the subject is itself eloquent, and he that feels it in his heart will be sure to know how sweetly living waters flow from it.

Now let us speak of the glory of God's grace, first noticing the qualities of that grace in which its glory may be seen. We will dwell on that first. There are certain qualities in divine grace which are its glory. And surely the first is its freeness. We are accustomed to say " free grace," and I have heard some quarrel with it because it is a redundancy. If it is grace it must be free. That is very true; but there are certain gentlemen that have a kind of grace that is not free. Therefore

I go in for the redundancy, and I venture to say " free grace,"
that there may be no mistake about it. We sometimes, in
common language, speak of a thing as " free, gratis, and for
nothing." Well, I will even take the triplet and say that of the
grace of God—that it is free, gratis, and for nothing, and that
is the glory of it—the freeness of the grace of God. Why, see
how free it is. It comes to men that never sought it. It came
to any of us, who received it, long before we sought it or could
seek it, for it came to us before we were born. Christ Jesus
died for sinners before they lived on earth, many of them. We
were certainly redeemed by the precious blood before we had
actually fallen into sin, so that grace had the start of our
existence—much more of our seeking it.

But indeed, brethren, when we sought the Lord, though we
did not know it, the Lord had sought us long before. There
had been a work of His Spirit upon our hearts when we did
not know it. We thought that *we* said, " I will arise and go
unto my Father." So we did; but there was another parable,
if you remember, before the one that speaks of the return of the
prodigal son, and that tells us of a piece of money that was
lost, which could not find itself, and the house had to be swept
and the candle to be lit that it might be found; we are told of a
sheep that never thought of coming back, as sheep seldom do,
but the shepherd had to go after it and find it and lay it upon
his shoulder. Yes, in all cases when we come to God it is
because God first came to us.

And the freeness of this grace is manifested from the fact
that it comes to very unlikely persons. That verse was most
truthful—

It is Thy boast,
Into unlikeliest hearts to come,
The glory of Thy light to find
In darkest spots a home.

Why, the grace of God has come to persons who have been
abandoned in character, and it has reclaimed them. It has
come to those who have been blasphemous and profane, and yet
it has renewed their hearts. It has come to persecutors, to those
desperately set on mischief and arrested them in their madness,
sobered and renewed them and made them to be servants of
the very Master whom once they opposed. It is free indeed when
it comes to such as these. And I count it very free indeed that
it should have come to me, for though, perhaps, I might put
myself, as many of you would, among those whose outward

lives could not have been considered to be so desperately wicked, yet, what with the pride of our hearts, the self-righteousness of our natures, and the stubbornness of our wills and the reluctancy of our souls to close in with Christ, having sinned against so much light and so much knowledge, the wonder is that God did not leave us to choose our own delusion. It was a marvel of grace that we should have become the subjects of it! And I think I speak the mind of my brethren and sisters in Christ if I say that if there were no other instance on record of the sovereignty of divine grace, each one of us would claim to be a record in the matter. It was sovereign grace that chose us and looked upon us.

I.

Now I am so glad to have this to say, because I do not see why the grace of God should not look on some here to-night —some of the most unlikely people. Did you come here to get something to laugh at? The grace of God may send you away weeping for your sins. I pray it may. Did you come in here after having misspent the rest of the day and many previous Sabbaths too, and do you think you are never likely to be converted? Come, Thou eternal Spirit, come. As the lightning's flash strikes the loftiest oak, come Thou and split the heart in twain with irresistible force! O God of love, Thou hast but to stretch out Thy sceptre and the most rebellious heart must yield to Thee. Let it be so, and glory shall be given to Thy grace. The first point, then, is its freeness.

But the next is its omnipotence, for, wherever the grace of God comes it is omnipotent grace. I do not say it is always put forth omnipotently, for the Spirit of God sometimes works without putting forth all His strength and then men resist Him, ay, and successfully resist Him too. " Ye do always resist the Holy Spirit, as did also your fathers," said Stephen of old. There is such a thing as striving against Him; and He will not always strive with men. But when the Spirit of God comes forth with the power of divine grace, then there is no longer any resistance. It is not that the man could not still resist if he would, but it is that he would not if he could, for when grace comes it changes the nature and transforms the heart. I suppose it operates somewhat in this way: the man is prejudiced, but when grace comes it takes away his prejudice. His understanding is darkened: he thinks that bitter is sweet and sweet bitter; grace comes and he sees clearly, knows the bitter to be bitter and the sweet to be sweet. Then at once, his understanding being enlightened, his will becomes affected, for a man does not naturally will towards that which he feels will be to himself evil; but now, knowing that such a thing would be evil he wills to leave it, and knowing now that such a thing is good, being taught by the Spirit, he wills to seek that which he knows to be good to himself. The will thus becomes tutored and trained. The bit is put into the mouth of the will—the most stubborn of all things. No sword can come at some men's wills. They are like Leviathans: they laugh at the spear: the sword comes not at them, but when the Eternal lays to His mighty sword, how he drives through Leviathan's scales and brings down his pride and glory. We have seen some great sinners that never trembled before shake like aspen leaves when the wind of the Eternal Spirit has blown upon them. There is nothing that the power of eternal grace cannot overcome. And when the will is subdued the affections go in a different channel.

If some traveller were to come home some day and tell us that while looking at the waters of Niagara he had suddenly seen the waters leap upward, instead of down, and the whole of the rivers began to flow towards the lakes, we should not credit it. But if it were true, it would not be so great a miracle as when a man's entire nature that has been rushing down to the sea of destruction with great leaps, with cataracts of evil, is suddenly turned the other way and made to seek God, the God from whom he so impetuously fled. Yes, the grace of God can do that, and that is one of the glories of grace. If a man be so bad that only the devil himself is worse, yet the grace of God can renew him. If his heart be as cold as an iceberg and as hard as an adamant stone, yet can the grace of God thaw him and break him; and though his nature be as a dreary Sahara with its burning sand, if Death has marched over it and destroyed whatever of life may once have been in it, yet God's Spirit may come and make the desert to blossom like Sharon, ay, like the garden of the Lord. This is, then, another part of the glory of that grace: it is free: it is omnipotent.

Another part of its glory lies in this, that it is always consistent with the other attributes of God. The grace of God never interferes with any other of the great characteristics of the Most High. You have heard some blunderers say that if God does not pardon sin without an atonement there is no grace in it. Poor fools! It is grace the more transcendently displayed, because, in the wisdom of God, grace full-orbed is not permitted to eclipse any other attribute of Deity. Observe, God is just. God might be merciful at the expense of justice, but I question whether it would be mercy, for it is not mercy to a community to let off a criminal. I am not sure that our lives are any safer because certain murderers of late, for whom I could not see any reason for mercy, have been exempted from the rights of justice. I am not sure your houses would be more safe at night or our brethren in the street if the judges were to suffer the burglars and garroters to go free without punishment. It would be a mercy to them, perhaps, but not to us. Now, God's mercy is mercy and truly so, and does not interfere with justice, for God is as just in the case of every forgiven sinner as He would have been if that sinner had been cast into hell. The vengeance on that sinner has been borne by Jesus Christ. The Son of God has paid the debt, and therefore the sinner is discharged. It was grace that gave the sinner such a Saviour; but it is the very glory of grace that it is perfectly consistent with the sternest justice.

So is the grace of God consistent with divine truth. If God had to take back a word He had ever spoken in order to save men, it would be a great misfortune; for God cannot be suspected of falsehood or of suffering His word to fall to the ground. If He were, the foundations of society would be loosened, and the world would be greatly the loser by it, however much the mercy might be praised up by some. But there is no threatening of God's justice violated; there is no single word which has gone forth out of His mouth but which has been met by its fulfilment. The laws, like the laws of the Medes and Persians, have never been altered, but a new law has come in over the rest of which God, without interfering with the former, has certainly been true.

And certainly it is consistent with holiness. If you meet with a man who says, " I have the grace of God, and therefore live in such and such a sin," the man speaks falsely. The grace of God never was the father of any sin, ay, and never will be ! The apostle says of some who declared that they lived in sin that grace might abound that their damnation was just—as if he meant to say, " Everybody knows, and everybody can see with half an eye that their damnation is strict justice." No, the grace of God has never in this world caused a man to do wrong to his fellow-men, nor to do wrong towards his God. It has a holy influence wherever it comes, and when it has full-play it sanctifies the heart that comes under its power and makes it perfect—taking it away to Heaven.

And let me say that the grace of God is always consistent with divine goodness. I mean this, that though the grace of God does not come alike to all men, that there are some men who receive it and are saved by it while others perish in their sins—yet the grace of God never has done an injustice to any man. There will be no man at God's bar at last that will be able to charge Him with partialities. It is very easy to fling that word about now, but it shall not be so then. There shall be no sinner with a valid excuse. There shall be no sinner that can lay his sin on God's back or his ruin at the feet of the Most High. Every soul saved shall glorify the grace of God, but there will not be in the salvation of that soul a single infringement upon the benevolence of God or His strict justice towards the sons of men. He knows how that may be done. We may not be able to justify His ways to men : we are content to give Paul's answer, " Nay but, O man, who art thou that repliest against God ?"

II.

Now, another point. It is a part, as I believe, of the glory of divine grace that it is immutable. Certain brethren think that God's grace comes to men and then leaves them. We have not so learned Christ. Where the grace of God begins— effectually begins and the heart of the man is really changed, the work which has been begun will be completed. There will be much opposition to that completion from the flesh and from temptations from without and from Satan; but he that began to build is not a vain builder who cannot finish. He that goeth out to this war is not one whose forces are too weak to encounter the gigantic enemy. Bless the Lord, O my soul! Thou hast to deal with an immutable Jehovah! " I am God! I change not; therefore ye sons of Jacob are not consumed." The grace that can be lost is a grace well lost. The only grace worth having is the grace which, when it takes hold of us, never lets us go, but lands us safely in glory, according to that ancient promise, " The Lord will give grace and glory. No good thing will He withhold from them that walk uprightly."

One other feature of this grace is its all-sufficiency. It is the glory of grace that it meets every want of the sinner. If the sinner is dead, it gives him life; if he be filthy, it gives him washing; if he be naked, it gives him clothing. Is the sinner hungry? It feeds him. Is he thirsty? It gives him drink. Do the sinner's wants grow even larger after he becomes a saint, or has he a deeper apprehension of them? Then the supplies are just as deep as his necessity. Bottomless mines are the treasures of divine grace :—

> Deep as our helpless miseries are,
> And boundless as our sins.

You will never get to a point where grace will fail you—never come to an extremity where you will have to say, " Here, at last, the arm of grace is palsied, and I must look elsewhere for succour." Oh, no, from this spot to the brink of Jordan and through the Jordan and up to the great white throne of judgment, and through the judgment, and until body and soul, re-married in a splendid marriage for eternity, shall sit down at the wedding feast above—till then there shall be no failures in grace, nor shall we ever have to think of it as otherwise than all-sufficient.

Thus we have briefly run over a few of the characteristics which are the glory of divine grace. Who would not have such grace as this?

And now, secondly, only a few minutes, we want to talk a little about where the glory of God's grace may be best seen. I think there are two or three places I could take you to. One is in the new convert. Just look at him. You see how joyous he is, full of gladness, and that gladness runs down his cheeks in glistening floods of tears. Do you know that man? A little while ago that man was wretched and unhappy. A little farther back than that he was happy, but it was a happiness like the crackling of a burning thorn : it blazes and it is gone. He used to enjoy the company of those who talked lasciviously. Possibly he was licentious himself. He loved the settle in the ale-house; he would be found amongst those who broke the Sabbath and profaned God's name. Look at him now! He tells you he is pardoned; he has looked to Christ, and his soul has been lightened, and you can see by the very look of the man that a very strange change has come over him. He is a new creature in Christ Jesus. I recollect when such a change came over me. Do not many of you remember that time? And oh! what the glory of God's grace was to you! You had been on the brink of hell, and you were saved; you had felt a sentence of condemnation in your own conscience, and there you were absolved. Every sin was gone; you were clean as the driven snow; you were accepted in the Beloved as much as if you had been a saint all our days, instead of a sinner, and you were perfectly saved by the simple act of faith—faith in the bleeding Saviour. Oh, there was glory in God's grace that day!

And now I will take you to another spot. The glory of God's grace may often be seen in believers. I have seen it in believers in their poverty—when they have had to bear much hardship, but they have not repined but thanked God for what they had. I have seen it in Christians in their temptations, when, like Joseph, they have said, " How can I do this great wickedness and sin against God?" I have seen it in believers when under very heavy trials. Their children have died; perhaps the wife or the husband has died also, and the one left behind has said, " The Lord gave, and the Lord hath taken away," and, though it choked them almost to say it, they have added, " blessed be the name of the Lord." " Though He slay me, yet will I trust in Him."

Now, that was the glory of God's grace, and I have seen this often, and I trust you have and felt it too. And how that glory has been seen in the hour of death! Many and many a time one has stood by the dying bed and envied the departing saint—envied him, because, though the bones were ready to start through the skin, he certainly had a happier portion than we had who were in health and strength. His mind was more resting upon Christ and more in peace, and he seemed more full of ecstasy and joy. I have heard things from the lips of dying saints which I never heard from living ones—I mean never anything so choice. Poets have never been able to rival the mysterious utterances of departing believers when Heaven has shone right in upon their faces, and they have begun to hear the singing of the everlasting choirs. Oh yes, grace has been glorious there! And you read, in the Book of Martyrs, and in other works, how the saints of God have died—have died on the rack, have died in the dungeon, or have died at the stake, and yet with all that have gloried in the God of their salvation. Are not these things written in the Book of the wars of the Lord! There can ye see what He hath done, making them strong and for the timid in making them brave. Recollect the name of Anne Askew, sitting down on cold damp slabs, when they had racked her till there was not a single bone in her frame but was full of pain.

I

I am not she that list
My anchor to let fall
For every drizzling mist;
My ship's substantial.

She felt that God was in her heart. She called the rack and all its mockeries but a drizzling mist, not storm enough; she felt such scorn for the cruelties they were able to put upon her. Yes, there is glory in God's grace in such a case as that.

But now I wish I had the power of a Dante or a Milton, and could bear you into the air away into the region where the Prince of Darkness holds his court. I would take you away at least to the brink of that drear pit, that awful prison-house of souls condemned by the justice of the Most High. If you could stand, and but for a moment see the smoke of their torment and hear the cries and moans of spirits for ever withered by the breath of justice, I should then say to you, " That would have been my fate and yours if it had not been for the grace of God." And as we started back from that dread abyss and dare not look upon it, and closed our ears to those terrific sounds, we should feel, " O God! how boundless is Thy grace that has kept us from those dark abodes of woe!" And then, if some seraph could bear us up to the seventh heaven, and place us there upon the sea of glass commingled with fire, and we could stand awhile upon that placid but lustrous deep and hear the harpers harping with their harps, and receive our own harp and have our own crown put upon our head, as surely we shall if the grace of God has looked upon us—if we could bow amongst them there and chant Emmanuel's praise, then too would this thought come into our souls, " Oh, the glory of this grace that lifts up spirits that might have been damned to become glorified, and makes immortals that might have been immortal in their agony to become immortal in their bliss. O glorious grace! Where are the words with which we can speak of thee! We want our harps, our golden harps, to sing thy praise; we want the freedom of a spirit that is perfected and gloried in order to be able to express thy majesty."

III.

And now we must close by just a few practical words, in the last place, as to how we can manifest the glory of this grace. And I would say to every believer here, the first thing is, let us take care to ascribe our salvation always to the grace of God. I am always glad when God's people can speak plainly; there are some of them that can't. I know they are my brethren and sisters, and I love them for all that, but I don't like to hear them go stammering and stuttering about the house as some of them do. For there are some people that cannot say " Grace," but somehow or other there is a sound of " Law " gets in it. They cannot say " Grace " outright; they mix up the Old Covenant along with the New. Some seem to know Christ after Moses, and mistake Moses's rod for Christ's cross. It is a very different thing. I believe in studying theology; the great necessity for a student is to know the difference between Sinai and Zion, between Sarah and Hagar, between Jerusalem and Arabia. I want to know what grace is and what works may be; but you cannot mix them. They are like oil and water; they won't mix together. If it is of works, it is all works, if it is of grace, it is all grace. If I am to get to Heaven by my own merit, I must get there purely and simply by my own merit : I cannot get there partly by merit and partly by grace. And if grace, it is all grace. A man may trust partly in works and partly in grace, but he has, as it were, one foot on land and one on sea, and he will go down certainly. He is between two stools and must go to the ground. It is grace to begin, grace to go on with and grace to end with, or else you must not try grace at all, but must try your own works and try to work your way to Heaven, which you will never do. It will be a grievous failure. Try to ascribe everything to your God. There are some of God's people who never will do that till they go to the college where Jonah went to study. A strange college it was in a lonely region in the depths of the sea. He was in a whale's belly; and there it was that he became a Calvinist, for he said, " Salvation is of the Lord." If we could send some of our friends to the same academy, it would be a great mercy to them. Do try to ascribe salvation—everything—to grace.

Next, let us glory in the grace of God before other people. Don't be ashamed to tell what God has done for you. Don't be ashamed to own that you know what grace is, and to tell it out plainly by your lives as well as by your talk ; and if you want to bring glory to the grace of God, live in the energy of it. I am afraid we are all getting into a sleepy state again. We did have a more lively time. Some little while ago revivals were pretty common. They were not all of them good for much, but some of them were, and the Church did seem to pray and be awake. But now there is a spirit of slumber almost everywhere. There are happy exceptions, but I am afraid they are few. If we want to glorify God's grace, we must glorify it in action. We must pray mightily that He will bring in thousands and tens of thousands into the Christian Church; for Infidelity is opening its mouth very wide. So, also, Ritualism is doing its very best, and what is wanted as an answer to both Rationalism and Ritualism is that the grace of God might be displayed in its mighty power. Oh, that the Lord would save some big sinner, some great member of Parliament, some priest, some man who has preached false doctrine! Would God that He would save some big sinner—I repeat the word—some thief, some drunkard and bring in some whose conversion would astound the sons of man and make them say, " This is the finger of God." The Lord send it, and He shall have the praise. But may we all live to the praise of the glory of His grace.

One thing more, and that is, if we would see the glory of God's grace, let us believe the truth, let us trust ourselves to it, let us cast our souls upon it. Sinner, if you will come to Christ, He will not reject you. If you were to come to God pleading your own works, you must be driven from His presence, but if you will come and appeal to His mercy and rely upon His grace, He cannot and will not reject you. He delighteth in mercy. God is more glad to give it than you will be to have it. It is His heart's joy to bless the sons of men. Seek mercy to-night through Jesus Christ, and you shall have it. Go to your chamber and cry mightily. Yea, on the spot may God incline you to put your trust in Jesus, and you shall find that grace most rich and free will come to you. Even at this moment perfect pardon for a life of sin is to be had for one look at the crucified Saviour.

God give us that look, that we may give that look to Christ. Amen and amen!

XI.

WHEN GOD SPEAKS.

I will hear what God, the Lord, will speak; for He will speak peace unto His people, and to His saints; but let them not turn again to folly.—(Psalm lxxxv. 8.)

IT would be difficult to say how low a true Christian might fall as to inward grace and as to consolation. I hope none of us will ever make the experiment; but certain it is that there are times with some Christians when they walk so carelessly that by-and-bye the joy of their religion departs from them, the confidence of their faith becomes weakened, their love becomes so dim as to be like an expiring spark, and they themselves walk in darkness and see no light. We have known them at such times entertain doubts as to whether they ever had any religion, whether, after all, they have not been deceived, if not deceivers; and then at such times their conscience will grievously lash them, reminding them of the joys they once possessed, of the days when the candle of the Lord shone round about them, and if they have been highly favoured saints before, so much the greater will be their anguish of spirit when they seem to hear the Lord saying, " I will go and return unto My place until they confess their transgressions. Surely in the days of their affliction they will seek Me earnestly."

It may be even, and it often is so, and it is a blessing it is so, too, that while the heart is thus brought down with anguish the hand of God also goes out against His erring child in providence. We have known the backsliding Christian's business begin to slack and to fail him. We have known, at the same moment, sickness come into his family, children have died, the wife has sickened. Or, perhaps, the hand of God has gone out against his body; there has been some disease in his person or some damage to his limbs; he has known what wearisome days and sleepless nights mean. Now, when two seas of inward trial and of outward affliction meet, the Christian will be awakened to cry unto his God. If he can continue to sleep then, ay, and if he become provoked against the Most High, and be led to go from one sin to another and from bad to worse, there will be in that man a sign of reprobation, not of election; but if he be a child of God when he feels first of all his own heart smiting him—that is a hard blow—and then feels God's chastisements smiting him at the same time, he will discover that he is in a very evil case, and he will lift his eyes up towards his God to know what he may do to be delivered therefrom.

The mercy is that out of this state there is a way of escape. No child of God ought to sit down contented in it. It is for every Christian that has lost his first love to seek it again, for every believer who has descended from his former lofty estate to pine and sigh and cry until the Lord shall bring him up again, yea, and lift him up to yet a loftier position than he occupied before. It is not the Lord's will that His children should be in bondage: it is not at His desire that they are brought low. Even their affliction He sends unwillingly, for " He doth not grieve the children of men for nought."

Now, this evening's text will be mainly useful to those who are in the condition I have indicated; but some of you who are not in that state may lay it by in store for the possibilities which you may have, and, perhaps, the word spoken to-night may be in readiness against some evil time which may be drawing near.

Notice that the text divides itself very naturally into three parts. The first part we shall call the resolution of wisdom :— " I will hear what God the Lord will speak." The second part is an expectation of confidence :—" For He will speak peace unto His people and to His saints." But the third is a warning of prudence :—" But let them not turn again to folly."

I.

First, then, we have before us in the text a resolution of wisdom on the part of one who desires revival, feeling that he is wandering from God and is suffering in soul. Notice the resolution :—" I will hear what God the Lord will speak." It is the man brought up to a dead stand. He has wandered; he has lost his way; he is in the thick darkness and he stands still. His soul had before been gadding abroad, and wandering after a thousand objects, but now in his deep distress he says, " I will wait upon my God. I will hear what God Jehovah will speak."

There is evidently upon the mind here a sense both of divine majesty, which awes him, and also of divine faithfulness, which encourages and attracts him. " I will hear what God the Lord shall speak." I ought to hear what He speaks. Is He not God? Is He not the self-existent Jehovah, the I Am That I Am? My heart, thou hast got into this low estate by listening to other voices; thou hast deprived thyself of comfort by forgetting His promises; thou hast brought thyself into sin by being unmindful of His commands; thou hast been negligent of His voice of love and of His voice of rebuke. Stand still now, and be ashamed of thyself, and be humbled, and from this time close thine ear to all other sounds and resolve to hear what God the Lord shall speak. You see it is a sense of the authority of the divine voice that comes over the soul, and therefore it resolves that to whatever else it shall be deaf it will certainly listen to the voice of God.

And then that same authority seems to prompt the spirit of confidence, for it saith within itself, " Now I am in this condition—that none can help me but God. No voice but God's can direct me; no voice but His has power in it to deliver me, therefore for this very reason I will not wait to hear what anyone else may say, but I will go direct to God and hear what He has to say. Perhaps if I wait upon the preacher he may not understand my experience, or he may come without being sent, and what are a mortal's words if there be no God at the back to inspire him? I will not run to Christian friends and ask their advice; that may be useful at some other time, but I have come to this position that nothing will suit me now but the voice of God. When I have wandered so far, no brother's voice can call me back: the Father Himself must call me. When I have sunk so low as to be like Lazarus in his grave, no disciple's voice can call me forth to newness of life; the Master Himself must speak. Therefore I will hear what God the Lord shall speak."

Oh, there is great wisdom in this resolution to anyone at any time, but especially to anyone who knows that he has come into a low state of grace. Dear brother, dear sister, I know you desire to get out of that condition. Now, sitting in the pew, let this be your resolve—and may grace sustain you in the carrying of it out—" I will now hasten to my God; my

spirit shall say to Him, 'Speak, Lord, for Thy servant
heareth.' I will get me to my first husband, though I have
wandered, for it was better with me then than it is now. I
will go back to my Noah, to my rest, as the dove did, which,
though it flew over the waste of waters, could find no resting
place for the sole of its foot. I will go back to that ark. I
will go back to my God. I will hear what God the Lord will
speak.''

That seems to me the first point in the resolution—the pro-
minence that it gives to the divine authority and the implicit,
though unexpressed, confidence which is placed in the voice of
God, if it be but heard.

Now, let us note, dear brethren and sisters, in trying to
carry out this resolution, that God speaks to us in various
ways, and if we will hear what God the Lord shall speak we
must be attentive to the many voices.

Of course, He speaks to us in His Word. This is the surest
light of prophecy, and we do well to take heed to it. This is
the chart of every Christian mariner. These are the commands
of the great captain of our Holy War, and we ought to be
more diligent in reading the Bible—not only in reading more
of it—perhaps we do not err there—but in reading it more
solemnly—not reading it with the eyes, as some do, but reading
it with the very soul, sucking in the Scripture as the sponge
drinks in the water, being filled with it to the very full, with
holy spiritual thought after the Word of God. If you have
backslidden, my dear brother, you cannot do better than
become a more constant searcher of Scripture. Say, " I will
hear what God the Lord shall speak. Perhaps I have become
discouraged because I did not hear His promises; perhaps I
have grown careless because I did not hear His admonition;
perhaps I have grown weak because I did not receive strength
through feeding upon the manna of His Word : I will, therefore, go to Scripture again and hear what God the Lord shall
speak.''

And, beloved, you must also hear that word as it is spoken
by God's servants. Alas, I am afraid there are many
Christians who do not care to hear God's word in the pulpit.
I mean this, that in the choice of a ministry they seek after
that which may be fashionable, or attractive, or pleasing to
the ear, whereas the true gauge of a ministry is, Does God
speak through it to the soul? If not, beware of it. Though
it be called your own Parish Church, it is no better to be

starved in a Parish Church than anywhere else. Though it may be the meeting house your fathers always attended, it is no better for your soul to be famished in the family meeting house than anywhere else. Seek not after the best garnished, not that which most charms your ear, but that which feeds your soul. Be resolved that Sundays are too precious to be wasted in listening to displays of oratory and say, " I will hear what God the Lord shall speak." " Take heed what you hear," and " Take heed how you hear," for both precepts are equally valuable. May that be our resolve that we will hear God's voice as it speaks to us from the ministry.

But then the Lord speaks to His people in another way, viz., in providence, and I wish we had an ear to hear there. Christians with little troubles should hear the twigs of the rod, for those that won't hear the twigs will have to hear the harder part of the rod. If we would hear God whisper we should not need to hear God thunder. No doubt many of our trials come upon us severely because lesser trials are of no service. A good physician does not administer to a patient the most violent drug at first, but, if there must be medicine, he begins with that which is weaker, for, perhaps, that may meet the case. But, if not, sooner than the patient should die, he will be sure to give the most violent medicines he can. And it is so with God. He dealeth tenderly with us. " Be not as the horse or as the mule which have no understanding, whose mouth must be held in with bit and bridle lest they come near unto thee." For many sorrows must be with the wicked. If we were not so prone to go with the wicked our sorrows might be less. Let us ask God in every providence, " Lord, what dost Thou mean by this?" for providence is like a hieroglyphic from God—only some eyes can make out the meaning. God writes to us in everything that happens to us through the day. Not without God doth anything happen, and God doth nothing without a meaning. Now, very frequently, if a man would read, he might read his sin in his chastisement. He might discover wherein he had erred by the very form of the chastisements that came upon him. May we have grace, then, since there are ways of understanding God's meaning, to find it out and to profit by it. " I will hear what God the Lord will speak."

Besides that, God has a voice in our hearts. There is a voice in His withdrawing from us. Have you lost the light of God's countenance? He need not speak: there is a voice in that. What doth He say but this, " I cannot walk with thee, for thou dost not walk with Me aright. Have I not said, ' With the forward I will show Myself forward? Can two walk together except they be agreed?' " The Lord, in leaving you to yourself, is saying, " Thou hast trusted too much to thyself. Thou didst try to do without Me. Now see how thou canst! I leave thee to thyself that thou mayest discover how weak a thing is an arm of flesh." And truly there may be often heard in the heart, if we listen to it, the voice of God's Spirit suggesting many things. I do believe the Spirit of God brings constantly to our view all the things within us and all the things of Christ for us; but, alas! there are some spirits that do not seem to be susceptible to the motions of the Holy Spirit at all. The Lord deliver us from that spiritual hardness of heart! " I will hear what God the Lord shall speak."

Now, as God speaks in different ways, so He also speaks in different tones, and it should be ours to desire to hear His voice in whatever tones He addresses us. Sometimes it is with rebuke, " My child, thou hast erred; thou hast gone astray; thou hast grieved My Spirit." Hear it! Hear it! Though the sound pierce through your heart, hear it. Who is there among you that desireth to be negligent at the rebuking voice of God? For if you are so, you will go into greater evil, and then, instead of rebukes, the Lord will have to use His rod to thee. It is always well for us to be willing to read and hear that which searches and tries us rather than that which continually comforts us. I know some hearers who always want sweet promises to be expounded. These are like little children that must always have sweets in their mouths, but wise men know that this is not the best of health. A tonic often does us good, and a soul-searching ministry is that which our soul should seek after. Be willing to hear God speak, though He speak no sweet things, but sharp things that go through and through your soul.

At the same time the Lord does speak very encouragingly and sweetly, and we ought to be just as willing to hear. You say, " Of course, we are," but I reply that there are some who are not; for there are children of God in a certain state who always put all encouragements away. Their soul abhorreth all manner of meat. If it be encouraging, " Oh," they say, " it can't be for me! It's too good to be true." Say not so, dear brother, but, rather, resolve, " I will hear what God the

Lord will speak. As I would have heard Him had He spoken roughly to me, much more if He speaks sweetly to me will I give my ear and my heart to Him: let Him say what he will."

And we ought especially to hear the Lord when we are in a sad condition if He speaks in a directing, teaching manner. No doubt many believers might rise into a refreshed state and again enjoy light and liberty, if they minded the directions of the Gospel. Sometimes a forgotten duty will be just like a decayed bone in the system, or a sin—perhaps a sin not known to be a sin—will be like a thorn in the foot which had not been perceived until it lamed the traveller. None of us know how much we may lose every day through neglecting to do the Lord's will in some point which we have considered to be non-essential. Every Christian duty is essential, not to salvation, but to consolation, and the omission of any known, aye, and I will say any unknown duty may involve great loss to us. It is ours, therefore, always to be saying, " Lord, tell me what I ought to be in any other point, and I will hear what Thou shalt have to say to me."

Now, I must note for a second or two how we ought to hear what God speaks to us. When the Psalmist said, " I will hear what God the Lord will speak," he did not mean, " I will casually hear it, as men hear a story in the streets," but, " I will hear it attentively, incline my ear to it, drink it in, hear it distinctively. I will detect the difference between man's voice and God's voice. I will not be misled by the human gloss, but I will hear the divine text; I will hear, separating as a sieve the chaff from the wheat, the precious from the vile, and I will hear with discrimination, and when I have heard it I will hear it with submission. If it be God's voice, I will not cavil at it. If the Lord shall say it, it shall not be for me to question. Has He said it? It must be right. And then I will hear it obediently. Whatever His word is, by His grace I will do as He bids me. If He saith, ' Go!' I will go; if He saith, ' Stay! ' I will stay."

I tell you, brethren and sisters, a man is not far from a very gracious state of soul-revival when he can use the words of the text in the sense which I have put upon them. If he be resolved now henceforth to be obedient unto the Word of God, it is not long before his brightness shall break forth as the morning and His glory as a lamp that burneth. He that stands in the thick darkness in the midst of a tempest in the mire, the deep waters all around him, yet standeth in a blessed and a hopeful state, if upon his heart and upon his tongue there are these gracious words, " I will hear what God the Lord shall speak." May that be the resolve of everyone here, for it is a personal resolve—" *I* will hear, if others do not : if there shall be no general revival of religion, no desire after it, yet *I* will hear what God the Lord shall speak. I will not be a mere talker; I will not merely enter into Christian conversation; I will not even work on with a deaf ear, but I will submit myself in quiet and bow before my Saviour. With Mary, I will sit at the Master's feet. This shall be my happy choice henceforth." So much for this wise resolve.

II.

Now, secondly, we have in our text an expectation of confidence—" For He will speak peace unto His people and to His saints." What a charming sentence that is ! How full of joy ! How it makes the heart leap ! " I will hear what God the Lord will speak, for He will speak peace." No dreadful things after all ! Though He speak rebukingly, though He speak in tones of thunder, yet the sum and substance, the drift and end of what He will have to say shall be peace to His people and to His saints.

I find that the word here might be rendered " prosperity." We will render it so, putting " peace " with it. " God will speak peace and prosperity to His saints ere long." And, dear brethren, is not this certain ? Must not God speak peace to His people, for is it not their portion ? Is not peace given to them in the covenant ? Let us go back again to where we were. Then God must give peace and prosperity to His children because it is guaranteed to them in the covenant of grace. Jesus Christ left it to them as a legacy, " Peace I leave with you ; My peace I give unto you : not as the world giveth give I unto you." And I cannot believe that the Holy Father will hold back from His people the legacy which His own Son has given to them. Oh, no, every drop of the blood of Jesus pleads for peace. All His wounds speak and plead for the prosperity of His people ; and, therefore, surely, the Lord will visit us again and bring us up even from the depths of the sea.

Moreover, is not it God's will that His people should be full of peace and happiness ? Think you He delights to 'see His people cast down and unhappy and declining and back-

sliding? Far from it. As a father delights in the healthiness
of his son, so does our Father delight in our prosperity. In
asking, therefore, for that which we know it will be His
delight to give, we may ask with perfect confidence. " He
will speak peace unto His people." And is it not for His own
glory? Can it ever be for God's glory for His people to go
downcast and weak and trembling, to lead useless and doubtful lives and to have " Ichabod " written upon the walls of
His Church? And shall His mighty Zion, which ought to be
the glory of all lands, become dishonoured, and His mighty
name blasphemed thereby? No, beloved, it is for God's
glory that His people shall arise and shine. The dead shall
not praise God ; those that go down into the pit shall not
give Him thanks. If He deliver the soul of His turtle-dove
to his adversaries, those adversaries will not praise Him. If
He forsake His people that will not enrich Him ; if He
withdraw His mercy, that will not honour Him. On the contrary, to lift up the hands that hang down, and to confirm
the feeble knees, will produce many a joyous song of praise
and fill both earth and heaven with hallelujahs. Therefore,
since it is for God's glory, we may rest assured He will speak
peace unto His people.

Now, Satan will be saying to some of you who have gone
astray and backslidden, " The Lord will never have another
good word for you. You have left Him, forsaken Him : His
wrath is hot against you." Beloved, believe not every spirit,
and especially believe not the evil spirit, for, be assured of
this one thing, that the Lord who loved His people once loves
them once for all. They say, " If a woman leave her husband and commit adultery, shall he return unto her again?
Shall not the land be polluted? " These are the words of
God Himself. " Yet," saith he " Return ! " Oh, glorious
grace ! He represents the soul of His servant as having committed the foulest of transgressions, and yet He says, " I am
married unto thee, saith the Lord. Return, ye backsliding
children ! "

Oh, may we feel that there is hope ; that however low we
may have fallen, there still is hope. Surely, if God meant
to cast away His servants, He would have cast away some
of us long ago ; but He has restored our souls, and He will
restore your soul and lead it in the way of righteousness,
for His name's sake. Go to Him, go to Him with the resolve
of our text, " I will hear what God the Lord shall speak,"

and He will speak to you—not words that shall say, " Depart, ye cursed," but He will put words into your mouth, and teach you to confess your sin and to humble yourself before Him, and then He will apply His promise with power to your soul.

III.

Now a third point of the text is a caution to prudence: " But let them not turn again to folly." Should your Lord visit you again, drive Him not away. Should you ever be restored to your former joy and peace, it will behove you to walk very carefully and guard your restored treasure with a double jealousy. It was folly, first of all, when you turned to sin. Sin is always folly. Now and then, men in business think that to do wrong will be a prudent thing under the circumstances; but sin is always folly. Sometimes it looks as if to lower the rigid standard of duty might, perhaps, be prudent for the occasion ; but sin is always folly—always folly—and they that sin find it to be so. When their God is gone, when the light of the Saviour's love is hidden, when the Spirit of God no longer quickens them to joy and strength, then they know that sin is folly. But let not the man that is restored from that folly go back to it again. When a child has eaten something which it has found in the fields which looked like a sweet berry and turns out to be poisoning, if after weeks of sickness it is still saved, even that child would have wisdom not to go back again to that. Master Bunyan represents young Matthew and others as eating some plums which grew in the devil's garden. The boughs hung over the wall where the pilgrims went, and he tells us how sick he was and long ill. We do not find that he went to eat of those plums again. " Let him not turn again to folly." We say, " a burnt child dreads the fire." There are some that burn their fingers first, and go and burn their arms afterwards. I know some professors who smarted under a sin at the beginning, and began to feel they were sliding little by little, and yet they have gone into it worse and worse, pursued it farther and farther, not only turning again to folly, but, as it were, being two fools in one, for he who, being a fool once, has learnt he was a fool, and then goes back to play the fool again is a fool with an emphasis. May we be delivered from ever turning again to such folly.

But I think I hear one of you say, " If ever I am restored and brought into full liberty, ever once again sit at the banquet of wine with the King and lean my head upon His bosom, I will never turn to folly again." " Thou art already foolish; thou speakest as one of the foolish women speak!" as Job said to his wife. Why, man, if God were to catch thee up into the third heaven, and then put thee down on earth again and leave thee one minute to thyself, thou wouldst play the fool with the worst of beings. There is no sin of which men would not be capable, if the Lord left them to themselves. The caution is needed: " Let them not turn again to folly." " Nay," says one, " I am cured of one sin; I shall never go into that." It is where thou thinkest thyself to be best cured that disease is most likely to break out again. Wherever thou canst say, " I am safe," be sure thou art in danger. Where thou hast a fear and trembling, there thou art probably secure, but where thou art carnally secured there it is that the evil comes. " Whereas thou sayest, I am rich and increased in goods, thou art naked and poor and miserable." From the very fact that thou boastest, thy glorying is not good, but is folly. " Let him not turn again to folly."

But there might be something plaintive in this in the dear Redeemer. When His sheep has gone astray, and He has gone weary miles to find it and brings it back upon His shoulders and puts it down, He might well say, " My sheep, turn not again to wander." To the prodigal restored to his father's house with a ring upon his finger and with shoes upon his feet, surely it might be said by a father's affectionate and anxious heart, " My son, turn not again to folly. Already thy follies have grieved thy Lord, have grieved His Church, have caused His name to be blasphemed, have robbed thee of the light of God's countenance and brought grey hairs upon thee here and there and spiritual debility. Wilt thou turn again to folly? Thou hast tasted the poisoned cup and thou knowest there is bitterness in the dregs thereof: wilt thou turn again to folly?"

I feel as if I could stand here and plead with the tears in my own eyes with some members of Christian churches who did once run well, and then slipped, but have been set up again and persevered for a long time, but begin to be slack again. Was not once enough? Why, the times past, before your conversion, might have sufficed thee to have wrought the will of the flesh: why wilt thou go back to work that will a second

time? Having been forgiven, wilt thou turn again to folly?
" Thus saith the Lord, What hast thou to do in the way of
Egypt to drink the waters of Sihor, or what hast thou to do
in the way of Assyria to drink the waters of the river? Turn
thou unto the Lord, for He shall give thee to drink of the
waters of life, clear as crystal! Why gaddest thou about
so much to change thy ways? Go to them not, but follow Him,
and keep close in the footprints of thy Saviour." " Let him
not turn again to folly."

What was the folly? I will hope it was not some gross
folly, some sin of the flesh. Oh, by the blood of Jesus, be
thou clean from that! And if it was thy pride, if it was thy
angry temper that broke loose, if it was thy self-reliance, if
it was thy worldliness, if it was thy love of dress—whatever
it was (I will not go into details)—turn not again to folly.
Oh, mark that sin! mark that sin. It has cost thee too much
already. Turn not to *that* again. Thou wilt not a second
time plead that thou wast deceived. " Surely in vain is the
net spread in the sight of any bird." Will the game come
into the trap which it knows to be a trap? The very birds
seem wiser than ourselves, if we turn again to folly; and yet,
dear friends, we need to turn this into a prayer, and while
God saith to us, " Let him not turn again to folly," we have
need to say it again, altering only one word, " Let *me* not turn
to folly." Oh, how grievous it is to think that those of us who
have borne an honourable character for twenty, thirty, or forty
years may, in five minutes, blast it all, though we may have
lived in the esteem of Christian brethren. One folly like a
fly in a pot of ointment may make the sweetest nard of the
apothecary to stink in the nostrils of men. " Hold Thou me up
and I shall be safe!" Infinite Jehovah, preserve Thy servants!
We will hear what Thou speakest. Thou wilt speak prosperity
to our souls. Oh, let us not turn again to folly!

We ask it for Jesus' sake. Amen!

XII.

IN GOD'S GARDEN OF REST.

For we which have believed do enter into rest.—(Hebrews iv. 3.)

" REST " is a blessed golden word. It is the one thing, surely, which the world seeks after. It may be true that every man seeks after happiness ; I question if it be not equally true that each man seeks after rest. There are some few fiery spirits who wish not to rest, who seem to be like thunderbolts that must speed on in their predestinated pathway, and only an incessant and morbid activity suits them at all ; but for the majority of us the expectation of rest is very sweet, and the enjoyment of it now in the poor measure in which we can get it is one of our greatest refreshments.

The present age needs rest abundantly. Our fathers travelled by the broad-wheeled waggon, but we are not content, or scarcely content even with the steam engine. " Faster and faster and faster " the demands of this world's commerce seem to be. What we have done we must do again, though it strained us once, and we must do twice as much, and then twice as much as that. All around us there seem to be louder cries and fiercer demands for yet greater speed. This it is, I do not doubt, that has filled our lunatic asylums, that sends many to a premature grave. We have forgotten our resting place, and become like a rolling thing before a whirlwind that does not rest, and I scarce know a greater curse that can fall on an age than this.

A great many things we are proud of are by no means improvements. If somebody would contrive an engine that would do as much and do as well and let us sleep a little longer and rest a little longer it might be just as well for the general good of poor flesh and blood. Mental rest the world craves after, for now-a-days everything seems unsettled. Moorings have been shifted, vessels that seemed to ride at anchor and had lain there many a day have found their anchorage yielding, and they are drifting out to sea. New

K

lights, instead of old, are constantly being demanded, and
he that used to teach out of the old Book is now requested not
to do anything of the kind, but to think out of his own head
and to give something better than God's thoughts, plucking up
the common flowers of earth and presenting them to men
instead of the stars of heaven, setting up the calf molten in
his own furnace and saying, " These be thy gods, O Israel."
Bondage !

Everywhere there is the same unrest. As for spiritual
unrest, it is discoverable by all those who really give any
attention to it. Certain grosser minds neglect their spiritual
needs, but those who think and seek after that which is high,
that which is eternal, that which is divinely pure, these are
crying still for rest. Noah's dove was one, but the others fly
as a cloud, these doves that seek rest and find none, and never
will find it till they come back to the ark of the covenant and
to the hand of that Noah who is God's rest as well as ours.
Do not we find in men's minds now the belief that they shall
get rest somewhere or other? To speak of common matters,
when we are yet young we consider our schoolboy days to be
full of slavery to books. We reckon that when we shall escape
from those we shall get some rest. We have been long unde-
ceived concerning that, and have found that the cares and
business of life make us almost envy the days when we under-
went the drudgery of the school.

I.

And now, it may be, we are looking forward. Many a
merchant expects when he has laid by sufficient, a competence
being realised, that he shall retire to some villa in the country,
and there get his rest. And yet we meet with aged men in
that condition, and do not find that, after all, they rest ; while
many never reach that mature old age in which they expect
to go beside the still waters. Those who do are still com-
plaining, still murmuring, wanting something else ; and still,
when their own cares are over, find the cares of children and
of grandchildren depriving them of rest. The notion of some
has been that rest was to be found in a country life. Get
away from the noise of traffic, from the multitudinous habita-
tions of men ; get away where nature was still in her virgin
simplicity ; and there would be rest ; and peasants have been

painted to us as being the very models and portraits of almost
beatific bliss. If you go there and hear their own story you
will soon be disenchanted of all idea of any rest being found
there.

Others with, perhaps, somewhat more practical sense,
have said, "No, not among the lowly and poor with very
many wants, shall we find rest ; but in the higher circles—
there where incomes are counted by thousands, and broad
acres can scarcely be numbered. There is rest." It has not
been found to be so, for the biographies of wealthy men,
famous men, learned men, statesmen, have gone far to show
that they were no more restful after their greatest success
than they were before, and that still they cried, " Who will
show us any good? " Still their soul, like the horseleech in
the Proverbs, cried " Give, give, give." Insatiable as the
grave, their spirit never could be satisfied with any of these
things.

Peradventure there are some here to-night who particularly ask for rest, for they seem to be inundated with trouble.
Wave upon wave, they have been tossed to and fro. They
seem to have only gone from one trial to another. " Rest,"
say they, " when is it to come? Working hard from morning
to night to earn a scant pittance, when shall I escape from
this drudgery? "

Now, my text is a word of consolation, for, first, it gives
the good news. It tells you that there are some who have
rest ; and on the strength of it I feel permitted to give you
advice, namely, to urge many here, and to direct them as
well, to the place where they can find rest for their souls.
Very briefly indeed.

First, here is good news. There are some persons
that have found rest. " For we which have believed do enter
into rest."

Who are these persons? The reply is, they are not
strangers ; they are not persons in some remote country ; they
are not a people in some ancient golden age long since past ;
nor are they the sort of persons who are to walk in the
millennial period. No, there are persons here who have
believed and have entered into rest—persons of your age, and
your station in life, and your capacity of mind, persons once
guilty of your sins and still subject to your infirmities. In
many cases, let me add, these persons who have entered into
rest are your own relatives. Some of you have a father who

K 2

has believed and entered into rest. Many of you have mothers in that happy condition, and brothers and sisters and kinsfolk of all degrees. They have believed and have entered into rest. And they are not enthusiastic persons who tell you what is not true, not fanatical persons whose imagination supplies them with facts. You know them and esteem them. You live with them ; you know that they are persons of credit ; you place every confidence in them ; in fact, you love them. And they will tell you to-night, when you reach home, if you wish to hear the story—and I trust you may—that they have believed and have entered into rest. There are many of us now present who without any exaggeration can declare that since the dear hour which brought us to the Saviour's feet, when grace enabled us to look to Him and trust in Him, we have, in very deed and of a truth, entered into rest.

Now, our text tells us that these people "entered." It points to the gateway, the pearly gate of this golden garden of the Hesperides. It tells the way to enter into this Paradise of rest. "We that have believed do enter into rest." The way to perfect peace with God, with conscience, and with our fellow-men, is the way of faith ; faith in God, faith in what God has revealed, especially faith in His Son Jesus Christ. He that will have rest must come to the cross-foot, must there confess his sin and leave it there, must look up and see the streaming wounds of Emmanuel, and accept the substitutionary sacrifice of the dying Son of God. He that has done that has entered into rest. He that shall do that shall enter into rest. Moses canot show you the gateway into rest. He can show you the gate through which Adam was driven when the flaming sword in the Cherubim's hands guarded the way. That Cherubim stands there still, and his sword is not sheathed. By the way of works no man can enter into rest, since the works of all men are deficient, imperfect, and fall short of the demands of God. But, by the way of trusting, there is an accessible road.

I am sure many here ought to be thankful indeed that there is such a way into rest, for had it been by the way of works they could not have entered ; but by the way of faith even the sinner can enter and, however defiled he may have been, he can approach unto the throne of God by the exercise of faith in the righteousness of another, even the Son of God. It is by believing that we get rest—by no other means, not by scheming and plotting and planning and thinking and criticising and judging and doubting and questioning, but by believing—the submission of the soul to God's truth, the yielding of the heart to God's salvation. This once done we lie down in green pastures, and are led beside the still waters.

II.

Now, I have thus spoken of the persons who have found rest, and of the gate by which they enter the golden garden. They shall tell you—and I will be their spokesman—something of the walks of that garden, something of those beds of spices whence they get the fragrance of rest. They will tell you that they find much of their rest in what they have experienced. They have experienced the complete pardon of sin, for those who have believed in Jesus are forgiven. A free pardon is issued from the King of Heaven to every believer in Jesus. Now, if sin be pardoned we are secure. Even death has no sting. Besides, that is a precious walk in the garden of rest. Once get sin pardoned, beloved, and how can you help resting? Your spirit must rejoice when Jesus Christ has washed your sins away. They have, since that, experienced acceptance in the Beloved, for whoever believes in Jesus is acceptable to God. God looks upon him with complacency ; He deals with him as a righteous person. And this is no small privilege—to be acceptable with God. Oh, this is a delightfully cool walk in the garden of rest, and happy is the man who can walk up and down in it. Pardoned of sin and accepted in the righteousness of Christ—that man has now experienced an acquiescence in the divine will. He feels now that the Lord may do what He likes with him. If He has forgiven him, He may do whatsoever He pleases with him. Now will he say, " Strike, Lord, for Thou hast forgiven me. I will have no questionings with Thee, since I have had such proofs of Thy love." And when the mind is perfectly willing that God should do as He pleases, it cannot but rest. Now this is no small blessing to have been brought into peace with God through the forgiveness of sin, through the clothing of the soul with righteousness, and by the spirit being made cheerfully to submit to the ruling will of God. Blessed walks are these in this golden garden.

And then they tell you that they find much peace from what they know by faith. Here are some of their secrets. They who have believed know by faith that God loved them before the world began. They believe in eternal love—love which never had a beginning. They rejoice to know they were chosen in Christ from before the foundations of the world. If you knew that, would not that give you rest? Well, it gives believers rest. They know also by faith that God loves them immutably ; that He cannot love them more and will not love them less ; that His love never changes, and cannot be removed from its present objects. The people of His choice He cannot, will not cast away. They know this ; they know that change as they may they have an unchangeable God to deal with. Think you, does not this give them rest?

They also know that the work which saves their soul is a finished work—that it is not half done, but all done. They are saved. For their pardon there is no need for a fresh ounce of suffering; for their clothing there is no need of a fresh thread of righteousness. They are complete in Christ —completely saved, and they know that, come what may, they never shall be lost. "For there is therefore now no condemnation to them that are in Christ Jesus." He has given to His sheep " eternal life, and they shall never perish, neither shall any pluck them out of His hands."

Do not these things give them rest, think you? Surely if they did not rest they must be acting inconsistently with the nature and with the reason of things. They also know by faith that they are one with Christ, joined to Him as the wife is to the husband, in bonds that never can be snapped, joined to Him as the member is to the head, for we are members of His body, of His flesh and of His bones. Oh, what joy there is in this truth! Surely he that knows it to be true of himself by faith cannot but enter into rest. How could it be that he should be disturbed in spirit? So I have shown you the things they experience and one or two of the things they know by which they enter into rest.

And there are some things implanted into believers' minds that make them enter into rest ; for, unless you change a man's nature, he won't rest, if you put him where you will. After all, our happiness more depends upon our own hearts than upon anything else. The believer has a new heart; he has a contented heart ; he has a heart submissive to the divine will ; he has a heart that does not live in the present, but lives in the future ; he has a heart that looks across the river of Death, a soul that rejoices to live upon invisible things and eternal things.   Scant may be his table here, but he eats the bread of angels; wretched may be his garments, but he wears about him robes of royalty.   He may be despised of men, but he knows he is a son of God.   He may not have a foot of land, a freehold of his own, but he knows that the whole of Heaven is his from its Dan to its Beersheba.   Such a mind as that cannot but be restful—as a mind made to conform to God and to rejoice in Him.   Such a man must have rest; it cannot be otherwise.

III.

Note again that these persons, though they have entered into rest, have to say to you, " We have only *entered into* rest; we don't profess to know all about it—we have only *entered* it."   They may have entered into rest, but they are still as it were in the first part of the garden.   They believe that there are inner walks where the fruit is more luscious, where the fountains are more cool, where the brooks flow with milk and honey more plentifully.   They have entered into rest.   They bless God for that, but they have only entered it. And this is one reason why you sometimes find Christians disturbed.   They have not got far enough into the garden of rest to lose the sound of dogs outside.   They can hear the howling of the hell-dogs at the garden gates, though they have come into rest.   They are like men in one of our ships covered with impenetrable armour, shot at still; and though they are not fatally wounded they can hear the balls strike on the iron outside and they are troubled somewhat.   And there are times when they don't live by faith as they ought, and then they lose their rest; for it is only as they believe that they enter into rest.

I know there are some Christians who do not believe about daily bread and are worried about it.   There are some who cannot believe.   They get wanting to drive their own horses instead of sitting in the chariot and allowing the Lord to drive.   They lose their rest.   I know there are some who want to carve for themselves, but they cut their fingers and get but a small slice upon their plates; whereas if they left it all to God and did their part to it, namely, were obedient to God's will and left the rest to Him, they would fare far better. They do not believe, and, therefore, do not rest; but you shall always find that in proportion as they believe they rest.   Did you ever hear of a more restful man than George Müller, of

Bristol?—a perfectly happy man with the care of an establish-
ment with more than two thousand children—no care at all
because he believes his Father about it and he leaves the Lord
to manage the orphanage.   I often wish I could do that.
Don't you wish so, too?   Who are you that should say, " I
have cast my burden on the Lord," and then go back and take
it again?   How is it you can talk of leaving it with Him, and
then, after all, try and bear it yourself?   But he that believes
has entered into rest.

I do not say that the believer's life is all peace, for his
condition is peculiar in this way.   When the children of Israel
entered into Canaan they were a portrait of a saint entering
into rest.   First, they had to cross the Jordan: the believer
has to cross the Jordan of his sin.   That is dried up, and he
marches through by divine grace.   Then there stand, inside
the promised land, the walls of Jericho, namely, his own
corruptions and his own sinful nature.   It takes time to bring
them to the ground, but after that, when the walls are
levelled, there are Canaanites still in the land.   Canaan was
not a good type of Heaven, for they were always fighting in
Canaan, always having to war against the adversary.   That
is a good type of the rest to which believers come.   They do rest.
They know that Heaven is theirs; that they are saved; that all
their troubles work for their good; that they are God's people.
Still they have to fight against sin, and that is no more inconsistent with their being at rest than it was inconsistent with
the fact of the holy land belonging to the Israelites, though
they had still to go on fighting against the Canaanites.   We
are like those at sea; the vessel is tossed but not wrecked,
and never shall be.   There is a great deal of water outside
the vessel that tosses her to and fro, but we are clean pumped
out.   We bless God that we can know the meaning of that
text, " Let not your heart be troubled."   The trouble is outside; it does not get into the heart.   The Lord has helped us
to get rid of that: we have laid our burden of sin and grief
and woe at Jesus' feet, and now that we have believed do
enter into rest.

IV.

I have, therefore, now to close with the good advice I
would wish to give ; and it is this.   The rest is to be had
by those that seek it in the right way.   It is to be had

by believing.   I know you have been for months trying to get rest from the burden of sin.   Young men, you may have rest to-night if you believe in Jesus.   At this very moment you may have complete rest.   But if you refuse this, and go about and try to mend your ways, and to find salvation for yourself by your own doings, you will never have rest.   You that wish to climb to Heaven by the way of Sinai had better look to the flames that Moses saw, and shrink and tremble and despair.   Calvary is an easier mount to climb.   When God gives grace to believe, rest is immediately obtained.   Oh, that the Lord would make some rambler end his ramblings now at the foot of the cross and find perfect peace!

Remember that the door to this sacred garden is an open one.   To believe in Jesus is not a matter that needs a great explanation from me.   " If ye be willing and obedient, ye shall eat the good of the land."   If ye would have it, " hearken diligently unto Me, and eat ye that which is good, and let your soul delight itself in fatness."   " Faith cometh by hearing, and hearing by the Word of God."

You have heard the Word of God, for this is the testimony of God, that He has given His Son Jesus to be a propitiation for sin, and whosoever believes in Him, that is, trusts in Him, rests upon Him, leans upon Him, depends upon Him for this faith—whosoever does that is pardoned, is a child of God, is accepted, is saved.   He shall never be lost; he shall enter Heaven as surely as he lives.   It is Christ's business to keep him and to perfect him, and to present him faultless before the presence of the Father with exceeding joy.   There is the door of faith.   Sinner, will you enter?   If you refuse to enter, know this, there is no other name given under Heaven among men whereby you can be saved or find rest.   Do you say, " I am unfit to enter "?   It is for the unfit that Jesus died. He died for the ungody.   Remember that!   He " came into the world to save *sinners*."   Catch at that precious word, and let your unworthiness rather console you than depress you, since your unworthiness is your claim to the promise through God's grace.   He came to save sinners—even the very chief.

" Oh that I had rest," saith one.   Why have ye it not? Turn not away from it.   Put not away your own salvation, but may God, by His sweet restful Spirit, lead you now to repose in Christ, and yours shall be the rest, and His shall be the glory for ever and ever.   Amen.

XIII.

THE DAY OF ATONEMENT AND THE FEAST OF TABERNACLES.

Also on the tenth day of this seventh month there shall be a day of atonement: it shall be a holy convocation unto you; and ye shall afflict your souls, and offer an offering made by fire unto the Lord. And ye shall do no work in that same day, etc.—(Leviticus xxiii. 27-40.)

THESE two festivals were both exceedingly instructive. Take either of them and you shall find them full of the richest meaning. Without any extravagance of spiritual ideas, or endeavouring to find teaching in every single detail, there is very much to be learnt from each of these; and, perhaps, the greatest lesson of all is this—that the Day of Atonement comes first with its sorrow for sin, and then the Feast of Tabernacles comes afterwards with its sacred joys and devout exhilaration. We shall have to speak of each of these as we go on.

And, first, let us speak awhile on the Day of Atonement— the Day of Atonement attended with soul affliction; and then afterwards the Feast of Tabernacles attended with its exceeding great joy.

I.

First, then, the Day of Atonement. The object was to set forth to all Israel that sin was a great evil, that God could not endure it, and that it must be put away. Once a year there must be a great demonstration of the putting away of sin before God. The first thing to be done on that occasion was that there should be brought a sacrifice, and a sacrifice by blood, for of all truths the most important for us to learn is that without shedding of blood there is no remission of sin. There never was a sin pardoned in this world by God apart from atonement by blood, and there never will be. Heaven and earth may pass away, but this rule shall always stand—"Without shedding of blood there is no remission of sin." God is merciful, but then He is also just, and unless His justice can be satisfied His mercy cannot exercise its function. It is of the nature of God that all His characteristics should be full-orbed and all-perfect. We know with regard to men that often one of their virtues will eclipse the rest.

No man can be in character perfectly balanced; there is always something in excess. We have known many a man whose strightforwardness has overcome his courtesy and tenderness, and many another man whose tenderness has been exhibited at the expense of his honesty and of his love of the right. To have all the parts of one's character balanced would be, of course, to be perfect; and that is what God is, and He would never allow one of His attributes to be glorified at the expense of another. God has devised a way in which He can be merciful without the violation of His justice, and that way is simply wrapped up in the person of Jesus Christ. Jesus bears the penalty due for sin. Mercy steps in and gives us Jesus. The love of the infinite Father gives Jesus out of His bosom. Mercy, therefore, has the widest possible scope in giving the unspeakable gift; and justice has full play after it sacrifices Christ for sin.

The question is, how could it sacrifice Christ for sins that were not His own? and the answer is a very easy one. Adam was the head of our race and sinned for us. Jesus Christ is the second head, and His people are one with Him. It was right, when they were in debt, that He should pay, for He was married to them. It was right that when they had sinned He should be punished, for He was their representative, and they were in Him. At His hand the evil was required, not because He had done it, but because He was the legal representative of those who had offended; and it was just and legal that He should suffer in their stead. He has done so. On the Day of Atonement the priest killed the bullock and the goat, and went with their blood into the mysterious presence of God within the veil and sprinkled the blood there. Dear friends, all our hope of pardoned sin must lie in Jesus, the great High Priest, having carried His blood within the veil. He was within the veil, I might say, in that thick darkness which hung over Calvary when He was pouring out His soul unto death on the cross. There in that inner circle of blackness and of agony where none could come at Him, for He was altogether alone—there it was that He made expiation, and sprinkled o'er the eternal throne. Let us bless and magnify Him to-night as we think over the Atone ment.

But then the next part of the ceremony of the Day of Atonement was the bringing out of the scapegoat. It was not killed. Killing it was not a part of the type, but sin was confessed over its head, and then the fit man led the goat out into the wilderness. There was a picture some time ago in the Academy of the death of the scapegoat. It ought not to have been painted. Whether the scapegoat died or not, however, has nothing to do with this. The whole of the meaning of this is that it was taken out into the wilderness and lost, and the sin was lost. There was no need to go farther. The goat was gone, and the sin of the people was gone too. Now, when Jesus Christ was taken down from the cross, being dead, our sins were gone. He cast them into His own tomb, and they are buried there, never to have a resurrection.

Brethren, it is most important that we should have well ground into our spirit these two truths—first, that our atonement, our salvation, is by the substitutionary death of Christ. No man is saved by what he does, but by what Christ has suffered. And it is equally needful we should know that, if we have believed in Jesus, Jesus took our sins, and our sins have ceased to be. They are no more to trouble us, for they do not exist. What saith the Scripture? " He hath finished transgression." What stranger term than that could be used? " And made an end of sin." Oh, what a magnificent expression—" made an end of sin "! It is gone. It is not possible for it to be laid to the charge of God's people any longer, for it does not exist—has no being. It is a nonexistent thing. A person is in debt: the debt is paid. Where is that debt? There is no debt. He cannot be summoned for it, or called to account. It is paid, and the moment it was paid it ceased to be. And our liability as sinners before the eternal God ceased to be when Jesus Christ " bore our sins in His own body on the tree." Oh, happy is that man who knows that his sins were borne there, and that he had a part in that great sacrifice when Christ laid down His life for His sheep.

A further part of the ceremony of the Day of Atonement lay in the burning of the relics of the goat and of the bullock whose blood had been carried into the holy place. A part of the fat had been put upon the altar, but the skin and bone and offal still remained. All these were taken away, and carried right out of the camp—a distance of some miles in so large a camp, and then taken to a lone place, the place of the lepers, the place of the unclean; and there these things were utterly consumed by fire. Furthermore, to set out to us how Jesus Christ, when He took our sins, became obnoxious before the Lord as our representative, He had to be taken outside of the gate of Jerusalem to the unclean place, the Tyburn, the Old Bailey, of Jerusalem, where the malefactors were ordinarily put to death, and there He had to suffer. And He had to suffer, moreover, away from His God, for He cried, " My God, My God, why hast Thou forsaken Me? "— a most instructive picture to us as well as to the Jews of old of how the Lord hates sin—that even when He sees sin upon His own Son He smites Him with the blows of a cruel one. " It pleased the Father to bruise Him. He hath put Him to grief."

I may also remind you that a part of the ceremony consisted in a very significant change of garment of the high priest that day. The high priest had to put off the robes of glory and stand in the place of the sinner; he had to put on the humblest array to appear before the Lord, just like our Lord, of Whom it is written, " He made Himself of no reputation, but, being found in fashion as a man, He humbled Himself unto death, even the death of the cross." And then, after the atonement was made by blood, the priest put on his beautiful garments again, just as our dear Master, having bowed to the humiliation of this mortal life and the agonies of death, has now resumed the garments of His glory. John in the Revelation, when he saw Him, saw Him with His countenance as the sun, girt with a golden girdle about the paps, and so lustrous and fair that our eyes have longed ever since to behold the glory of that vision, the beatific sight. The atonement is made; therefore He has gone into His glory. One sacrifice for ever, offered up by Him, put away all the sins of His people. Their sins have ceased to be, and therefore He puts on the robes of glory and rests from His toil.

But the great point I want you to notice is that during the Day of Atonement, the time set apart for these ceremonies, every Israelite was commanded to afflict his soul. Read the 27th verse: " Ye shall afflict your souls, and offer an offering made by fire unto the Lord. Whatsoever soul it be that shall not be afflicted in that same day, he shall be cut off from among his people." That is to say, no man ever receives the atonement of Christ unless sin be loathsome to him. I dare not preach, as I have heard some do—I think they err greatly in so doing—a faith that is apart from repentance. I am persuaded there is no faith that can save a soul which is not accompanied by affliction of soul for sin. Can it be possible that Christ took my sin and suffered for it, and yet I can think of sin without any detestation of it. Do you believe that man to be a pardoned man who was never a repentant man? Does he ever know, or can he ever know, the joy of the Lord who has not first of all felt the godly sorrow on account of his transgression? And, dear brethren, every one of us, when we come to the cross again, should come with an afflicted soul. I know some will think I mean they ought to doubt whether they are ever saved. I do not mean that. The Israelite was to afflict his soul when he knew that he was forgiven; and it is for that very reason the soul ought to be afflicted because it knows it is forgiven.

Now, the legalist won't understand this. He will say, " If my sins are forgiven there is no need for me to repent." I tell thee, soul, thou canst not repent aright unless thou hast, at any rate, some faith in thy forgiveness, for it is when we are forgiven that we begin to feel the smart of sin.

> I know they are forgiven,
> But now the pain to me
> Is all the grief and anguish
> They laid, my Lord, on Thee.

"*On Thee.*" To have transgressed against One who is so good and kind, and who has already forgiven me—this is the bitterness.

> My sins, my sins, my Saviour,
> Their guilt I never knew,
> Till, with Thee in the garden,
> I near Thy passion drew.

We must see the sweat drops bloody, and mark the wounds in His dear flesh, and see what it cost Him to redeem us, before we shall have, in very deed and truth, in an evangelical manner afflicted our soul. Why, it is a bitter and a sweet thing to be always repenting. Do not imagine that we have done with repenting when we begin believing, for the more we believe the more we repent; and in our dying moments, it is probable, our repentance for having committed sin will be deeper and more pure than ever it was in our lives before; not conviction of sin, mark you—not terror of conscience— not doubts and fears, but a true childlike faith and grace, to think that one could have offended against so good and gracious a God. You would never see the atonement so well as through your tears. Believe me, John Bunyan was right when he put Mr. Wet-eyes to go with the petition from the town of Mansoul to Prince Emmanuel; and I believe that Mr. Wet-eyes is clearer-sighted than most, and when the tear-drop is in the eye it acts like a telescopic glass.

> Oh, let me weep for naught but sin,
> And after none but Thee!
> And then I would (oh, that I might!)
> A constant weeper be.

At some time on the Day of Atonement the Jews added to this affliction of their soul a cessation from all work. I will read the 28th verse: "Ye shall do no work in that same day"; and in the 30th verse: "And whatsoever soul it be that doeth any work that same day, the same soul will I destroy from among his people." When we come to Christ we see all the work is done. When we behold His atonement and see the High Priest come out in all His golden garments we know that it is finished; and if it be finished there is nothing more for us to do, and we cease from all our legal works. Now, those that will work for salvation may take what comfort they can out of the solemn verse I read just now. That soul shall be cut off from Israel. By the works of the law there shall no flesh be justified, for "by the law is the knowledge of sin." I believe that verse in one of our Revival hymns is perfectly true:—

> Doing is a deadly thing,
> Doing ends in death,

if it be with a view to obtaining the favour of God, or the blotting out of sin. There may be as much doing as you like out of motives of gratitude because you are saved; but to do anything by way of merit to salvation is to destroy your soul. You give up God's way of salvation: you set up a way of salvation of your own: you will perish in your impertinent rebellion against God. Now, he who receives the atonement ceases from all servile work and rests in Christ, so that though there was an affliction on that day there was a measure of joy at the same time.

But, then, notice that though they ceased from servile work, it is said, " Ye shall offer a sacrifice by fire unto the Lord " (27 v.). That is what the child of God does. He knows his Father, and he now brings his sacrifice willingly and cheerfully; he brings his own heart, body, soul and spirit, which are but a reasonable sacrifice. " I am redeemed," saith he. " I am not therefore my own, but I belong to God. Now, since I have seen my sin put away by my Substitute, for the love I bear His name, He shall have all I have and all I am and all I hope to be, and I will spend and be spent in His service."

That the child of God does do, but it is a very different thing from servile work. Altogether, the Day of Atonement, though it was a day of affliction, was a day of Sabbatic rest. It is said, " Thou shalt keep it as a Sabbath unto the Lord." O, dear hearers, do you know anything about this Sabbatic rest ? Did you ever enjoy it ? Did you ever come to this : " Now I have seen my sin laid on the Son of God; I have seen the Son of God bearing all the punishment of that sin, and now for me there remains no fear of hell " ? " There is therefore now no condemnation to *him* that is in Christ Jesus," so the old version of the Bible runs, and correctly enough. He has no fear of being cast away from the Divine presence. " I will be their God, and they shall be My people " has put it beyond all fear of that, and he has come into a state of perfect contentment—a restful state, in which he finds Christ to be his all—all that he can desire and even more.

Now, if you ever came there, I know how you came there. You came there by the work of God's Spirit leading you to look right away from yourself to the dear Saviour standing in your stead. And if you have never come there, I will tell you this : you have missed the greatest joy this side of Heaven; you are in a state of danger, and as long as you live as you are, be you who you may, the most moral and the most amiable persons in the world, there is but a step between you and death and between you and hell. God is angry with you every day, and as you have not believed in Christ you are condemned already, because you have not believed on the Son of God. God gives you this testimony, that He has given unto us eternal life, and this life is in His Son. If you accept not His Son and trust not in Him, you make God a liar because you have not believed His testimony concerning His Son. You cannot have peace. You may have just now a flush of joy because your conscience is not awakened, but if it ever should be you will be full of anguish, and I pray you may be, that your soul being afflicted you may fly to the atoning sacrifice. But mark this word : if you should die without that atoning sacrifice, " There is none other name given under Heaven among men whereby we must be saved. If he that despised Moses' law perished without mercy, how much sorer " —mark the extraordinary question—" punishment shall he be counted worthy who hath trampled under foot the precious blood of the Son of God." Bear that in mind, for you trample on it when you seek some other way. This much concerning the Day of Atonement.

II.

Now, secondly, let us turn to the Feast of Tabernacles. When the Day of Atonement was over Israel was commanded to gather in the fruit of the land. And they were to take boughs of trees and willows and make themselves booths in which they were to dwell so many days, and make themselves as merry as they could be. After the atonement is over, then comes the joy. After the soul has seen its sin put away, then comes the blessed mirth which is wrapped up in that expression of Christ, " My joy shall be in you, that your joy may be full."

Now, why did they bring these booths ? They were to remember that they dwelt in booths when they first came out of Egypt to Succoth. So God would have His people when they receive their pardon in the precious blood. Already, if you have only been saved the last hour you have much to look back upon for what God has done for you in bringing you out of the House of Bondage and setting you free. Your gratitude ought to cause you joy. Has the Lord done so much for us, and shall we not be glad ? We will be, till those round about shall say, " The Lord hath done great things for them whereof they are glad," and we shall say, " He *hath* done great things for us." It was, then, a remembrance of mercy received.

But the booths were also a token of the peace they felt. Men in times of war dwelt in castles and fenced cities; they do not go in fields and dwell in booths. None dared to make them afraid. They were quiet and happy. That is just the same under the atonement. Now each sitteth under his vine and fig tree; his doubts and fears are all over; he is not afraid of sudden death, hell, nor anything. Why should he fear? The Lord is reconciled to him, and he can sing, " I will praise Thee every day now thine anger is turned away." That, I think, is another reason for their dwelling in booths.

And then, again, this feast was connected with harvest. It came at harvest time, so it was a time of plenty, a time when they could afford feasts beyond any period of the year. And so the child of God, when pardoned, finds plenty of grace. The fruits of joy and love are very plentiful in his spirit, for he is enjoying the love of his espousals, and therefore it is that he is exceeding happy and the Feast of Tabernacles, after the atonement, has with it a harvest of thanksgiving. I am told, too, that this time of the Feast of Tabernacles was in September, a season of the year which in the East is uncertain, subject to disorder, and therefore they had some discomforts while they were in these tabernacles. But that was to remind them that that was not their rest. Now, to the sinner that is a very comfortable idea. He wishes it might be his rest. But the child of God, when he has received the atonement, knows he is living in a booth, not in a house, and knows that if this earthly tabernacle be dissolved he has a house not made with hands, eternal in the heavens. I believe—and I think there is good reason for believing it—that our Lord Jesus Christ was born on the day of the Feast of Tabernacles, or somewhere in that month of September. There is no earthly reason for believing that He was born in December, but there are a thousand reasons for believing that it was in September He was born. There are reasons that may be gathered from His age and from the whole circumstance of the Jewish festivals that He was born about this time. And if so, right well might they keep the Feast of Tabernacles, when He was come—the Word made flesh and tabernacled among us, and we beheld His glory as of the only begotten Son of God full of grace and truth.

No doubt their dwelling in tabernacles would lead those who were instructed believers among them to think of Christ's coming in the flesh, to think of the time when the tabernacle of God should be among men, and " how amiable," I may say of Christ's body, " how amiable was Thy tabernacle, O Lord God of Hosts, my king and my God !"

And I have no doubt that the booths would carry forward the minds of those who were believers to that happier period which is prophesied as yet to come—the Millennial time, when it shall be said in very deed and truth, " The tabernacles of God are with men, and He doth dwell among them." These tabernacles would make them think of the day when He shall wipe away all tears from our eyes, and lead us unto living fountains of waters, and this earth shall have upon it the New Jerusalem which shall come down out of Heaven in all its glory; the earth itself shall shake off the curse, and the mantle of mist which sin hath spread shall be rolled up, and put away, and this planet shall shine in its pristine lustre.

There is one thing about this Feast of Tabernacles I would mention in closing, and that is this: it does not appear ever to have been celebrated from the days of Joshua to the days of Nehemiah. I do not understand it, but if you will read in Nehemiah you will find the people who returned from captivity kept the Feast of Tabernacles, and it is said it had not been kept since the days of Joshua, the son of Nun. What was David and what was Solomon about, and all the others that this rich festival was forgotten? There must have been great wrong about that. But it seems to me to be typical of this fact that there are many believers in Christ who have received the Feast of Atonement who don't ever care to keep the Feast of Tabernacles. I mean they are saved but do not rejoice. I wish they did. God meant they should, and it is their own fault that they do not. There are many believers resting in Christ who have a cloudy notion about the atonement. They do not believe that He was literally their substitute. If they did, they would be as happy as the days of summer. If they did but know their sin was gone and never could return; that as far as the East is removed from the West God hath removed transgression from them, surely they would begin to rejoice, and they would sing some of those noble psalms and some of those grand utterances of Paul would be upon their lips. They might even get so far as that hymn which we have at Communion :—

> My name from the palms of His hands
>   Eternity cannot erase;
> Impressed on His heart it remains
>   In marks of indelible grace.

> The terrors of law and of God
>   With me can have nothing to do,
> My Saviour's atonement and blood
>   Hide all my transgressions from view.

Yes, I to the end shall endure,
As sure as the earnest is given,
More happy, but not more secure
Are the glorified spirits in heaven.

That is the way to keep the Feast of Tabernacles. God grant that we may come to keep it now, with all our hearts and souls glorying in that atoning sacrifice that was not offered in vain, that precious blood that was not spilt in vain. I believe all Christ died for He will have. Nothing was paid for by Him but what He will have. I cannot understand the Son of God pleading all that He has suffered in our stead in vain. God cannot cast into hell a soul whose sins were visited upon His own Son. Oh rejoice, and be glad ye that believe in Him and keep the feast this day. Go from the Tabernacle to the Temple and keep the feast of your dear Redeemer.

XIV.

HELD AND KEPT.

Nevertheless I am not ashamed; for I know whom I have believed,
and am persuaded that He is able to keep that which I have committed unto Him against that day.—(2 Timothy i. 12.)

AN interpretation has been put upon this passage which I
think is not its meaning, but still, it may be. Paul had been
speaking to Timothy of the trust which had been committed
to him, namely, the preaching of the Gospel, and the word
here used might be rendered, " I know that He is able to keep
my *deposit.*" The Gospel was a deposit put into the hands of
Paul. He was very careful of it, and anxious about it. Just
then he was persecuted, and was likely to die. All the fury
of the Roman Emperor was put forth to crush Christianity;
but Paul said, " I know that Christ is able to keep my deposit;
He is able to keep that Gospel which He has committed to
my charge. I shall not labour in vain. Though I be cut off,
others will be raised up to continue the good work. Christ's
cause is safe enough in His own hands, for He is able to
preserve it, and He will."

Now, we certainly have the same consolation at all times.
We meet with persons who say that Popery is coming back,
and that there are coming all sorts of evil days. Well, I
believe that Christ is able to keep His own Gospel alive in the
world; that He is stronger than Satan, and that the victory is
not doubtful. The day shall surely come when, in spite of the
efforts of adversaries of truth, King Jesus shall reign throughout the earth. Let us banish our dark suspicions and be of
good courage.

Still, I do think that that is a far-fetched meaning, and
that it would not strike a reader. It seems to me that the
Bible was intended for common people's reading, and that
its meaning lies generally upon the surface, except where the
truth taught is exceedingly deep and mysterious. Would it
not occur to anybody reading this that Paul meant that he
himself, his body and soul, had been committed by himself
in faith to the hands of Christ, and that he felt quite safe

there; that, whatever occurred, Jesus was able to keep him until
that day. Well, we will take that as the meaning, and we
shall notice in our text, first, what the apostle had done: he
had committed his soul to the keeping of Christ; and then,
secondly, what he knew—he knew whom he had believed; and
then, thirdly, what he was sure of—that Christ was able to
keep him, and, fourthly, what, therefore, he was—he was
not ashamed.

I.

First, what Paul had done. He had committed himself to the keeping of Christ. He felt that his soul was very
precious. Do you all feel that? Do we, any of us, feel the
preciousness of our immortal natures as we should? Are we
not too often asking, " What shall we eat, and what shall
we drink, and wherewithal shall we be clothed?" as if spirits
whose existence is coeval with that of God, that shall live
throughout eternity, were to make these the main enquiries,
eating and drinking and clothing. I am afraid we do not,
any of us, value our souls as we should. Still, if by grace we
have been taught as Paul was, we do value them: we want to
see them in safe keeping. But Paul knew that his soul was in
danger. He perceived the evil within him and the temptations
outside of him. Do we feel that as we should? Are we aware
of our many dangers? Some men act as if they were not in
an enemy's country at all, but as if the temptations of the
world which would destroy them were really their friends, as if
sin were no injury, and to bring upon one's self the anger of
God were no peril whatever. Paul, however, saw that his
spirit was in danger, and, valuing it much, he desired to see
it safely housed. He felt also that he could not keep it.
Alas! how many think they can. Where the apostle trembled,
there are some that will presume. They feel as if they could
well enough preserve themselves without divine help; but ah!
it is not so. Left alone, the priceless treasure of our soul will
assuredly be lost: it will become the prey of Satan. How
shall a man be able to preserve his own soul? Paul, knowing
all this, had, therefore, gone and committed his soul as a
sacred deposit into the sure keeping of the Lord Jesus Christ
the Saviour.

This is the great act of faith. This is what some of us did
—what all of us did when we were first brought to Christ. We
had done henceforth with trusting in ourselves, and we trusted

in Him. And this is what we are doing every day, if we are believers. I love every morning to put myself again into the dear hands of the Crucified with all that concerns me and all that belongs to me, for when I feel that everything is there, this church there, and all the work of God there, then I feel it is safe. But 'tis ill to live an hour as your own keeper, or to have anything that you are to keep yourself. It is sweet and blessed and happy living when you have left everything in the hand of Christ Jesus, and are, therefore, free to serve Him, and joyfully to go about doing His will. I suppose, if Paul had to explain what he meant, he would tell us that he left himself in Christ's hands, as a sick man leaves himself in the hands of the physician. "There," saith he, "my disease is grievous, and I do not understand it, but, good Master, Thou hast much skill in anatomy and also in medicine: do as Thou wilt with me." This is what a Christian has done— he has left himself as a sick soul in the hands of the Good Physician.

Then, mark you, he takes the Good Physician's medicine. Some divorce faith from works in such a way that it is not faith at all. For if I trust a physician I take his medicine, I follow his prescriptions. My soul is left with Christ as a physician, and I desire, therefore, to do what He bids me. Our soul will be healed assuredly if we are really thus trusting to the Great Physician's care.

Paul meant that he trusted himself again as one trusts all his needs in the hands of another—as the sheep trusts itself with the shepherd. It is not the sheep's business to provide for itself; the shepherd does that. So do we. If we are as we should be, we are trusting ourselves as to all our soul's needs in the hands of Jesus. He is our shepherd, and we shall not want. But you know the sheep follow the shepherd whithersoever he goeth. They keep at his heels. And so must we (if our faith be true and real) keep close to the dear Redeemer and follow where He leads the way. If we have not truly committed ourselves to His keeping; if we pick and choose our own pathway and run hither and thither, we are self-willed, but if we have indeed the desire to follow closely where He guides us we have committed ourselves to Him as to a shepherd.

Then Paul had committed himself to Jesus as a captain commits his vessel to a pilot. "This is a new river to me," says he. "I have never traversed it. There are shoals and

narrow channels. Pilot, thou knowest the way up to the city.
Take the helm and steer my vessel safely." So amidst the
shoals and quicksands of this mortal life we know not our
way, but we leave ourselves in our great Pilot's hands—the
Pilot of the Lake of Galilee, the Lord High Admiral of the
Seas, with whom there were many other ships in the day of
storm. He guides us and leads the way. Then in trusting
Him we do His bidding—reef sail and do whatsoever He
commands us; and we are not truly trusting if we are not also
obedient in the trust.

And, brethren, we have committed ourselves to Jesus in
the same way as a person who has a case in law committs
himself to his advocate. If he be a wise man and hath a
good advocate he never interferes. You have heard, I know,
the story of Erskine. When he was pleading for a man upon
a capital charge, the man wrote upon a piece of paper—" I'll
be hanged if I don't plead for myself," and Erskine simply
wrote upon the paper, " You'll be hanged if you do." This is
much the case with us. Jesus Christ pleads for us and, if we
think we can plead for ourselves, we shall lose our souls, but
if we leave Him to speak for us, He knows how to baffle all
the devices of Satan. The Lord that hath redeemed us will
rebuke our adversary, and we shall come clearly out of every
suit before the bar of God, if we leave our souls in the hands
of Christ Jesus.

We have also left ourselves there as a defenceless nation
may leave itself in the guardian care of a great captain and
his soldiery. We cannot resist our spiritual foes. If we go
out against them, we shall be as stubble to the flame. Our
shield is God's anointed, and the breaker is gone up before us.
He clears the way and smites our foes hip and thigh with a
great slaughter, and though they come against us like a flood,
His blood-stained hand uplifts the cross and backward they
fall before Him. For who can stand against the Christ of
God? Committing our souls, then, to His keeping as the
defenceless to the care of the guardian, the great act of faith
is done. But then the defenceless abide in their city. They
are obedient to those who protect them. And such must our
faith be if it be at all the faith of the Apostle Paul.

I should like to ask of all my audience to-night—as I
have already asked of my own heart—each one, " Have you
trusted your soul in the hands of Jesus? Have you committed
it to Him to keep as a sacred deposit?" If you have not, I

pray that you may do it this night, ere your eyes be closed
in sleep. But if you have done so, do it again and continue
still to do it. You will, if you have done so before, have
learnt already how sweet a thing it is. Do it again, and trust
your Lord with all that has to do with you. Cast your burden
upon Him—your little burdens as well as your great ones.
Commit all your wants and all your cares, for time as well
as for eternity ; commit your body and your soul, your children
and your goods and all that you have into the same hands ;
for where your treasure is there your heart will be. If you
will trust all with Christ, you will love Christ better than all,
and all you love you will love because He keeps all for you.
You will, if you be rich, find Christ in all, and if you be poor
you will find all in Christ, and the difference is not much.
Only commit all to that dear, faithful hand. This is what the
Apostle did.

II.

Now, the second thing is what the Apostle knew.
"I know," said he, "whom I have believed." How often we
hear Scripture misquoted ! For instance, we hear persons
say, "I know in whom I have believed." That is not Scripture. What do you want to put in that little word "in" for?
It is "I know whom I have believed " ; and there is a difference there. It is not to know that we trust in Christ, but to
know Christ Himself. That is the great thing. Paul did not
trust in an unknown Saviour. He knew the Christ he trusted
in ; He was a personal acquaintance of his. Do we know
Christ? For you may say you trust Christ, but that is not
the faith that will save. It is really trusting ; it is trusting
in Him as one you know to be real—a real Christ, a real
Saviour. How did Paul know Christ? He knew Him, first,
because Christ had met with him on the way to Damascus.
Christ has never met with us precisely in that way and spoken
to us out of Heaven, but there was a time when He met us.

> Dost mind the place, the spot of ground
> Where Jesus did thee meet?

Yes, peradventure, you know it well to-night. You remember
when first He unveiled His lovely face, and you saw lines of
love in that dear countenance.

Paul knew the Saviour, next, because no doubt he had
gathered all he could about Him ; he had intimate acquain-

tance with Luke ; he had the means of knowing—did know—
Mark, and no doubt he spoke with Matthew ; and with John
he was familiar. Though Paul had not been with our Lord in
the days of His flesh, yet he treasured up all the incidents
which he might have heard from others ; and with such as
might have written in his day he was no doubt familiar. Well,
even in this way, we know whom we have believed. I hope you
are close students of God's Word, beloved, if you have trusted
Christ. Try and know all you can about Him Whom you
trust. You must trust Christ because He is revealed in Scripture ; but, the more you know Him, the more easy it will be
for you to trust Him. The employment of a Christian should
be to make his acquaintance with Christ more full. Knowing
something of Him, he should every day add something to
what he knows, till he can with greater emphasis say, "I
know whom I have believed."

For Paul knew the Lord, next, by personal communion
with Him. Many and many a time had the Lord spoken with
Paul. In his secret chamber, in prayer, Paul had risen up to
the heights of communion with Jesus. In sacred praise and
rapt devotion I have no doubt that oftimes the Apostle felt
that whether in the body he could not tell or whether out of
the body, for Jesus Christ had revealed Himself so fully to
him.

Dear Christian brethren, I am afraid we do not give time
enough for communion with Christ in these days. Our Puritan
forefathers had their hours of devotion every day. We are
so busy now—so very busy ! Is it not a busy sort of idleness
that neglects the Saviour? We are getting rich, perhaps ;
but is that a true richness which does not make us rich
towards God? We seem to know everybody now-a-days but
Christ. And there are some·Christians that I wot of who
know doctrines but do not seem to know Christ. They can a
hair divide between the west and north-west side in theology,
but yet in their spirit they seem as if they had no love, and,
therefore, do not, cannot know Him. And some there are
that know biographies, and know about the various sects of
the Church, and know the history of the Church, and know
I know not what besides. But the main thing is to know *Him*.
It were a life-long study to gaze upon His blessed person, and
to know Him as God the Man, to know Him from head to foot,
from glory to shame, to know Him in Bethlehem, and to know
Him on Calvary, to know Him in glory and to know Him in

His second advent. This is the sciences of sciences, the highest of all attainments. Would God we stuck to this. The Christian should make Christ his classics, Christ his crowning study. Christ should be the very soul of poetry, the very essence of philosophy—to know Him. How can this be except we have more fellowship with Him?

The Apostle knew Christ, moreover, by experience. He had tried Him and had tested Him, and there is nothing like this. "I know whom I believe. I remember," the Apostle might have said, "when I was in the deeps and the ship was near being wrecked. I know how the Lord stood by me in the chill midnight. I know Him: He forsook me not. I know how He cheered my heart on the way to Rome when He sent the brethren to meet me at Appii Forum. I know He stood by me when I faced the lion-like emperor, and how I was able to speak the right word, and so my life was then preserved." Such a one as Paul the aged shivering in his loathsome dungeon, yet with his heart warm with love to his Master, writing his epistle and bowing his knee every now and then unto the God and Father of his Lord and Saviour Jesus Christ, feeling that his dungeon glowed till it was infinitely brighter than the golden house of Nero with the glory of the Crucified —he knew his Master; he knew He was a firm friend, knew He kept His word, knew that that sweet word, "Lo! I am with you alway, even to the end of the world," was fulfilled, and therefore he said, "I know Whom I have believed."

Now I speak to a great many that have believed in Christ. I hope the most of you have; but do you know Him? Do you *know* Him? It is not necessary when you trust your money to a banker that you should know the banker. If he is a man of good repute, it does not matter about personal knowledge, though I daresay, if you knew him personally, you would feel all the more confidence. But in the matter of Christ Jesus an unknown Saviour is to a great extent a doubting Saviour. Your faith will lack force, it will be sure to become weak, unless ignorance be chased away and you know your Lord. "I know Whom I have believed." Do seek to know Him; and may this table to-night help you to know Him better. When we eat of the bread and drink of the cup, may those instructive emblems bring Jesus near to us, and may we know Him even better than we have known Him at the best before.

III.

And now, thirdly—here is the point—what the Apostle was sure of.   He was sure that Christ was able to keep that which he had committed to Him.   And I suppose Apostle was sure of.   He was sure that Christ was able to keep that which he had committed to Him.   And I suppose every one of us would say that we are sure of it, too.   But we act sometimes as if we were not so sure.   We are full of doubts and fears and mistrust, which ought not to be.

Now mark, first, Paul knew the ability of Jesus to keep souls that were committed to Him.   He knew that He was God : who can defeat the Deity ?   He knows that as Man and Mediator all power was given to Him in Heaven and earth, and, if all power be with Christ, what power can there be that can stand against that ?   Nay, what power is there, if He hath all power in Heaven and earth ?   He knew that if our danger arose from our past sins Christ could meet that, for He had offered an all-sufficient atonement.   He knew that if the danger arose from the demands of the law Christ could meet that, for He is "the end of the law for righteousness to everyone that believeth."

He knew, moreover, that Christ was so infinitely wise that He could foresee and remove all dangers.   If it was Paul's lot to be sifted in a sieve, he knew that Christ would pray for him that his faith fail not.   The prescient eye of our great High Priest foresees the evil, and provides for it ere it comes.   He is able to save us in a thousand dangers, and He is able to keep far from us all foes.   The keys of death and hell swing at His girdle, and the government is upon His shoulder.   We need not fear, therefore, all our enemies, whether they be men or fallen angels, or death itself.   Christ, having all power, is able to keep us against all such dangers.

This Paul knew; but the point about it was not only that he knew Christ could keep souls, but " that He is able to keep that which I have committed to Him."   You remember Bunyan's expression where he says, " These are but generals : come to particulars, man."   And, oh, it is grand to come to particulars in the Gospel.   It is a general fact that Christ can keep souls, but it is a particular fact and a precious fact for me to know that He is able to keep that which *I* have committed to Him.   I can believe for everybody sometimes; but faith to believe for myself—*that* springs   out   of   personal knowledge of Christ, for he that can say, " I know Whom I have believed," can say, " I am persuaded that He is able to keep that which I have committed to Him." Your soul, what-ever its peculiarities, your case whatever its dangers, is safe enough in the hands of Jesus. Do you believe this?

If so, note again, the Apostle believed that Jesus was able to keep him then—" that He *is* able to keep that which I have committed to Him "—able *now*—now that I am in this dungeon, now that I shall soon have to be executed : He *is* able to keep me. Do you know it is so easy to say that He was able to keep us years ago, and so easy to hope that He will be able to keep us by-and-bye, but to rest on Him now, to believe that *this* billow will not swamp the ship, that *this* fire will not consume me, to look at this present trial and to feel that *now* by God's grace one could " break through a troop, or leap over a wall "—this is the grand thing.

I used to know a countryman who told me this. He was an aged man, and he said, " Sir, all through the winter I wish I could have a job at reaping. I feel that if I had an oppor-tunity I could reap against any man in the country. But somehow," said he, " when the autumn times comes and I get my sickle I find that Tom is an old man." And so often-times it is with us. We think we have got no end of faith—perhaps a little to spare—but to have the faith when you have the trouble—there is the point. The good practical faith is that which believes whatever the circumstances may be, that " He is able to keep that which I have committed to Him."

But then he also knew—that Christ was able to keep him " till that day." I often marvel at the unbelief of old people. When I think of some of them getting on to seventy and having doubts and fears, after having known the Lord for fifty years perhaps, and having been kept by Him all that time, I am indeed surprised. How long do you expect to live? Cannot you trust Him the other ten? Has the Master carried you so long and can you doubt Him now? Surely all those years ought to rise up and upbraid you for unbelief. When I see an aged Christian close on the borders of the grave, sitting on the banks of Jordan with his feet in the stream and saying, " I do not know yet whether I am saved," I hope I shall not be in that condition. I pray God I may not. It must be a very wretched state, for He that has kept you so long surely can be trusted to keep you to the end. It is a bad example for young people for you that are growing

old to be getting doubts and fears.   But may not a man be
an excellent Christian and have doubts and fears?   He may
be a Christian: I won't say anything about his excellence.   Is
assurance a necessary thing as a Christian?   Well, brethren,
a man may be alive that cannot speak, but I think speaking is
a necessary thing to a man for all that.   That is to say, it is
generally necessary—necessary to his comfort, and I should
not like to be without it.   I will say this much to-night, if I
did not know in whom I have believed, and if I were not persuaded that He is able to keep that which I have committed to
Him, I would not dare go to sleep this night till I did know it;
or if I must through weariness fall asleep the first work of
the morning should be to cry out to the living God till I knew
I had passed from death unto life.   I can understand your
being doubters, but I cannot understand your being comfortable doubters and continuous doubters.   The natural condition of a child of God should be that of full confidence in
Christ Whom he has trusted, a joyous assurance that all is
right because the hand that keeps us is a hand that never
wearies, a hand that never palsies.   If you have not trusted
your soul to Christ, well then, come now as a lost soul; but if
you have, why fret and worry and question and dispute?   You
must be safe: you are safe now and you shall be safe if that
is where you are trusting.   How can you doubt your Lord?
How can you mistrust that hand that holds up Heaven and
earth?   Oh, go and repent of this great sin and rest in that
dear Saviour from this time forth, even for evermore.

IV.

Now, the last thing was what the Apostle was.   He
was not ashamed, he says, for he knew whom he had believed.
By this he meant to teach us first that he felt happy.   He was
a prisoner, despised, calumniated, but he was not ashamed
of that.   He knew Christ, and knew how safe he was with
Christ, and, therefore, he was not ashamed.   If some people
I know of that hide their colours and seem to go sneaking to
Heaven did but know Christ a little better they would be
happier in their souls and then they would be braver in their
actions.   It was a happy sight to see Paul expecting to die
and yet not regretting that he brought himself to death by
preaching Christ—nothing to alter, no wish to go back and
retrace his steps and be a Jew and a pupil of Gamaliel to save

his life. No, not he! And so if we have been resting in Jesus, we have no wish to go back to the beggarly elements of the world. Therefore, I pray you trust Him better so that you may be happier in Him and less likely to be ashamed in Him.

We want now-a-days more of Paul's courage. You working men, I know, have to work in shops where religion is at a great discount. If a man in some of our large factories be known even to attend a place of worship, he becomes at once a speckled bird. Well, I hope that you who belong to this Church, at anyrate if you be ridiculed for Christ, will not only bear it patiently, but joyfully. What is there, after all, to be ashamed of in it? The shame is on the other side. Reply boldly, though meekly. Give a reason for the hope that is in you, and inflict upon every person who ridicules the penance of hearing what the Gospel is. They will be less slow to ridicule when they see you are the braver in confessing the more they persecute you. Oh, for a generation of lions once again. Swifter than eagles may they be in strong passionate love for Christ, and braver than lions with a determination to avow Him and to fight for Him to the death. Let none of us, whether we be poor or rich, illiterate or educated, ever from this hour think of concealing one sentiment we hold, or ever think of keeping back the fact that with the Crucified we take our part in the shame and spitting that we may take our part in the glory with Him hereafter.

I will close with a story. There was once a king who sent his son into a province of his dominions that had revolted; and this son came there not in princely robe, but dressed as a common peasant of the country. And the men of that land despitefully used him, and they set him in the pillory. While he stood in that pillory of scorn, there came one who stood at his side, and when the filth from ungracious hands fell on the prince it fell also upon him. He stood there seeking to screen the prince, if he could, glad to bear contempt and share it with him. All men counted him mad; but there was a day in after times when the great king of that land held his levee, and the courtiers were gathered round about his throne, and the prince that day, returned from the land where he had received such treatment, put on his silken robes of glory and of beauty. And there stood amidst the throng in the palace halls many princes of great estate, peers of the realm, and nobles of the blood. But the prince, when he had come to his glory, looked over the whole scene and, spying out the man that had stood side by side with him in the pillory of shame, he said, " Make way, princes and peers, for this man was with me in my dishonour: he shall now be with me in my glory."

It shall be so at the last when Christ shall sit upon His throne.   Do you know the interpretation of the parable? He shall cast His eye over Cherubim and Seraphim and the glittering ranks of angels and see the man that was despised for His sake, and He shall say, " Make way, ye angels! " and they shall ; " Make way, ye cherubs !" and they shall ; " Make way, ye seraphs !" and they shall ; and there shall come the once despised and persecuted man and Christ shall meet him and say, " Thou shalt sit upon My throne, even as I have overcome and am set down with My Father upon His throne."

May that be your case and be mine!   Amen.

XV.

A COMPREHENSIVE PRAYER.

Behold, O God our shield, and look upon the face of Thine anointed.—(Psalm lxxxiv. 9.)

David longed to be in the courts of the Lord's house, and he conceives himself to be already there. His wishes seem to have carried him upon their wings: at any rate, he acts as if he were there, and he falls to offering prayer. He feels as if he had already come near to God, whether he had come to the tabernacle or not; and, therefore, he pours out his prayer into the ear of Him Whom he knew to be present and ready to hear. Peradventure this may serve us for a prayer to-night. Indeed, I think jit should; for there is scarcely any condition of heart which this prayer would not suit, if that condition of heart be at all right, or if there be a longing to be right.

I think we may regard these words as a prayer in three ways. They appear to be, first of all, a prayer for king David; then they might be read, I think, as a prayer for all the saints; but then, mainly and lastly—and, in truth, though last in order, this is first in importance—they are a prayer concerning our blessed Lord.

I.

First, then, they are a prayer of David. "Behold, O God our shield, and look upon the face of Thine anointed."

David pens these words for the people to pray for their king. God is the true shield of Israel, and hence the verse may be read thus: "Behold, O thou God Who art our shield, and look upon the face of Thine anointed." There are some critics who hold that that is the true reading; and, indeed, whether it be the true reading of the place or not, it is a truth. God is the shield of His people—their only true shield. From all evil doth He defend them. They are badly defended, nay, they are exposed to a thousand perils if they rely upon

any other defence. But should they be defenceless apart
from God He is their castle and their impregnable tower of
defence, and they are secure in Him. Therefore, the prayer
is, " O Thou Who art our shield, look down upon our king,
and cover him in the day of battle! Shield him, and shield
Thy people." Or, if the reading should be, " Behold, O God
our shield," and by the term " shield " a person is intended
who is afterwards called the " anointed," then it is true in
the secondary sense that kings become the shields of the
nation; and such a king as David was, in the hand of God,
a shield to the people Israel. It was for Israel to cry to
God for David, as it is for us to cry to God on the behalf
of any through whom we receive blessings from the Most
High. The text says, " Look upon the face of Thine
anointed." Does it not mean, " Comfort and cheer the king :
support and strengthen him; let him have a sense of Thy
favour. Hear his prayers; give him acceptance with Thee.
Enlighten his countenance. Let him see the brightness of
Thy face that his own face may shine."

It is a large and comprehensive prayer of a people for a
king who is well beloved; and, brethren, it teaches us just
this, that we ought to pray for those who are in authority over
us. We too often forget the duty. I am well persuaded that
if we had for a short time a taste either of despotism or of
anarchy we should prize the blessings which we now enjoy,
and should be more mindful of that Christian statute that
prayers should be made for kings and all who are in authority.
But, indeed, it is not kings merely, but God makes other men
to be a shield to us, and He anoints them for certain ends.
Are not all God-sent pastors in very deed the shields of the
Church of God; and are they not anointed to preach glad
tidings—anointed of God to bear His messages? Indeed,
what is their ministry worth, if it be not in the unction of the
Holy One? What power is there in it unless it be the power
of the anointing of the Holy Ghost, Who shall be with them?
Pray, therefore, for our brethren whom God may call and set
apart to be teachers for Him, and to be His mouth to the
people. Pray for us. Pray for all godly ministers, and say,
" Behold, O God our shield, and look upon the face of Thine
anointed."

How much better we might preach if our people prayed
more for us! I stand here to confess frankly that from my
inmost heart I attribute the large prosperity which God has

given to this Church vastly more to the prayers of the people than to anything that God may have given to me.   I know it is so.   I am sometimes—I hope not superstitious, but I do think I am sensitively conscious of the amount of prayer there is in this Church.   I seem to feel—I know not how it is, but the Spirit of God that worketh in us makes us feel—when you are prayerful, and to feel when the spirit of prayer begins to grow at all dull among us.   Oh, never let us slacken in prayer!   Do plead that everyone whom God anoints to any service may have strength given him.   Take up the case of those of God's servants who are not successful.   They need much to be upheld in labouring, perhaps where their non-success is no fault of theirs.   Pray for them; and pray that the time of their sowing may not last for ever, but may it be followed by a blessed reaping.   If we could but once get the entire Church to pray we might rest quite assured that God would bless the entire country.   We often wish to see enquirers, but we must be enquirers ourselves first.   " For this will I be enquired of by the House of Israel to do it for them."   A prayerful Church is a powerful Church.   I think there will be less fault to find with the ministry when there shall be less fault to find with believers in their closets.   You shall find yourselves edified when you have brought your quota of prayerful anxiety with you to enrich the Church of God.

I will leave, then, this first thought.   It is a prayer for David, which may be a prayer for all who are anointed to rule and all those who are anointed to preach the Gospel.   Lord, send an answer of peace to the prayer in that form.

II.

Secondly, shall I strain the text if I say that it appears to me to be a prayer for all saints, or may be so used at any rate, for all saints are anointed of God?   Is it not said of our Lord that He was anointed with the oil of gladness above His fellows?   It follows, therefore, that His fellows were anointed, too, in some measure, though He was anointed above them.   Is it not most certainly said, "Ye have an unction from the Holy One, and know all things "?   Brethren, doth not the anointing which was poured upon the head of Christ descend even to the skirts of His garments, as the sacred ointment went to the skirts of Aaron's robe, and we who are, as it were, the skirts of the robe of Christ have

participated in the divine anointing, and we rejoice in it
to-day. His name is as ointment poured forth, and in the
sweetness of that name we have a share.

Well, then, may we not ask that all the anointed of God
may have a look from God? Behold them, O God! Look
upon the faces of all Thine anointed. Some of them want a
look of sympathy. They are suffering in secret, pining in
obscurity. If somebody would say half a word to them they
would be cheered. If but some brother in a happier condition
would but whisper a word of consolation they would be
rejoiced. But, oh, if God shall look upon them, and they shall
know it—if they shall understand the sympathy of Christ, and
that He is touched with the feeling of their infirmities, and
feels at His heart all their sighs and their groans, will it not
be a great joy to them? Remember those that are in bonds,
as bound with them ; and remember them by praying devoutly
to-night, as you think over their separate cases, " Lord, look
upon Thine anointed! "

They want not only a look of sympathy, but they need to
receive from God a look of love. Oh, the love-looks of the
Eternal! Do not some of us know what they mean? We
have been in doubt, fearing, trembling, scarcely knowing
whether we were saved or not. We could not find that love
in our hearts which we desired to find there, and we began to
doubt whether He loved us. But some promise has been laid
home to our soul, and that promise has been like a glance
from the eternal eye, and it has spoken to us. That eye has
spoken far more clearly and sweetly than words could do ;
and in our inmost soul that glance has said, " I have loved
thee with an everlasting love; therefore, with lovingkindness
have I drawn thee." What raptures all divine our spirit has
experienced when the Lord has thus looked upon His
anointed!

And then many of God's people need a look that shall
give them real help and strength, for there is power in the
look of God. He looked upon the Egyptians out of the cloud,
and their chariot wheels were taken off, so that they dragged
them heavily. But when He looks upon His people that same
look gives power to the weak ; and to them that have no might
that same look increases strength. Many of the hands that
hang down, and the knees that are feeble need to be con-
firmed by an omnipotent glance from the eye of the everlasting God Who fainteth not, neither is weary. Let us pray

for many of our fainting churches—our brethren that are growing weary in the ways of God, that they may be helped, supported, sustained, invigorated by a look.

And surely, dear brethren, we should pray for all the Lord's anointed in this way. We are very apt, I am afraid, in our prayers to pray for all God's saints nominally rather than really. " Behold, O God our shield," Thou Who art our shield, " Look upon the face of Thine anointed," as if it were only one face. Look upon all Thy Church as though she were what, indeed, she is in Thine eternal covenant—only one, and make her one. And look upon her—the whole of her. Let all parts of her be revived and refreshed. I am sure that when we live near to God we never desire the prosperity of our denomination of Christians at the expense of another, nor even in preference to another save only and except so far as we believe that more truth may be there. May anything that we hold of error be blasted with the breath of the Almighty, and anything that is held that is error in any other church be withered and dried up as the grass before the mower's scythe! May it fall and utterly perish. But every truth everywhere, and every truth holding man, may they be immortal. And grace anywhere, grace everywhere, wherever it is; if it be the grace of God, may it go on to wax stronger and stronger, and may it conquer. I would earnestly pray for every true believer in Christ, even if he were in the Church of Rome— pray that he might have grace to get out of it at any rate, and out of some other churches I could mention too—pray that he might have grace still to love and fear God and rejoice in Him, notwithstanding all the difficulties that would surround him. Lord, if Thou hast a child of Thine that is sitting on the very doorstep of hell, lift up the light of Thy countenance upon him. Wherever he may be, or into whatsoever state he may have come, and however crotchety he may be, however cross he may become, and however often he may drive across all my notions and all my ideas, and however objectionable a person he may be, favour him with Thy presence notwithstanding that. So we ought to pray.

I must confess that it takes a deal of grace to pray much for some people. They seem as if they were not a prayable people. One does not object to the hope that one may live with them for ever in Heaven, but to live ten minutes with them here on earth takes a deal of grace. Well, the Lord change them or change us! No doubt sometimes our imperfections jar, and one set of imperfections may be unsuitable to come into contact with another set of imperfections. So let us, nevertheless, pray that God would bless the whole of His people, bringing them to Himself, looking upon them, and shedding His light upon them.

III.

But now, to detain you no longer over these secondary meanings, does it not seem to you that the great meaning of the text is concerning our Lord Jesus Christ? Of whom can it be properly said with emphasis that He is our shield and the Lord's anointed—of whom, I say, but of the Lord Jesus Christ, Who stands between us and God—Who shields us, and has been anointed of God that He might do so?

Beloved, we will not dwell upon these two titles of our Saviour since they at once suggest their own meaning. What shield have we from justice with its fiery beams? What shield have we from Satan with his malicious machinations? What shield have we from the world or the flesh, or from any of our myriad foes? What shield that we can stand behind with perfect security, save Jesus Christ our Lord? Well, let us rejoice in Him as such, and feel ourselves perfectly secure when we are hidden in Him. But He is the Lord's anointed, and there seems to be much consolation in it. Though I will not go into the world I will just refresh your memories; for if God has anointed Christ to save us He must accept Him as our Saviour. If He has anointed Christ to be a priest, He must be an acceptable priest. If he has anointed Him to stand for us the representative, the intercessor, and the mediator, He must have whom God Himself appoints. Jesus Christ is no amateur Saviour. He has not volunteered to take the work upon Himself without a commission; but the Spirit of the Lord is upon Him, and He hath anointed Him to be a preacher of righteousness and a Saviour of sinners. Let us rejoice in this—that we use with God a name which He has Himself set forth to be a saving name, and bring before God the remembrance of an offering which He has Himself appointed. Thou art our shield, O Saviour, but Thou art also God's Anointed; and this we plead when we lift up our souls in prayer to God.

Now the desire of the prayer is that the Lord would look upon Christ. And what does that mean? Why should we

desire Jehovah to look upon Christ? Is it not in order that
He may look upon us with favour and love? Christ is to us
an Elder Brother. We are erring; we have been prodigals.
Father, accept the family for the Elder Brother's sake. He
has never at any time transgressed Thy commandments, and
all that Thou hast belongs to Him. Look on Him; then look
on us; and remember Him, and for His sake regard us.

Christ is more than Elder Brother, however. He is our
representative and our head. When God looked upon Adam
He saw the race in Adam; and Adam's fall was the fall of us
all. When God looks upon Christ He sees His elect in Christ,
and the standing of Christ is the standing of all believers, of
all His people. In Christ we died; in Christ we were buried;
in Christ we rose again. In Christ we are raised up together,
and made to sit together in heavenly places even in Him;
so that when God looks upon Christ He is looking upon all
His Church, looking upon all His people, with the same glance
with which He regards the face of His Anointed.

And then, moreover, the Lord Jesus Christ is one with us.
There is a marriage union between our souls and Christ. I
must confess I often feel overpowered when I have performed
the marriage ceremony here, and then have read that passage
in the Ephesians where the apostle speaks of the husband
leaving his father and mother and becoming one flesh with the
bride, and declares that we are members of His body, of His
flesh, and of His bones. It seems such an extraordinary
union, so that Paul when he speaks seems to be speaking of
marriage, and then he says, " I speak concerning Christ and
His Church," as if the same words would do for one as for
the other. To think that all believers are married to Christ—
have entered into an indissoluble union in which eternal love
is the bond that never can be broken! My soul married to the
Christ of God! Oh, there is a heaven slumbering within that
single thought! 'Tis enough to make the spirit dance like
David before the ark to think of being married—married so as
never to be divorced—to the Son of the Highest, even to the
Christ of God.

Now, we would have the Lord look upon our Bridegroom's
face. We have no comeliness, but He gives us all His beauty.
When He took us He took us as we were, but He made us to be
as He is. He took all our foulness, but He gave us all His
righteousness; and we therefore say, " Lord, when Thou
lookest on the family, do not come and look at the spouse.

Come not and look at the weaker vessel, but if Thou regardest the house look at the house-band, the husband, the head, the lord, the master. He is our strength ; he is our representative.''

IV.

And now when the Lord does look upon Christ what does He see in Him? I want you to think this over. I won't try and put it in many words, but leave it for your own private meditation. It is a subject of that sort. I, being in Christ, desire God the Father to look at Christ instead of me. Why? Why, because, first, when the Lord looks at Jesus Christ He sees in Him His own self, for the Lord Christ is God and one with the Father, and by a wonderful and mysterious union not to be explained; so that when He looks upon His Son He must look with ineffable love and affection because He is looking upon the godhead—the perfect godhead—in the person of Jesus Christ. There is something delightful in that —that the godhead stands for me, and God in looking at my representative sees Himself. He cannot see anything there but what shall be to Himself well pleasing. But then He sees in Christ perfect manhood. When the Lord thinks of manhood is not there enough to make Him feel weary at His heart of the very name? Remember how, before the time of the Flood, it repented Him that He had made man upon the face of the earth ; and many a time, surely, if the Lord had been as we are, we should have been destroyed. Manhood! It must be coupled in God's mind with everything that is ungrateful, unnatural, vain, foolish, wanton, wicked. Shocking word, the word manhood! But now when the Lord looks upon His Son, He sees perfect manhood—manhood that never had a trace of sin about it—manhood the same as ours with this one exception, that it has never gone astray in thought or word or deed. God sees there what manhood can accomplish —manhood that has obeyed His law without a single flaw— manhood that has suffered for God's glory, suffered even unto death. And God loves man because there is such a man as Christ Jesus—that there should be a possibility of a creature being made like man who should be able sinlessly to suffer, which I suppose angels could not do. God looks, therefore, upon manhood on account of what Christ has been and is, and looks upon it still with love.

But, then, beloved, there is special relationship between Jesus Christ and His own believing people, so when the Lord looks upon Jesus He sees in Him perfect obedience. That is what He expected to have from His people, and He sees it in His people's representative. Christ stands for His people, and when the Lord calls for obedience Christ presents it: there it is. God cannot ask more from man than Christ the man presents to God. There is everything in Christ that satisfies God's holy attributes. It cannot be said that He is not pure in Jehovah's sight, or that He charged Him with folly. No, but the thrice holy One takes a delight in the obedience of His only begotten Son. And so, too, when God looks upon Christ He sees in Him a full atonement for all the dishonour done to His holy law. For all who have believed in Jesus there is in Christ the man, the sufferer, a sacrifice presented to God which for ever puts away all recollection of sin. " This Man when He had offered one sacrifice for sins for ever sat down at the right hand of God; for He hath by one offering perfected for ever them that are set apart." So that the remembrance of Gethsemane is to God most sweet. The recollections of the flagellation, the shame, the spittle, are upon the mind of the Most High, and He sees the sin of His people no more. It is washed out by the atoning blood of Jesus Christ. The Lord looks into Christ's face, and He sees me there. He sees in that face the memorials of Calvary. He looks upon His hands and sees the scars ; He looks upon His feet and sees the open wounds ; He looks upon His side and sees there still the gash that reached His heart ; for Jesus looks like a lamb that has been slain, even upon Mount Zion, and wears the memories of His priesthood still. Oh, this is delightful to think of—that God sees in Christ a perfect sacrifice, and a perfect obedience, and a perfect nature, and a perfect man.

And then, remember, He sees in Jesus Christ our justification, for though He died for our offences He was raised again for our justification. He sees in Christ the new life—such new life as we also have received in our regeneration ; and He sees in the resurrection of His dear Son that He has given a pledge to us that He will save us, and preserve us and bring us to our resurrection, too. In fact, when He looks into Christ's face the Father sees the covenant, for has He not said, " Behold, I have given Him as a covenant to the people " ? He sees the seal, the covenant seal, the covenant

sacrifice, the blood that ratified the covenant. He sees in
Christ every promise made yea and amen and secure to all
the seed. But, indeed, I cannot enlarge upon what the Lord
God sees in Christ, for, I might truly say, God alone knows
all He sees in Christ, but when He sees Him He is full of love
to us because of what He sees in Him. It is well for us to
recollect that our salvation does not rest upon our seeing
Christ so much as it does upon God seeing Him. We are not
saved except we see Him, truly, but then the real foundation
of our salvation lies in God seeing Christ. The type of the
passover brings that at once before us, for the Lord said,
" When I see the blood I will pass over you." The blood was
not put inside the house for them to see. It was on the door,
but not on the inside of the door: it was on the outside for
God to see it—for the angel to see ; and when God saw the
blood He passed over His people. And when God looks upon
Christ then it is that He hath mercy upon His people. At the
same time we must not forget that we also look unto Him
and are saved. This is our realisation, but the real fact which
is the basis—the fact which we realise—is God's having
looked upon Christ, so that we say truly,

> Him, and then the sinner see :
> Look through Jesus' wounds on me.

Now, to gather up all in a word or two. When God the
Father looks upon His Son it is with ineffable affection ; it is
with intimate union ; it is with infinite delight. So when we
are in Christ He looks upon us, and there is a union between
us and Him ; there is a love from Him to us ; yea, there is a
delight in us. The Lord delighteth in His people when He
sees them in His own Son.

So now I will just entreat you present to make use of this
as a prayer. Perhaps there is a sinner here who feels his
need of a Saviour, and wants to know how he is to come before
the Most High God. Beloved friend, I put this prayer into
your mouth ; may God put it into your heart. Say, " O God,
I am vile and sinful: look not on me, but look on Thine
anointed. I shelter in His wounds. Be not angry with me,
though I deserve it, but let Thy love to Him constrain thee
to show Thy love to me !" O sinner, if you search your nature
through you can find no plea which you can use with God ;
but if you take Jesus Christ's person to be your argument
for mercy you have prevailed. God will never deny His Son.

There is that in Jesus which at once brings to the sinner mercy when Jesus Christ is pleaded before the throne. Say, "Oh, for His sake, by His agony and bloody sweat, by His cross and passion, by His precious death and burial, by His glorious resurrection and ascension, have mercy on me, O God!" You are heard, sinner, if that be your prayer. Such a prayer cannot be unheard of the Most High.

But might not any backsliding child of God use just the same prayer to-night? O wanderer, thou who hast lost all sense of life and love, come back. Take with you words, and come to your God in this way, and say to Him, " My Lord, I have changed, but my Redeemer has not. I have been unfaithful, but my Lord has not. I have deserved Thy wrath, but He deserves Thy love. Behold, O God my shield. I hide behind Him. Look upon His face, and then look upon me." Backslider, by the love of God, I pray you, use that prayer to-night and come back to your Saviour whose heart you have grieved so much.

.V.

And might not this suit any Christian here who has been hard at work for Christ? You know, brethren, I believe those who work hardest for Christ are those who are most conscious that their work is not fit to be accepted in itself. If you find a man who rejoices in what he does, he does not do much ; for he that does much has such a high idea of what he would wish to do, and what he should do, and of how he should do it, that he is always dissatisfied, and he never brings anything in his hand of his own ; but he says, " Lord, establish the work of my hands. Bless it to sinners. Glorify Thyself. Make Jesus' dear name to be sweet in the world. But I pray Thee hear Him, not for my sake, but look into His face, and say does He not deserve to be honoured ; does He not deserve to have precious souls? If I have sought even in the humblest way to promote His Kingdom am I not one with Thee in this desire? Dost Thou not will that He should reign? Behold, then, the face of Thine anointed, and for His sake let the blessing come upon my poor services, unworthy though they be."

And might not any child of God who is pleading for the conversion of others use this prayer? I will suppose that you, dear wife, have been urging upon the Lord that He would have mercy upon your husband ; or you, sister, have been seeking the conversion of your brother. You have not yet prevailed. Have you tried this argument, " O God, look on the face of Thine anointed. Hear me by His name Who was full of tender compassion and wept over Jerusalem ; by His love Who would not let the sinner die ; by His heart which even after His death poured out a stream of blood and water for the sins of men. Lord, hear me, and save my brother ; save my husband ; save my child." Would not that be good pleading? And will not this do when we come to die? I scarcely know a prayer that would better become our lips when they are praying their last prayer on earth, and getting ready for their first song in Heaven, than to say here, " Behold, O God our shield, and look upon the face of Thine anointed," and then the moment the prayer was over to have to say, " My God, I also have looked upon the face of Thine anointed, and now that the beatific vision has charmed me into bliss I have forgotten all the pains of dying ; I have reached immortality and life ; for I see the anointed of the Lord Who is for ever now my shield from death."

Oh, yes, we might well die with this prayer upon our hearts, and then turn it into a song for ever, and say to angels and Cherubim and Seraphim, " Behold our shield, and look upon the face of God's anointed. Gather hither all ye saints who have been redeemed by blood. Come hither all ye hosts of ministering spirits, and ye worlds afar with all your varied races of creatures. All things that have sense and intelligence and wit and eyes to gaze and hearts to love, come hither, and look upon our shield, and behold the face of God's anointed. Was ever brighter glory? Was ever more transcendent love?"

And He is our brother still. A man—a man sits on the throne of God. " Unto which of the angels said He at any time, Thou art My son ; this day have I begotten Thee." He took not on Him the nature of angels, but He took on Him the seed of Abraham ; and now between God and man there is no gap, for the man is one with God, and the Lord may truly say, " The man hath become one of us," and we in Him have become unto the eternal God in communion and fellowship that shall last for aye.

God bring us there in His own good time ! Amen.

XVI.

SATAN WITH THE SONS OF GOD.

There was a day when the sons of God came to present themselves before the Lord, and Satan came also among them.—
(Job i. 6.)

IT is no use enquiring what day it was. The Jewish
Rabbis, who like to waste time over difficult questions—questions of no profit—say it was the Sabbath ; and that is very
possible. But I am afraid that Satan does not only go abroad
on Sundays, but that he will be found in congregations that
meet on week-days, and that when the sons of God at any time
come together it will generally happen that Satan is among
them. The question has also been raised, Did Satan go into
Heaven, then? I do not see anything about Heaven in the
text. The sons of God came together. They may have been
the sons of God on earth—the descendants of them, or other
godly men who were in the habit of meeting together for
prayer and praise. They may have been the angels in Heaven;
and I sometimes like to think that Sabbath is kept in Heaven,
as well as on earth, and that when we come together with
special gatherings below, the saints are keeping special festival
above, for though it be always Sabbath with them, there
may be a Sabbath of Sabbaths, and they may have their high
days and holidays keeping time and time with us below, only
excelling us in the volume of their praise. Satan could present
himself before God without being in Heaven. The whole
universe is God's audience-hall, and when He mounts the
throne and summons all His creatures together, they are there
and then before Him, whatever their position as to place may
be. Satan seems to have intentionally, however, mingled,
as far as he could, with the sons of God, wherever those sons
of God were found in the presence of the Most High.

Is not there something to be learned out of this? Let us
see if there be not some teaching in it.

And the first fact, I think, which is very clear is this—that
mere coming up with God's people is of no value whatever,
for " Satan came also among them." I hope none of you

have ever received the notion, though I am afraid it is common, that if you attend a place of worship regularly, and especially if you have a seat of your own, you have done something exceedingly meritorious, although you should never give your heart to God and never repent of sin or believe in Christ. Some seem to fancy that they stand on a vantage ground because they are regular hearers. They observe the Sabbath ; they are church-goers and chapel-goers. Now, see what a mistake such persons have made, because Satan kept this holiday, whatever it may have been, and Satan appeared with God's saints. Satan mingled in the throng. And it was not only once that he came, but as far as the Book of Job is concerned, there are two days when the sons of God came together, and Satan was there both times. He seems to have been a very regular attendant, to have been constantly there. And yet of what service could it have been to him? And of what service can it be to anybody unless there be spiritual worship, and unless the heart shall be given to God? "Who hath required this at your hands that ye should tread my courts?"

There is no value whatever in a mere bodily attendance upon the means of grace ; for, in the first place, it is certain that Satan's attendance at divine worship could not be acceptable to God. Could anything be acceptable that that false spirit did? Did not his polluted nature profane the whole? So in the case of ungodly men, their attendance with the people of God cannot be acceptable with God. Do they bow the head in prayer? If you do not pray with your hearts you do but mock God ; or if you offer the prayer of the Pharisee, and say, "God, I thank Thee that I am not as other men," you do but provoke the Most High. You have not brought to Him anything that He can receive. And when the song rises up to Heaven, and no doubt some think that that is good singing which is very musical—which is after the best style of art—yet, oh, it is not so with God. What doth He care for your concords and your harmonies, such as delight human ears? He reads the heart, and unless the soul blesses Him whose mercy endureth for ever, and unless the heart adores the Creator and the Benefactor, there is no song such as He can receive. Hosannahs fall short of Heaven if they do not rise from our hearts. Only that praise which comes from our heart will go to God's ear. If we do not bless Him from within, neither will He receive us.

I.

I would like some of you to think of this—that you have been twenty or thirty years, perhaps—possibly forty or fifty —constantly attending before God, and have never once offered any sacrifice that He can accept, for until you believe in His Son there is nothing about you that He can look upon with pleasure. Till you have repented of your sins, till you have trusted Jesus, till you are born again, you are condemned already, and the condemnation which is upon you personally is upon all that you do. Even your prayer becomes an abomination unto God, viewed as coming from one whose heart is not right with God. Oh, do think of this, I pray you, and henceforth never rely upon the outward use of the means of grace. Get farther than that, or else you stop short of acceptance and salvation.

Moreover, it is quite certain that as Satan's presence was not acceptable, so Satan's presence there was not beneficial to himself. He never repented of any ill that he had done. It does not appear that he ever slacked in his diligent rebellion against God. His proud heart was not humbled; his lustful mind was never purified. He remained the same devil after he had mixed with the sons of God as he was before. And do recollect, I pray you, that in the mere exercise of sitting in a pew and listening to a sermon, or joining in prayer, there is nothing that can benefit you. "Ye must be born again." If it does not come to that, no impression has been made. You may take the Ethiopian, and wash him as much as you will, but unless a miracle should change his skin he will remain black. And all the preaching in the world is no better than the washing of the Ethiopian until the Spirit of God shall apply it to the heart, till a divine power shall beget faith in the soul. Do remember this. I am sure there are some who pride themselves that they attend on the Church which they believe to be the only authorised one. Well, Satan was in a very authorised assembly, but remained Satan still.

Some, on the other hand, will boast that they belong to the most simple sect in the world, that their worship has nothing at all of adornment. It is as plain as possible. Perhaps they are Baptists ; perhaps they belong to the Society of Friends. We may as readily be hypocrites in an informal worship as in a formal one. We have as great reason to guard ourselves against trusting in our simplicity, as others have to guard against trusting in formalities, for if we rest in anything short of the work of the Spirit in the soul, and a real reconciliation to God by the blood of the atonement—in fact, a new creation within our heart and a saving faith in Jesus—we shall no more be benefited by our hearing and our attendance than Satan was by joining with the sons of God. It is a spiritual business. Oh, that all recollected this! In vain your sacraments ; in vain your gatherings of any sort. If God the Holy Ghost be not in you it falleth to the ground.

And note, once more, that Satan's attendance with the sons of God even gave him an opportunity for the commission of greater sins. So far from being accepted with God, or being benefited by his attendance, he even went from bad to worse, for there it was that he dared challenge God with regard to His servant Job, and go forth into the world to do more mischief than he had done before.

I fear me there are some that grow Gospel-hardened! They have heard the Gospel till they never mind it now. They have heard the law preached till there is no terror in it now. Good Rowland Hill used to say they are like the blacksmith's dog that goes to sleep under his master's anvil, though the sparks fly about him. They have learnt to sleep when the very sparks of damnation fly about them. It matters not how it is put ; they cannot be aroused. And you know these persons often become the raw material for making the very worst of people. When the devil wanted to make a Judas, he was obliged to take an apostle for the raw material, for you can always make the worst thing out of that which is akin to the best. Those men that miss virtue, as it were by an inch, are prepared to go out and out in all manner of vice. I do think that some could not sin as they do if they were not well acquainted with their duty, but they are able now, having a tender conscience, to sin greatly against conscience. Having light, they sin greatly against light. Knowing much of God, they are able to brave that knowledge, and to defy God more than others could do.

O dear hearers, are some of you getting worse? Am I preaching some of you into hell? Am I rocking cradles for you that I might rock you into eternal sleep? Is it so after all the care we take to try and adapt our discourse to your mind? Do we only, after all, make you fitter heirs of wrath because you continue to despise the message? I hesitate to come and speak in this pulpit when I think of some of you, for I despair of you. I fear that, after all, you will never be brought to Christ. You will remain as you are, and all that I shall be able to do will be to increase your condemnation. God forbid it by His infinite mercy! But this I am sure of, if there are any people against whom the woes which our Lord pronounced upon Capernaum and Bethsaida will fall with a sevenfold vengeance, it will be those people who have been plainly told their sins in words that never minced the matter, and have been earnestly pointed to Christ, and commanded over again in the name of God to repent and turn unto the Saviour that they might find salvation.

Well, that first point is solemnly clear. It proves that, as Satan came up with the assembly, the mere coming up with the people of God is just nothing ; but as his worship was not accepted, as it did not benefit him, but even gave him an opportunity to be even yet a greater transgressor, so may it be with some who frequent the courts of the Lord's house.

II.

But now, secondly, another topic. Our text teaches us that the best assemblies of saints are not free from evil persons. The sons of God came together, "and Satan came also among them." What does this teach us?

First, that we should not leave the assembly of the saints because unworthy persons happen to be there. I believe this to be a practical observation that may be useful to some present. For instance, I have known at the communion-table a person say, "I cannot sit down there, because in my judgment such a person is allowed to sit down who is unworthy." Now, dear friend, your course is plain. If you are aware of anything wrong in a church member—grievously wrong— there are the proper authorities of the church to whom, not in a spirit of gossiping, but in a spirit of righteous love for the purity of the church, you ought to communicate this fact. But you are not infallible yourself, and therefore it may happen that you have misjudged this individual, and your responsibility will cease when you have done what you believe to be your duty in that matter. If, then, it should seem to those who are set over the church that it is not a fault as you think it is, or that it is not proved, or if they think it not such a fault as should exclude the person, you have nothing further to do with it. It is your business to come to the table of the Lord, and to observe His command, whoever may be there; for, believe me, if you never come to a communion-table unless you feel sure that everybody there is perfect, I think you ought to stop away if for no other reason than this—that you are not perfect yourself. You will make one unworthy person; and therefore do not try to carry out that rule. Remember the first communion supper. Our Lord was there, and twelve apostles, but one of them was a devil. I hardly dare to hope that we have a larger proportion of true saints than Christ had among His apostles. I should not like to say that I believe that one in twelve of all professors will turn out like Judas, but I should feel very happy if I did not think it was more than one in twelve. It is not for us to judge, but there are many things that cause us justly to suspect; and therefore since Peter and James and John did not rise from the table and say, "Master, Thou hast said that one here is a devil, and we will no longer sit down with him," but as they continued there, and put the warning He had given them to quite another use, I would say to you, dear brother, dear sister, come up and meet with your Master and keep the feast, even though you should have to feel there is someone there who ought not to be there.

And then, again, seeing that in every assembly there is some unworthy person, turn it to the account the apostles did. Examine yourselves whether you are the unworthy person. If one of you be a devil, all should say, "Lord, is it I?" We cannot do better than always take the points of censure and of caution, and use them upon ourselves. Oh, to think that there should be here a company of God's people, and some of us should be hypocrites! Do not let us look across the gallery and say, "I see someone there that I think is one." Look at home and say, "Lord, am I one?" To think that we should meet around the table to commemorate our Saviour's death, and that it should be morally certain that there are some persons there who are as the devil is! I beseech you do not begin to say, "I am afraid that my neighbour, So-and-so, may be such." How goes it with your soul? What about yourself? Try your own gold. Test your own silver; and if you be clear there you may very well leave these matters to your Master.

And do you not think, once more, that this fact, that in every holy assembly there will be some evil person, should make us long for those blesse'd assemblies above where Satan cannot come, and where no evil persons will ever intrude? We have to walk with caution here, for there may be some evil eye fixed upon us even in these sacred chambers of God's house where we act like familiar children and unbosom ourselves ; but up yonder there shall be no Judas-eye to detect our inconsistencies, and we shall have no inconsistencies to be detected.   There shall be none to suspect and to impute wrong motives ; there shall be none there to charge us with sins of which we are guiltless.   We shall be quite free and clear from all contamination when we shall be permitted to stretch our wings and fly to those blessed assemblies where we shall feel ourselves eternally at home.

So much upon the second topic.

III.

Now a third and more important one.   It is this: You will find that whenever God's children desire to draw near to God Satan will come among them.   I believe this is so with each individual.   My experience leads me to remark that if ever I desire to pray more earnestly than at other times I feel temptation to be stronger at that particular season. I am morally certain that if I want to be quite alone the devil will send somebody to knock at my front door whom I must see ; or if he does not do that, and I can get the time to myself, then he will come in without knocking, and begin to bring all sorts of thoughts into my mind, stagger me with recollections of some old sins, bring before me, perhaps, quaint and pithy passages that I would rather not recollect at all, for they are unseasonable then, make me remember what I would fain forget, and forget what I desire to remember.   Have you never felt, when you were flying up to the throne, your face full upon the Eternal Sun, desiring only to behold its light, and to fly right into the fulness of its blaze, as if you have heard a mutter at your side, and, turning round, you have seen that the heel of the dragon wing has been equal with you in its flight?   No, he seems as if he would disturb you, and come right before you, and blot out the vision of God's presence from your eye, and, when you are nearest to God, would come into conflict with you there?   When the people of God, the sons of God, came before the Lord, Satan came also among them.

N 2

And this is a lesson to those who are seeking to come to
God for the first time—you with troubled consciences that
desire reconciliation—awakened sinners that long that their
Father should fall upon their neck and kiss them and blot
out their sins. Now that you are trying to come to God you
are very likely to be subjected to temptations you never knew
before. Possibly you will be tormented with blasphemous
thoughts. Many are. And you will find sin to be more
active in you than ever it was. Satan knows it is "now or
never" with you. He is afraid he shall lose you, and he
stirs up all his force. I think I hear the Black Prince say
to the spirits that surround him, "Empty out your quivers
upon that man. Spare him not. He begins to desert us. He
will leave us, and he will turn away from the pleasures of sin
to follow after our enemy Christ. Now, tell him Christ won't
receive him. Tell him his sins are too many. Remind him of
his old transgressions ; pierce him with your barbed shafts ;
put venom into all his blood. Torment him ; make him, if
you can, commit suicide, or abstain from listening to the
Gospel. Don't let Christ have him. Do keep him away from
God." When the Lord's people are coming to Him with
penitence, seeking mercy, then Satan presents himself and
stands in the way to seek their destruction.

Keeping, however, to the subject closely, whenever our
assemblies come together, brethren, do you not find that Satan
also comes among us? He will come with the minister. He
will come into his study, he will come with him into the pulpit ; and he incites the minister to say those things that will
strike—to put them in very pretty language ; and he will
suggest, as soon as it is so stated, "How well you put that
point—uncommonly well!" Or he will say, "You were very
faithful to the people over that head, now. You are doing
your work exceedingly well." Seldom enough does the
preacher want to be told that he has done his work well. If
there is one that stands behind, that pats him patronisingly
and saith to him, "Well done! well done!" it is another voice
than that which will say "Well done!" at last. Meanwhile,
if Satan is busy in the pulpit, he is busy in the pew, too.
Did he not just now make one of you recollect that sick child
at home? When there was something that might be beneficial to you he brought before your mind where you left your
keys when you came away. A thousand little things will
come just at the moment you do not want them.

I cannot, of course, mention these, but Satan is a great hand at leading people into distracting thoughts which prevent their worship of God. And I have known him to go and stand at the front gate, and, if he can, make some trouble in your coming into the pew ; and when you get there something will happen that makes you feel uncomfortable and get into a vexed state of mind. And then, when the word is being preached, he will come and insinuate doubts about this and doubts about the other. If there is a choice promise, just as you hope you are going to get the flavour of it he will pluck it out from between your teeth and away with it before you can feed upon it. And if there should happen to be a word of rebuke, he will tell you that that does not mean you ; you are superior to the necessity of receiving such a word as that ; or he will even make you rebel against the word when it comes home to you, as if, after all, it was not the preacher's business to speak very pointedly to your conscience.

Oh, the ways in which Satan will spoil our best services ! He is ever busy, and I believe where there is the best spiritual meat, and God feeds His children best, there the devil will be most active. When there is a very nice, prim, natty sermon which is read very nicely to the people, and the devil rides down the street, he never goes in there. He knows there will be no hurt done by that. But if there is an earnest preacher, he says, " I must stop my chariot here," and in he goes and begins to put forth all his strength, if by any means he may spoil the worship of God's people and prevent the Gospel coming with power to their hearts. Watch, dear brethren, watch and pray and resist him, for he will flee from you. And let it be our endeavour never to come to this Tabernacle as a matter of form, and never to go away satisfied unless we have seen Jesus, never contented unless we have bathed our souls in Heaven, and have had the dew of the Lord upon our foreheads.

It ought to be a wretched Sunday evening with us when we feel that we have not worshipped and have not fed upon spiritual meat ; and if there is a Sunday in which you have not got good and done good too, you should feel, " Well, I could lament that I have lost, not a day as Titus did, but a Sabbath day, which is ten times worse." What a dreadful thing it is to have barren Sabbaths, formal Sabbaths. The

Lord save us from this great calamity! Satan will come and make it so if he can ; but may the Spirit of God come too, and He will soon put Satan to the rout, and we shall worship God in His strength.

Now, if Satan comes into an assembly of saints, we may expect him to come into a mixed assembly like this, in which there are saints and sinners too ; and if there should be a word in the sermon that is likely to be blessed to a sinner, Satan will be sure to distract his attention if he can. I have told you several times of that simple-hearted little boy that used to lean forward and put his hand to his ear to catch every word the minister said, His mother said to him, " Why are you so very attentive?" " Because, mother," said he, " the minister once said that if there was a sentence in the sermon that had a blessing in it for us, Satan would be sure, if he could, to prevent our attending to it ; and I am anxious not to lose a sentence that God may bless to me."

Oh for hearers like that! Beloved, there would be no fear for conversions if our congregations were made up of people who sought for the blessing, who would take every sentence like a cluster from the vine, and press it with anxious foot to get the wine from it, that they might drink and be satisfied. The Lord give us to feel that, since the enemy will distract attention if he can, we will hear, and take heed how we hear.

Then I have known him do much mischief by suggesting criticisms of the preacher. Many come merely for that very reason. Well, they will compare one preacher with another preacher. " Paul, well he is very argumentative, but he has not at all the brilliance of Apollos, and Apollos—well, he is a rhetorician. Cephas is my man—rough, plain, blunt Cephas." And another says, " Well, Cephas is almost vulgar. Give me Apollos. He is the man for my money." But is that the way in which we should hear the word of God? Well, as George Herbert put it, " Judge not the preacher ; he is thy judge." If there be anything in God's ministry at all it is not meant to be looked at, and examined, and turned over as if it were a work of art. Sirs, I care nothing of what you should think of the hilt of my sword. I want to strike right through your souls, and cut and wound with it ; and surely I have failed utterly to do that when you are able to think about the style of the sermon. When anyone says, " That was a famous sermon," the preacher may conclude that that was a sermon lost ; it was a useless sermon ;

for that only will be famous with God that will affect men's consciences.   Oh, how busy Satan is to engage men with the niceties of phrases, when, instead, they should be looking at the inner sense, and receiving meekly the word of God.

Then Satan has a great art of taking off people's minds from the word of God when it is delivered.   When the seed was scattered on the stony ground the birds of the air found it and took it away.   Oh, those birds of the air!   Yes, when you get down the Tabernacle steps there will be one of those birds of the air waiting for you.   You will be taking an evening walk, and then the chat will take away any impression that may have been produced on your mind.   Oftentimes one no sooner crosses the threshold of the door than topics are suggested for conversation that effectually put out of memory any good thing that may have been heard.   I believe this to be one of the devices of Satan, and that he comes into our assemblies to see in which way he may best destroy the power of the word in men's hearts.

Brethren and sisters, pray for us.   If this enemy be so busy, how much we need the gracious spirit to be ever at work to make the truth " the power of God unto salvation."

IV.

And now, lastly, Satan came up with the people of God, but he was never more Satan-like than he was then; and so we close with that observation, that there is a possibility that there may be in the midst of the people of God those who will develop their character, their evil character, all the more terribly because of their association with worship and with the Gospel.   Satan at once began to find fault with one of God's best servants; and many who join in the assembly of the saints amuse themselves by pulling to pieces the characters of God's people, and if they cannot find anything to fix upon in their characters, they usually impute motives or make suppositions as to what such persons would be if they were in a different position.   Oh, do not come into contact with God's people merely to oppose them!   He that touches them touches the apple of Jehovah's eye.   If he be a bad man, better let him alone than injure the character of one true child of God.   Touch a man's child, and you will see the colour coming into the man's face at once. He might have forgiven a blow upon himself; but a blow upon his child—it shall go hard with you if you provoke him so. Never, I pray you, come up into the midst of the assembly, and there sit and indulge hard and bitter and cruel thoughts against those that seek to follow their Master. Satan was very satanic, for even when he had accused Job he went away to persecute him and torment him. I pray that husband not to go home to-night to ridicule his wife as he has often done. You can get to hell very well and very surely without going post haste there by persecution; for if any man wants to make his destruction infallibly sure, and his being driven from the presence of God certain beyond all doubt, he has only got to begin to persecute his children or his wife, or his friend because they will follow the Lord. Why, if you do not want to go to Heaven yourself, let other people go. What is the good of being a dog in the manger? Let them have their way: you have yours. Wherefore should you, as an Englishman, oppose their liberty; and as a man of sense and a man of decency, why should you attempt persecution? I speak thus because I know there are some that have to smart very severely under the cruel things that are said about them and against them when they reach their homes. Satan came also among the saints, and he came there to do them mischief. It is enough for one Satan to do that. Let none of us imitate Satan lest we should fall into his eternal condemnation.

And now I send you away, but not till I have stated again, for the thousandth time, the simple way of salvation. Whoever in this audience desires to be reconciled to God, whoever desires the pardon of his sin, this is the way of salvation. It is that you stop in your career of sin and repent of your transgression, and then listen to this word, which is the word of His Gospel—" He that believeth and is baptized shall be saved." To believe is to trust; and if you would know what you have to trust, hearken to these words. " Hear, and thy soul shall live." Christ, the Son of God, became man, and as man suffered and died upon the cross. On Him were laid the sins of all who believe in Him, and He was punished for their sins, that so God might be just, and yet might receive those for whom Jesus died—as many as believe in Jesus, the Saviour; " for God so loved the world, that He gave His only begotten Son, that whosoever believeth in Him should not perish, but have everlasting life." If you trust Christ, then know your sin is forgiven, for it was laid on Christ; your iniquity is put away, for Christ put it away by His death. You are pardoned and saved. Go your way, and rejoice in such a Gospel.

May the Lord grant that many of you to-night may seek mercy through Jesus, may not delay and procrastinate, but may seek and find now pardon through the precious blood of our redeeming Lord! Amen.

XVII.

PLAYING THE FOOL.

And as thy servant was busy here and there, he was gone.—
(1 Kings, xx. 40).

IT was the excuse which the man in this prophetic parable
made. He had been entrusted with a captive of great importance. He had been told to take care of him, and that if he
suffered him to go his life should pay for his life. He accepted
the charge, was put in the king's commission to take care of
the prisoner, and he suffered him to escape, his excuse being
that he had other things to do. He was busy here and there,
and lo, the captive was gone.

I suppose a man must be very hard driven before he would
not have some excuse. We are, most of us, excellent hands at
excuse-making, and we carry this business of ours into religion.
There, if we happen to be without God and without Christ,
we make a capital policy for ourselves. A great many persons excuse themselves with the same plea, the same stale
plea, which we have now before us—they are so busy, they
have so much to do; and one of these days when they come
to die I expect they will say that they were busy here and
there, and while they were so doing they somehow or other
lost their souls. Now, this excuse is a very common one, and
I purpose for a short time to try and deal with it to-night.

I.

And, first, let us observe that it is one which a certain
class of persons could not in any conscience make. Young
people cannot very well say that they are pressed with business, and therefore cannot think of an eternity, or seek reconciliation with God. As yet you have no business ; you are
not surrounded with the thousand cares which your parents
plead ; all that you want is provided for you. You have
certain duties which occupy a portion of your time, at least

I hope you have, for it would be a very unfortunate circumstance for you to be left with nothing to do, and your friends
must be very unwise if they are exposing you to that temptation ; but still, you have not so much to do that you could,
even with any sort of face, say that you have no time for
prayer, no time for reading the Word of God, no time for
solemn consideration, no time for repentance, and no time for
faith.

Dear young friends, you will be busy by-and-bye. Perhaps some of you are about entering upon business for yourselves. Is it not a suggestion which your common sense
approves that now, *now*, the great business of life should be
seen to? Have you not a special promise that they that seek
God early shall find Him? Do not lose that by postponing
the seeking of your Saviour. Is not the morning often the
very best time for solemn consideration—when the dew, as
yet, has not been brushed from the lawn, and the smoke has
not yet gathered on the sky? And so is the morning of life
a sweet and fair season in which to come and give yourself
to the Saviour. We have heard many regret that they came
to Christ so late, but never once did we hear it said that any
mourned that they came to Him too soon.

> 'Twill save us from a thousand snares
>   To mind religion young.

I speak here from personal experience, and I hope I shall
have all the more weight in my pleading with you. Just
when I was about sixteen years of age, I began to preach
Christ Jesus, but ere that I had confessed my faith in Him
by baptism—just when I was fifteen years of age. I wish
it could have been many years before ; but I bear my witness
that He is a good Master, that His service is good, and His
wages are good, and Himself best of all. Might I have the
privilege of being the instrument to-night of persuading some
young heart to say, " We, too, will give our soul to Jesus
lest in after-life our thoughts should be smothered amidst
the tares of a thousand cares and worldly concerns. We will
give our hearts to Jesus even now." You see, if you do not,
you cannot plead the excuse that you were so busy, for now,
at least, you have the time.

Neither can some say this whose occupations are light.
There are persons placed in such a condition now (not so
many as I could wish) whose hours of labour are not grind-

ingly long, and whose occupations themselves are not so altogether absorbing to their minds that they cannot think. There is many a man who can perform his trade with his hands, and yet his heart can be in heaven. We have known many such. There are handicrafts that leave the soul unfettered while the hands are busy. I grant you that these grow fewer and fewer, and the rush of the world's business becomes stronger and stronger every day, and like a mighty cataract bears men's minds along with it ; but there are some of you who have good pauses, and intervals, and periods of thought. Especially you have your Sabbaths ; and those sweet Saturday evenings that some of you get when you should prepare yourselves for the holy day; and then the long Sabbath from the first break of dawn till after the sun hath gone down. Oh, these are times when the world is shut out, and hushed, and still, when surely your spirit should say, " I will arise and go unto my Father." God has given us these respites from toil that we may not say that we never have a space of time in which to think of Him. He marks out and sets apart these Sabbaths not for Himself only, but for ourselves, that in them we may find our richest good, may commerce with the skies, and do the great business that shall make us rich for eternity. Some of you, then, could not say that you are so busy that you have no time to think about your souls.

And I do address, I know, to-night, a few persons who are still unconverted who could not say this for another reason. God has spared them now to a considerable age, and they have given up business and have retired. Beloved friends, you used to reckon that when this time came you would set it apart for solemn consideration. You have to be very thankful that you have been spared to see that time. You might have been cut down as a great many others have been. How many times, now, within these last thirty years, while you have been in business, have you heard it said, " So-and-so is gone," and " So-and-so is gone " ? Why, if you think a minute, the persons whom you did trade with when you first commenced—where are they now? With the exception of a few like yourself who have been spared, they are gone, and there are new names on your ledger and your day book now. Well, you have been spared in the mercy of God to get out of business, and to shake off most of its toil and turmoil ; and yet for all that you are living a prayerless and a thoughtless life. Oh, I could burst into tears over such a one as you

are, because you really have seen such wonderful mercy. When
you reflect how you have been spared, and the remarkable
way in which God has favoured you in business, and now
has given you this quiet opportunity in that retreat of yours
to think of Him, are you resolved to perish? Are you determined to be lost? Have you made a covenant with death and
a league with Satan that you will perish, despite all that
God's providence can do for you? Oh, I trust it is not so.
And if it be, my prayer shall be that God's Spirit would
come in and disannul your league with death and break your
covenant with hell; for if not you will not be able to say
in eternity, "Good Master, I was so hurried that I could not
repent; I was so pushed for it that I could not seek Thy face;
I had not time to learn the Gospel, because I had to keep my
face to the grindstone with such severe toil. I never had
rest." Why, that little villa of yours will stand up against
you, and these quiet days in the autumn of your life will all
impeach you, for having been wilfully a transgressor against
the infinite love and sovereign mercy of your God. Thus,
young people, and old people, and persons placed in circumstances in which they are free from pressing toil, will be quite
unable to use such an excuse as this, though I should not
wonder, such is the impudence of the human heart, that even
they might venture upon it.

II.

But now I pass on to the second remark—that those who
do make this excuse, and think that they can well make
it, ought to remember that it is not a valid one. I will try
to show it is not. You say that you are too busy. My first
reply is, Why were you so busy? What was the reason of it?
You were so busy because you had such-and-such a quantity
of money to make. But why needed you have made that
money? I do not see that it was a very important matter after
all that there should have been such a quantity of Probate-
Duty paid from your estate. It does not seem to me, whatever it may seem to you, such a mighty fine thing to be lost
for and to be damned for, and to have it said, "He died
worth £100,000." To me it seems a mere trifle, a ridiculous
thing which only shows what a fool the man must have been
to have thrown away his best part and his eternal happiness.

for the sake of paying so much more into the Exchequer, taken from his heirs when he came to die. There are other ways of finding the revenue of the country without finding it out of the woe of immortal souls, surely.

Oh, but you are not occupied with money-making, you say ; you are occupied with scientific studies. Certainly a somewhat nobler pursuit ; but was there any great need that we should know a little more at the expense of your soul? What have you found out? Anything very remarkable? You have classified beetles, have you? You have arranged ferns; you have tracked a river somewhere; you have studied the law of storms; you have found out a new machine, have brought out another notion that may save toil and promote domestic economy. Very well. We are much obliged to you; but was that what you were sent into the world to do? Were you created on purpose for that? And, having done that, if your soul is lost, was there absolutely any need for the world to get a new machine that should be stained blood-red with the blood of a soul for ever? We could have waited a little while. If it had been put to the humane portion of mankind they would not have liked to have the best invention at the expense of a single immortal spirit. There was not any need for you, then—I believe there was no necessity—that you should have been so busy, even if the excuse be true.

But you say, " Oh, but in my case it was absolutely needful that I should fight for it, to provide for myself and a little regiment of little ones." Oh, I know how hard some are pressed ; and 'tis grievous when we see men working from early morn till late at night with no time whatever for mental improvement or for spiritual thought. It used to be so. I do not think it is so much so now, nor will it ever be so again. I should hope it would not, but there may be cases in which it is still so, and, if so, let me remind you that your having found a Saviour would not have rendered it more difficult to find the bread that perisheth. Your having given your heart to Christ would, in fact, have eased you of much care. You would then have felt that you had a Father to provide for you—a Father whose care over sparrows and ravens would be a guarantee to you that He would take care of you. Why, your toil would have been lighter. It might have cost you as much sinew, but it would not have cost you so much discontent and wear and tear of heart ; and this is the main drain upon a man—that wear and tear of his inner soul. O, you labouring man, if you had loved your God, you would have worked to music instead of working to groans. If you had thought Christ to be your Friend, you would have toiled cheerfully, doing it as unto Him, and therefore the yoke would have been easier about your neck. Therefore it is no excuse, but rather a call upon you, because of your labour, to come to Him, for He hath said, " Come unto Me, all ye that labour and are heavy laden, and I will give you rest."

But now let me put it to you. You say you were so busy that you could not attend to religion. Had not you time to attend to the other necessary things? I do not see many of you in the streets ordinarily without your coats or without your dresses. You have time to dress. Then I am sure God has given you time in which to put on the robe of righteousness. You sometimes hurry your meals, but still you do get them. There is the breakfast, and there is the dinner ; and I cannot believe that God gives us time to eat the bread that perisheth and has given us no time to eat the bread of life. All of you usually get to your beds at some time or other, and get your sleep ; some get quite enough of it, and if they cut off a little for their devotion, it were well for them ; they would be none the more weary for that. But you *do* sleep, and he that hath so much time for sleep must surely have time for the things of God. But permit me to add, I find in this country and in this city most people have time for recreation. Somehow or other they will get an outing now and then (and I would not rob them of it) ; they have times in which they spend their diversion (I do not blame them) ; but do they not say they have no time and are too busy to think of God and their souls?. That is a stark naked lie when a man says that he finds time for fun and merriment, and cannot find time for prayer and for seeking the Lord.

Moreover, although some of you do not hoe your own gardens, occasionally you find time to hoe your neighbours', aye, and to hoe up their flowers as well as their weeds. We find persons who are too busy to be saved, but are not too busy to pick holes in the characters of Christians. They puzzle their heads about Predestination and Free Will ; they do not mind sitting down over some problem that the archangel Gabriel could not solve, and pose themselves over that ; but the simple truth, " Believe and live "—they have no time for that; and to forsake their sins and turn to Christ—they are too busy for that ; but yet not too busy to have political speculations, and radical theories, and I know not what be side. O, sirs, I think the thing does not hold water. It is a leaky vessel. Let us put it away. The excuse is hardly worth the combating. It yields as soon as we give it half a stroke. There will I leave it. It is a broken thing.

III.

But I will remind you now, thirdly, that this is an excuse which accuses. It is an edge tool which cuts the person who defends himself with it ; for when men say that they have had much business and have not had time to think of their souls, then it is clear if you have had much business you have had much mercy. You must have seen a good deal of God's goodness in the course of these many years. Others have been bankrupt ; you have seen many wrecked in the sea of life ; and you have escaped. Man, have you had all these mercies, and never thanked God for them? You say you are busy. That means that God has given you much, sent much of His goodness to your door. And have you never returned thanks to the great Giver of all good? "Ah!" say you, "but I have had much trouble, too." There I have you again with another argument. Have you had so many troubles, and never sought God in them? Yes, perhaps you have sought Him in trouble. But, then, why have you forgotten Him when the trouble has been removed? How was it you wrung your hands in despair and said, "O God, help me out of this," and, when you were helped out of it, you still remained a stranger to Him? Your many mercies and your many troubles are both calling against you. Why, surely they should have drawn you or have driven you to your God. With a favourable wind and a fair sheet you ought to have made for that haven, or, with a rough wind, you ought to have worked for it and laboured for it with all your might. You have had much business, you say, and been very busy here and there. Then that looks to me as if you were not a fool —as if you were a man with brains beneath that forehead, a man that could think. Now, if you were a downright simpleton and lost your soul, some might say, " Poor fool, he knows no better." But you, sir, you take a prominent place in the city, and you are on the Exchange ; you can always hold your own, your opinion is always worth hearing ; and will you be wise about everything but your soul and eternity ? Have you wit for everything except for that which concerns judgment ? Do you save your foolery for your God ? Are you a wise man everywhere, and then play the idiot before Jehovah's face ? If you live with heaven's gate wide open before you, and seek not to enter, if you have the dear wounds of Jesus streaming with atoning blood, and yet never seek a share in the pardoning efficacy that comes from them, you are playing the fool with a vengeance—a comedy before God which will end in a tragedy as you are a living man, unless the grace of God prevent it. The very fact, then, that you have been busy here and there is an excuse which does accuse you. Mention it no more lest it increase your condemnation.

Again. This excuse that we have been too busy to think of divine things is an excuse which will cost us terrible wounds to our memory when we come to die. I cannot somehow ever try, for I know I never should succeed, in painting the death-bed of a man who with sound health and good judgment and grand opportunities, and education, and the like, has spent all his time simply upon the things which concern him, and then comes to die without any preparation whatever for the eternal world. It seems to me of all things beneath the sky the most monstrous. Why, to have one's self prepared for the eternal dwelling-place might well become so absorbing a pursuit that we might forget the things of time. I could comprehend a mental abstraction that should make us absolutely foolish from day to day as to ordinary affairs if the mind were set upon superior and spiritual concerns ; but I cannot comprehend this raving madness of humanity that men seem to be utterly abstracted from spiritual things, and rapt and taken altogether away about these bubbles, these trifles, these children's toys.

I passed the Lake of Thrasymenus one evening, in travelling from Rome, and I marked the spot right well, for it is said that there when the Romans and the Carthaginians were engaged in deadly war there happened a terrific earthquake which shook the ground beneath their feet, and heaved the lake in waves, and tossed the mountains about on either side, but the combatants were so desperately set at slaughtering one another that they never observed the earthquake and did not believe it on the following day when they were told of it. It seems so strange, does it not, that they should be so taken up with it? And men seem to be so taken up with the concerns of this life that even were God to set up His throne of judgment, and it did not interfere with the Stock Exchange, and the corn market, and the coal market, I believe men would still go on buying and selling and getting gain, and if the last thunderbolt were even now to be rushing through the sky, they would be so occupied with the things of time and sense that they would not be startled even then until it came in even closer proximity to their own souls. Oh, what perversity of intellect is this! May God rouse us from it. When a man comes to see how all his lifetime he has been busy about these things and lost his soul, what a look it will be in looking backward! "I gained that money, scraped it together, for my heirs—used the rake, and used the shovel. I pinched myself, fool that I was! Why did I? I pinched myself for nobody. There I was up early in the morning, and late at night still at my business, my Bible covered with dust, the House of God forsaken, or, if I went to it, too sleepy to attend to what I should have heard ; meanwhile no private prayer, no cleansing of myself in Christ's blood, no seeking reconciliation with God ; and all for what? Just that I might leave this heap of money to those who will forget me and probably be glad that I have gone, so that they may inherit what I have scraped together. What a fool I have been to live for that which I must leave, and to scrape together the thick clay which I must now renounce for ever."

If I have lived for God there is something worth living for. If I have brightened the home of sorrow, if I have cheered the mourner, if I have helped the orphan and made glad the widow, if I have been the instrument in the hands of God of teaching the young the way to Heaven, and guiding wanderers to the Saviour, and if my hand is linked with the hand of the Eternal, and I am resting in the precious blood, then what matters it if death comes? But if I have lived for just these things that perish in the using, O Death, O Death, thou dost shake my palaces and pull down my towers. O Death, thou fell destroyer, thou hast blasted me, and I am blasted, and that for ever and for ever. Sirs, awake, I pray you! May God awake you! No more use this excuse which will certainly tear your heart like a serpent gnawing at your very vitals. I pray you, turn from ever using it again.

IV.

And now, lastly, it is an excuse which cannot, even if it could be proved a valid one, restore to a man the loss which he has sustained. I may say I was busy ; I may moan it over as I clutch the sheets of my dying bed—"I was busy, I was very busy. God knows I was busy from morning till night. I could not go to the house of God ; I made my ledger up on a Sunday. I could not read my Bible. I was too busy with the day book. I could not pray : I had enough to do to be thinking of how I should meet my bills, and what I should do to get custom, and to get trade. I was all for that which concerned getting my boy out into a trade or trying to get a connection together. O God, Thou knowest I was so busy!" Yes, but though the poor wretch may hiss that between his teeth it will not give him back his soul, and when he is in hell, banished from God's presence, *that* will not undo the bolts that shut the iron door ; *that* will not give a drop of water to his parched tongue ; *that* will not shorten eternity; *that* will not kill the worm that never dieth, or quench the fire unquenchable. . No, but that thought, "I was busy," "I was busy," shall only add to the eternal unrest of the spirit that can know no repose.

There are certain birds about Constantinople that they say never rest. They seem to be always on the wing, poor things, and the common name by which they are known (I am afraid profanely) by many is that of "damned souls." And truly if men were wise they would look at that metaphor of the birds that never rest. They must not light upon the sea: even there they shall find no chance of repose ; nor on the land, nor on the tree, nor anywhere ; but flit on, on, on, with wings for ever weary, and that shall never rest. This looks to me like the fate of souls too busy to find rest in God —to fly for ever and for ever and get no rest, no rest for the sole of their foot. Poor Noah's dove was plucked into the ark by Noah when she was faint ; but once let this life be passed, O souls that will not rest in Christ now, and you shall never rest. You shall have appetites you cannot gratify, desires you cannot satiate, ambitions to which you never can attain. You shall blaspheme God, and yet will He not be blasphemed by you ; nor will His holy name be injured by your curses. You shall long for death itself, and it shall be denied you.

Oh, wherefore, wherefore, will ye inherit this? Why will you run these risks and cast yourself into this woe? "Turn ye, turn ye, why will ye die, O house of Israel?" To-night, whatever be your business, put it aside till your soul is saved. I would fain say the most pressing engagement ought to give way to this. I must become a friend of God; I must be washed from sin; I must be delivered from going down into the pit. Oh, it does not matter what my engagements are; if I am slipping down a precipice, and there is a chance of escape, I must escape, engagements or no engagements. If I have accidentally taken poison it matters not though I have a call to go to business on the spot. I cannot go. I must take the antidote first and have my life preserved. Necessity has no law, and the stern necessity of souls being saved demands that anything and everything should go on one side and be pushed to the wall, to make room for solemn consideration and earnest thought concerning the things of God.

I have done; but I wish that I had an opportunity of speaking these words into every unconverted man's face and heart. It is one of my regrets that I cannot come round to speak individually to so many; yet I would fain post myself at each one of yonder doors, if I were divisible, and say to each thoughtless busy man, each thoughtless family woman, I beseech you do let other things have their place—their right place; but let God have the first place; let Christ have the first place; let your soul have the first place; and do not have to say, "While I was busy here and there my soul was gone, and I was lost."

God save you! Amen.

XVIII.

OPENING THE STOREHOUSES OF GRACE.

And Joseph opened all the storehouses.—(Genesis xli. 56.)

PERHAPS the history of Joseph is to many persons the most interesting narrative in the whole of the Old Testament. It is full of pleasing pictures. Poets, painters, writers of all kinds have revelled in the matchless scenes which that story presents. To us as Christians it is perhaps chiefly delightful because Joseph is such an eminent type of our Lord Jesus Christ. All through his life you see touches that remind you of the story of Jesus of Nazareth ; whether it be in the dungeon or on the throne, whether it be as rejected of his brothers or as receiving them to his heart, or reigning in Egypt for their good and providing for all their wants. It needs no ingenuity—it is a very simple matter indeed— to say, " In this, Joseph is like to Jesus, and in that, and in the other ; and in hundreds of points he becomes one of the chief types of the Old Testament—types of our divine Master."

Now you see in the present text that Joseph is rightly made a type of Jesus Christ. There is a famine in all the earth—a famine after the bread, not of the body, but of the soul ; and behold Jesus has provided for that famine ; and it is true in these latter days,—especially and notably true— that, as Joseph opened all the storehouses, so has Jesus opened the rich treasuries of grace that famished souls in all regions may come and eat even to the full. That, then, will be the topic of to-night—to work a parallel between Joseph of Egypt opening the storehouses and Jesus, head over all things to His Church, opening the storehouse for perishing souls.

There will be four or five points upon which we shall briefly touch.

I.

And the first is this: Joseph was empowered by the king to do what he did. When Pharaoh saw the extraordinary wisdom which dwelt in that young man Joseph, and the evident favour of God that rested upon him, he selected him to carry out his own project, and to enable him to do so he made Joseph to be viceroy. He was the grand vizier of Egypt—was to stand in the place of the king, and attend to all the business of the land; so that, in the first place, nobody could approach to Pharaoh except through Joseph. When the people petitioned the king he said, "Go unto Joseph. What he saith unto you, do it." There was no coming to the throne except through the mediation of the king's prime minister, even Joseph. Well now, at this day the Lord God is not to be approached by us except through Jesus Christ. Prayers addressed immediately to God apart from the mediator will be unacceptable. We can only hope to succeed with the Most High by pleading that name which He has given to be a pass-word to the courts of glory, which He has given to be the seal to our prayers and the pledge of their acceptance with Him.

Dear friend, are you beginning to desire peace with God? You can only get it through the blood of Jesus Christ. Do you want to be reconciled to the Father? It must be through the Son. Do not indulge in any sentiments which lead you to think little of the Lord Jesus Christ, for God will not receive one who will not receive His Son. "No man cometh unto the Father but by Me," is Christ's own word; and so it must be. If you will not go to Jesus, the Father can not—will not—accept you. That is the way of access: there is no other. Come then, I pray you, if you would approach the great God and find mercy at His hands—come with the name of Jesus upon your tongue and upon your heart.

The king's order was moreover that Joseph was in all things to be obeyed. "Whatsoever he saith unto you, do it," says he. Now it is the order of the great King of kings that Jesus is to be obeyed in all respects. "That at the name of Jesus every knee should bow, of things in heaven and things on earth, and things that are under the earth; and that every tongue should confess that Jesus Christ is Lord, to the glory of God the Father." I want every sinner that would have peace with God to submit to the sway of Jesus, and to say in his heart, " What He bids me do, by His enabling grace I am prepared to do. Whatever of self-denial He shall ask at my hands, that would I endeavour to render, but I long for salvation through the Mediator."

But note that in Egypt there was nobody else in power but the king and Joseph; so is there nobody appointed to intercede between God and man save the man Christ Jesus. Do not be beguiled by anybody to seek another mediator. The virgins and the saints can have no power with God. He has put all power in Christ. If He pleadeth, the intercession will avail, but seek no other. And do recollect that you do not want any mediator between you and Christ. Very simple as this statement is, there is need often to repeat it. You may come to Jesus just as you are whoever you may be. The poor, needy, hungry, famished, Egyptians were to go to Joseph. They did not want any great man to introduce them to him, but if they went to him, then they came practically to Pharaoh. You do want a mediator between yourselves and God, but you want no mediator between yourselves and Christ. Priests, clergymen, ministers—they are all altogether unnecessary in the matter of approaching to Jesus Christ. Come to Him simply and humbly just as you are, and He will accept you, for God has appointed Him to be a ladder between earth and heaven. He is the secret link between a needy sinner and the all-sufficiency of God. There is the first parallel then. As Joseph was put in power so also is the Lord Jesus Christ King of kings and Lord of lords.

II.

Secondly, the text says, "Joseph opened all the storehouses." The fact is Joseph had filled the storehouses. He was the man to open them, for he was the man that filled them.

And Joseph had filled all the storehouses before the famine came. Glory be to the Lord Jesus that before Adam fell He had prepared the way to restore the fall. Before sin was born, or Eden had been blasted by the breath of treason, the Lord Jesus Christ had entered into a covenant with the eternal Father that He would redeem His people from the fall, which, as yet, had not happened. In that covenant He had filled the storehouses by His promise. Then came

the fulness of time, and though as yet you and I were not
born, and our time of famine had not come, the Lord Jesus
by His life and death filled all the storehouses. What heaps
of grace, what stores of heavenly food, He gathered together,
reaping not with the sweat of His face as we do, but with
the sweat of His very soul, sweating " as it were great drops of
blood falling to the ground." Vast granaries of mighty
grace He filled with every pang His body and His soul endured. Gethsemane heaped up the bread of Heaven: its wine-
press was full. And Calvary can tell how the body which
He gave to bleed and die became for the world food, of
which if a man eat he shall live for ever. Joseph filled the
storehouses before the famine came, and Jesus has made
provision of grace before you and I were born—certainly
long before we had any idea that there was a famine in the
land.

And then note that Joseph had filled the storehouses
sufficiently full to last through seven years. So much wheat
did he gather that he ceased to keep account of it. Some of
the vast storehouses are still remaining in Egypt, and we
have on the tombs of Egypt representations of the great
underground granaries which Joseph built. So much was it
that he could not count it. O beloved, Jesus has made such
provision for the sons of men as to be quite beyond all calculation. His granaries are deep as our helpless miseries
are, and boundless as our sins. Not only is there sufficiency
in Christ, but all-sufficiency. There is no measuring, for there
is no limit. When God Himself takes human flesh and bleeds
and dies, the merit of that sacred passion is not to be set
down in figures or conceived of by the mind. So, poor needy
souls, however ravenous your appetites, you will never exhaust
the store of sovereign grace which Christ has laid by for
such as you.

But He alone did this. When the famine was fully come
there was nobody in all the world that could feed men but
Jesus. He had filled the storehouses, and there they were.
And Joseph had them all under his own lock and key. And,
mark you, there is salvation in Christ, but there is salvation
in no other. The Gospel of Jesus is divinely intolerant. It
does not say, " There is salvation here, and also there and
there, for it courts not the approbation of being charitably
false." It speaks the truth and declares that " other foundation can no man lay than that which is laid "—Jesus Christ

the righteous. "He that believeth and is baptised shall be saved : he that believeth not shall be damned." It does not flinch matters. Joseph knew that they must come and buy corn of him, or starve. They might work as hard as they pleased, but it was no use working where money wages would not buy a piece of bread. They might dig and toil and till the soil, but as the time of famine had come the land would yield nothing to them. There was nothing for any man in the known world, but to go down to Egypt to Joseph and buy corn. And such is the famine which has fallen on our entire humanity that there is no possibility of your salvation in any way by your own doings, by your own feelings, by the help of priests, by multiplying ceremonies, and the like. You must go to Christ and get bread from Him or you will perish as surely as you are born. May the Holy Ghost make men know this that they may decide to go to Joseph—to Jesus at once.

III.

This brings me to the third remark, which is this : Joseph opened those storehouses which he had filled all in good time.

And here let us notice that Joseph had filled the storehouses on purpose to open them. He did not put a bushel of wheat in there for his own keeping and lock it up. What was the use of having it stale and musty for the mice and the rats? He put the wheat in on purpose to take it out again. When the Lord Jesus gathered all the merit of His life and death together, He did not do it to keep it useless. He gathered it on purpose to save sinners with it, on purpose to give it away. Whenever you think of Jesus Christ and think highly of Him, dear heart, say to yourself, "All this is meant for needy sinners." There is not anything in Christ for Himself. It is all for you and for me and such as we are. If we are guilty, that fountain which He filled is to wash us. If we are naked, that robe of righteousness was meant to clothe us. I will put it very plainly : there is not a bushel of wheat in Christ's granary but what is meant for hungry souls to eat. You have but to come for it and take it, for He has put it there on purpose for such as you.

Now, if Joseph had kept the grain, it would not have been to his credit. His profit and his honour both lay in getting rid of the wheat that he had gathered. If he had kept it there in the granaries, of what good would it have been to collect it but to mock and to insult the people? Jesus Christ's honour and glory never lie in denying mercy to sinners, but they lie in giving to those that need it. How you ought to catch at this, you that feel your need of Christ. I think this ought to cheer you very much. O Lord Jesus, if Thou deny me Thy grace, it will not make Thee more happy nor more rich, nor more honoured. On the contrary, if Thou give me Thy grace I shall be greatly benefited, but Thou wilt be honoured. It will be to Thy glory to distribute that which Thou didst gather on purpose to give us. Is not that good reasoning—sound argument? Be sure such a man as Joseph means to distribute what he collects, and be sure that such a one as Jesus means to distribute among poor and needy souls that rich, free, grace which by His life and death He has stored up on purpose for them. There is much encouragement in the parallel to those who seek the Lord.

Notice again that Joseph opened the storehouses when the famine was sore in the land. He did not open them during the seven years of plenty. If people could have come and had the wheat then, they would only have wasted it. He kept the door shut till there was need to have it opened, and then he opened it. If there is anybody here that is exceedingly good, righteous, excellent, and can get to heaven by his own works, the granary is not open. There is nothing for you. But if there is a poor soul here that has nothing to trust to of its own—no good works, no good feelings—if you feel that you are utterly lost by nature and by practice—then the granaries are open. The famine is in your land. And as Joseph opened all the storehouses, so does Jesus Christ. Famished soul, the promises are for you. Hungry soul, the blessings of the covenant are for you. Do but prove your need, and you have proved your right, for there can be no other need, no other right, for the poor soul except its own dire necessity. The advertisements of Joseph were not put out until the corn was all eaten. Then he made the people know that they might come and buy of him. Jesus Christ publishes His Gospel to every creature, but the point of it is, "Come unto Me, all ye that labour and are heavy laden, and I will give you rest." You that know your need—you sinners, you lost, you ruined ones—it is to you that the invitation is most pressingly given. Come and welcome to Jesus Christ!

Now, when Joseph had opened the storehouses, he kept
them open. As long as the seven years lasted, the granaries
lasted ; they were never exhausted. What a mercy that is,
for children of God that have been His people these twenty
years! The granaries are open still. Have you got grace?
He giveth more grace—grace upon grace. Has He blest you?
He will bless you twice as much. Have you been enabled to
be strong? He will make you stronger. He never shuts the
granary while there is a hungry soul to be fed. Dear saints,
if any of you to-night are straitened, you are not straitened
in Him. Come and welcome ; come and take all that you
possibly can out of the great storehouses of grace.

Once more. These granaries were all over Egypt. Up
the Nile, down the Nile, everywhere where there was a city,
there were the granaries. Where the people lived there were
the storehouses. What a blessing this is—that, wherever there
is a sinner, Christ is handy. You will find Him, you work-
people ; you will find Him if you lift your eye towards Him
in the work-room. You will find Him, you poor sick folk,
when you are in the hospital ; when you are lying in the bed
you expect to occupy before long. You will find Him, dear
mother, at home with the little ones. Christ is near to you.
You may find Him there. And you that pace the streets,
you that are watchmen of the night, you that have scarcely
a home to call your own, go where you may, you will find
Him there. And I would say to the prisoner, if he were lying
in his cell in the jail—ay, and to him that is in the condemned
cell—Jesus is to be found even there. Where there is hunger
there there is the granary ; and wherever you are, needy,
hungry one, say not, "Who shall climb to Heaven to bring
Christ down, or who shall descend into the deep to fetch Him
up?" He is "nigh you—in your mouth and in your heart."
If with thy mouth thou wilt confess the Lord Jesus, and
with thy heart believe in Him, thou shalt be saved. So
Joseph opened all the storehouses.

But I should not wonder, dear friends, if the type would
fail if we were to look closely into it, because he, very likely,
only opened them during some hours in the day ; and if you
got too late you must go without your dinner. Now, our
Lord opens all the storehouses at all times. From morning
till night—when you are young and when you are old—there
is not one single minute of a man's existence but that, if he
seeks the Lord, he will be found of Him. The storehouses

are always open up to the eleventh hour. Ay, and if a soul shall seek the Lord at the very last—sincerely seek Him—He will still be found.

> While the lamp holds out to burn,
> The vilest sinner may return,

and, returning, he shall still find the good Lord ready to receive him. Joseph opened all the storehouses, but he could not keep them always open. He had his hours, and if he had, I suppose when the crowd was gathered together to get their morning meal, if it was anything like the shops in Paris, when the people went to be served, each one with his ration, there would be a deal of pushing and squeezing, and many poor women would get pushed against the wall and have to go home with nothing. But it is not so with Jesus. He has so opened all the storehouses that the poorest, weakest, most trembling and obscure shall be served as soon as ever He comes. No fear of too great a multitude. He has enough for all that come, and He has an open pathway from the very ends of the earth for all that draw near to Him.

IV.

So that brings me to make the fourth observation. "Joseph opened all the storehouses"; that is, he opened them to all comers. Joseph had an eye to his brethren. He said, "God sent me before you to keep your souls alive." Yes, there is an election of grace, but, at the same time, Joseph served everybody that came, for so we find it. "All countries came into Egypt to Joseph for to buy corn because that the famine was so sore in all lands." And the Lord Jesus has a people for whom He shed His precious blood, for whom the whole work of grace is wrought out from top to bottom; but, for all that, it is quite as true that whosoever comes shall be received, come from what land he may. Here are two truths. It is not everybody that will believe two truths that look a little different, but here are the two in the Bible. "All that the Father giveth Me shall come to Me." There is sovereign grace. "Him that cometh to Me I will in no wise cast out." There is the freeness and richness of the word of God addressed to every soul that comes to Him. Now, some came to Joseph a great many miles across deserts, over the sea; but he did not ask where they came from.

They might have the corn. Free trade then. And so some
of you may come from very far-off places to Christ. Perhaps
you have been in character something unmentionable. Possibly you may so have sinned that, if your story were written,.
your own friends would blush to own you. But if you will
come to Christ, He will ask no questions, but will " blot out
your sins like a cloud, and your iniquities like a thick cloud,"
and feed you with the bread of heaven.

Some, however, came to Joseph from near at hand. No
doubt they had, comparatively, a little way to come, but,
if they had not come that little way, they would have perished.
So you that are near to the kingdom, take heed of perishing
near to the kingdom. The people in Egypt had to get the
corn from Joseph as well as the people in Canaan and Arabia.
It would have been a horrible thing for them to die of famine
with all those great storehouses bursting with grain ; and yet
they would have done so if they had refused to go to Joseph.
You people in the Tabernacle that hear the Gospel continually,
if you perish, you will be like Egyptians that lived next door
to a granary, and yet were starved, if such there were. I
should suppose there would be none such, but there are such
spiritually. The bread of life stands on the table before
them every day, and yet they are dying of famine because
they refuse the appointments of the Lord. I say again,
Joseph opened the granaries to all comers ; and Christ has
opened the doors of salvation to all sorts of people, of every
colour and language and character.

> None are excluded hence, but those
>   Who do themselves exclude.
> Welcome the learned and polite,
>   The ignorant and rude.
>
> While grace is offered to the prince,
>   The poor may take their share.
> No mortal has a just pretence
>   To perish in despair.

Joseph opened all the storehouses, and so does Christ. We
never read of one that Joseph sent empty away ; and you certainly will never hear of one that Christ sends empty away.

However, the parallel does not run all through, because
Joseph, though he opened the storehouses, did not give his
wheat away. No, those who wished to obtain wheat must

bring their money with them. They could not have it without; and you know that, after all the money had been spent, they offered their lands; and when the mortgage had all been eaten up, then the poor Egyptians offered themselves to become henceforth Pharaoh's servants. Then they had to be fed right through the rest of the time.

Now, our Lord Jesus Christ makes no such bargains as the son of Jacob did, but He gives without money and without price. I cannot blame Joseph, because very likely if he had proceeded to feed the people without their paying for the food, they would never have worked any more. After the seven years were over they would wish to be still fed in the same way. He would have demoralised all the people. As it was, they were ready enough to work, for a part of the bargain was that they were to have seed-corn as soon as the years of the famine were over, each man intending to get to his land again and work as Egyptians will do. Well, the Lord Jesus acts on another principle. Rowland Hill used to say, " You know, we ministers who have Christ to present to you are very different from other dealers, for all the other dealers have a difficulty to get people up to their price. Our trouble is to get you down to our price, for ours is 'without money and without price.' " The moment you preach Jesus Christ, the sinner begins to fumble to see if he has not got a shilling's worth of merit somewhere, and when he finds he has not, he puts his hand into the other pocket to see if he cannot find at least sixpennyworth of good feeling. When he feels nothing of the kind there, then he begins fumbling in his waistcoat to see if he has not got at least a halfpennyworth of something or other that can recommend him. Now, as long as ever he does that, he cannot deal with Christ. The terms of Christ are no terms at all: everything for nothing. That is Christ's bargain—all things freely given to the man who, with an empty hand and a humble heart, will simply take. O soul, thou art not asked to be, or do, or feel, but simply to let Jesus be and do and feel, and be to thee all in all—thy Alpha and thy Omega, thy entire salvation. What sayest thou? Art thou willing? If thou sayest " Yes, willing: I shall be rejoiced to have it so," trust thou in Him, and it is so.

V.

Now, the last point of all is this: Although Joseph and Jesus in the dealing out of the bread acted on different principles, yet Jesus brings the thing to the same conclusion. Before Joseph had done, Pharaoh had got everything in his hand—people, lands, houses, everything. It was a wonderful speculation in corn, indeed, and he had become the master— the absolute master—of the whole country. Probably, that was a good thing for the people ; but now they had only one landlord, and he was a great one and a king ; and the little petty landlords all over the country that used to grind them to death were all sold out. Everything was now held as crown-land on a lease, and the payment was by no means an unfair one. Though somewhat rigorous, it was nothing approximate to what is paid in rent and taxes in that country now.

Well, the Lord Jesus Christ acts on quite a different principle, but He brings it to the same result. At this moment it is the joy of a large number of us now present here to say that we belong to the Lord—our money, our lands, if we have any, and our persons. Oh, it is to us an intense delight that body, soul, and spirit now belong to God. We do not wish henceforth to think a thought for ourselves, or say a word except for His glory, or breathe a breath but for Him ; nor would we wish to have a hair on our heads that did not belong to the Lord. Take my goods ; take my talents ; take myself, my time—all that I have. I surrender them to Thee. I do not say that all Christians keep to this. I am afraid that many of them do not, but they ought ; and this is the point that the genuine Christian wants to come to. He says :—

> If I might make some reserve,
>   And duty did not call,
> I love my God with zeal so great
>   That I would give Him all.

How came we to this position, then ? Did Jesus bargain with us ? Beloved, we have given ourselves to Him because He did not bargain—because He said that His love would take no price, for it was priceless ; because He was so generous and gracious ; because it was all giving on His part and not receiving. We feel that we must be His: we love Him so. Oh, those dear wounds !

I remember seeing a picture once of Magdalen kissing the bleeding wounds of Christ upon the cross ; and, though it was a ghastly subject, I thought that, had I been there, I would have carried out the painter's strange idea. O blessed person, even of the dying Saviour. But oh, how blessed is He in His glory! and what a joy it will be to see Him when He comes, as soon He will, and every eye shall behold Him. O beloved, do not your hearts burn within you at the very thought of seeing Him? If suddenly He were to appear on this platform, is there anything you would deny Him? If He were to look at any one of you and say, " I have loved thee with an everlasting love," is there any pain you would not bear? Is there any sacrifice you would refuse to make for Him? You will not be put to the test, but I am quite sure many of you would bear it, whatever it might be. If He were to say, " My sister, My spouse, I take thee by the hand, and thou and I must walk to burn at Smithfield's stake," you would go gladly along if you knew that He grasped your hand. O dear, dear Saviour, Thou art worth ten thousand of us, and we give ourselves up wholly to Thee from this time forth even for ever, for Thou hast saved our lives and fed us with the bread of Heaven ; and henceforth we are not our own, but are " bought with a price."

That was the conclusion of Joseph's opening the storehouses. That is the conclusion of Jesus Christ's opening the storehouses for you and for me.

The Lord bless this word for Christ's sake. Amen.

XIX.

"WHILE THE LAMP HOLDS ON TO BURN."

I have sinned. What shall I do unto Thee, O Thou preserver of men?—(Job vii. 20.)

JOB battled well for his own character against the unjust remarks of his friends. When they said he was a hypocrite, he would not have it. When they declared that he must have been indulging some secret sin, he was somewhat tart in his own defence, as well, indeed, he might be, for God's own witness concerning Job was that he was a perfect and an upright man.

And how should he who possessed such a character willingly endure to see it torn to pieces by his envious friends? But, mark you, he who could afford to be thus brave before his fellow-men, and to stand up for his character as judged by them, adopted a very different tone when he came to deal with God. Then he was all humility; then he laid his mouth in the dust; then he put forth no self-defences; but he came before God with broken-hearted language and with the accents of contrition. "I have sinned," said he; "what shall I do unto Thee, O Thou preserver of men."

We do not intend, however, speaking about Job to-night. This language might well become the mouth of any Christian under sharp affliction who is asking God, "Show me wherefore Thou contendest with me," and who, by the light of God's Spirit, begins to discover that there were evils within his heart which he had not seen, but which it was intended by affliction to bring to his knowledge that they might be put away.

Beloved, many a time through life some of us have had to cry, "I have sinned. What shall I do unto Thee, O Thou preserver of men?" But this morning I turned my text into a sermon for seeking souls, and I feel in that mind again to-night, as if I could leave the godly to look after the ungodly—leave the ninety and nine in the wilderness to go

P

after that which has gone astray, and forget the pieces of money that are in the treasury to light the candle and sweep the house yet again to find that piece which has been lost. Pray for me, my brethren, that if I was unsuccessful this morning, though I am sure I was not, yet we may be doubly successful to-night, and that some may be reconciled to God this evening. I cannot bear the thought of your coming and going—continually coming to this house in such crowds—unless you are converted; and when I am every now and then laid aside, and compelled to be silent for a little while, oh, how I bite my tongue that I cannot preach to you, and feel to fret within my spirit that ever I should have wasted any opportunity, and counted it to be wasted unless I have addressed myself to the unconverted and warned them to lay hold on eternal life and escape lest they perish for ever.

It may not be long that we may be spared to address you, and it may not be long that you may live to be addressed by anybody. Therefore, with deep concern for your souls would I speak again to you unsaved ones. We will give the Sabbath up to you, and count it well used if some of you be led to bow before the Saviour and to find life in Him.

Our text contains three things very clearly: a confession—" I have sinned "; an enquiry—" What shall I do unto Thee? "; a title—" O Thou preserver of men."

I.

There is, first, a confession: " I have sinned."

Now, observe, when I take up the words of this confession, there is nothing very particular in them. " I have sinned." There are only three words. Anybody could use them. The worst of men have used them. Saul, the king who was cast off of God for ever, once said, insincerely, " I have sinned." And you remember that Judas, the son of perdition, took the pieces of money for which he had sold his Master and threw them down in the temple and said, " I have sinned," and went and hanged himself. There is nothing in the words. You may remember the publican's prayer, and yet not be justified like the publican. The best form that was ever written, or the best extemporaneous effusion that was ever poured forth from the lip, may have nothing at all in it. There are many things in this world that are like sacks that are labelled, but they have not the goods within that they purport to hold ; and what is the value of them? In your shops you have many dummies, perhaps, and nobody knows that they are such ; but oh, what thousands of dummy prayers there are ! They are exactly like prayers : they are the very same words, word for word, which the best of men would use in the most accept-able prayers ; but for all that they are only dummies. We cannot learn much, then, from the mere words of this con-fession, unless you look deeper, and look into the inner sense of it ; but this much I do learn from it. " I have sinned." It was an acceptable confession, but it was very short. There-fore, I gather that length of words will never be necessary to true confession of sin. " Short and sweet "—let me alter it : short and bitter let the confession be : bitter with true re-pentance, and then as short as you will. Many words are seldom associated with much heart. Prayers can often be measured, but they must be measured backwards. The longer, frequently, the worse, and the truer, often, the more brief. " I have sinned."

Now, there is nobody here that can have an excuse for saying, " I cannot go to God and pray ; I cannot go and confess because I am no orator." It wants no oratory. Why, sirs, if none but orators could be saved, where would many be? Where would the members of the House of Commons go to? Where would many go to of those men who speak, but have not the power to do anything but weary men with their long sentences? No, God wants no rhetoric. He wants you but to say what you feel, and pour your heart out as men pour out water. How it bubbles and gurgles as it goes. Well, let it do so ; let it make much noise, or no noise : it matters not. And so let the heart run out of the mouth in that way : that is the best praying in all the world. Shout, if you like. None, therefore, can be excused for want of utterance.

Now, let us think about this prayer of Job ; and the first remark about it shall be that it was very personal. "*I* have sinned." Oh, how easy it is to join in a " general confes-sion," and, then to feel, " Oh, yes, I have only confessed now what everybody else in the church has confessed too, so I am not particularly bad." But that man truly confesses who says, " Whatever others may have done, *I* have sinned." Charity makes excuses for others, but sincerity makes no excuse for itself. I can see the imperfections of my neighbour, but I will shut my eyes to them as far as I can. My own imperfections I desire to look upon with both my eyes steadily, and so to see them that from my very soul I may say with emphasis, "*I* have sinned," whether anybody else in the world has sinned or not. "I have sinned." Oh, I hope there are some people standing about in this Tabernacle to-night who, unnoticed by anybody else, are saying in their hearts, "Ah, true, I have sinned. If there is nobody else in the upper gallery that has sinned, I have. If there is nobody else anywhere in the house that is a transgressor, I am one. I have sinned. I have sinned." Personal confession is that which God accepts.

In Job's case, again, it was confession made to the Lord. "I have sinned," he said to that God whom he called the "preserver of men." The very point of confession is to feel that you have sinned against God. Many a man is sorry for having offended his neighbour who was never sorry for having offended his God. It is a curious thing that, if I call a man a sinner he is not angry, but if I called him a criminal he would be ready to knock me down, because a crime is a thing against my fellow-man, and we think a great deal of that ; but a sin is an offence against God, and therefore we think very little comparatively of it. It should not be so. We should look upon sin against God as the highest form of criminality, for such, indeed, it is, and in every disobedience there is a direct attack upon the person of God. Hear how David puts it : "Against Thee, Thee only, have I sinned, and done this evil in Thy sight,"—as if sin, though it hurt others, had not the virus in it in that aspect, but it came to its full poison as being an offence against God Himself. O sinner, canst thou say this ? Thou hast neglected thy God ; thou hast lived as if there were no God ; thou hast despised His reign ; thou hast forgotten His will ; thou hast violated His law ; thou hast refused His mercy ; and this it is that will damn thy soul except thou repent of it. Therefore in thy confession make sure that thou go unto God and say, "My God, my Father, I have sinned against Heaven and before Thee."

Now, next, Job's confession was wrought in him by the Holy Spirit. And this is necessary to every true confession. "No man can call Jesus Lord but by the Holy Ghost." So says the Scripture. And I will utter a saying that is quite as true as that: no man can truly say "I have sinned," but by the Holy Ghost. Confession of sin is as certainly the work of God as the creation of the world. Man will not acknowledge his guilt. He is proud, self-righteous. He says, "Who is the Lord, and what is it that I have done if I have broken His law? I care not for Him." But from the soul to say, "I have erred; I have done amiss: my God, I do confess it"—this is what only the Spirit of God can give. Oh, may the Spirit of God grant that to each one of you! It shall be a sure sign of everlasting life in your soul.

Job's confession, hence, was deeply sincere, and accompanied with a great amount of feeling. I think I can see the patriarch's face now. He had not shed a tear through all his losses. From that brave man's face not one single tear had trickled, although he had seen all his wealth suddenly melt away; but I think I see the big drop standing in both eyes when he turns to God and says, "I have sinned. What shall I do unto Thee, O Thou preserver of men?" Bunyan truly puts Mr. Wet-eyes as one who carried the petitions to King Shaddai when the city of Mansoul was besieged; and although I stand not here to speak for actual and for literal tears, for some eyes have but few of them, yet that man whose confession has no feeling in it, I think I may guess that it has no life in it. Can I, if God has quickened me, think I may sin without being grieved? God forbid I ever should. I loathe from my soul to hear some people talk about their sins. Why, I think I have known even some evangelists who, talking to others about their sins, have spoken of what they used to do as if they were almost proud of having been the blackguards that they said they were before they were converted, and talked about their sins as Chelsea pensioners might talk about their battles. Oh, God forbid that we should ever do that! Whenever we think of what we have been, let us blush, or else Satan has taken away from us a very precious thing, which is not a grace, but it is half of one; I mean shame. There ought to be a blessed shamefacedness about Christians when they make confession of their sin. And if you do not cover your brow and tremble when you do say to God, "I have sinned," then surely that forehead of brass of yours is appointed to be a target for the eternal thunderbolts in that day when God shall come to avenge Himself upon all the proud and stout-hearted among the sons of men. Yes, Job's was a sincere and feeling confession.

And I shall close this by saying it was a believing confession, for, note, he says, "O Thou preserver of men," and, as I shall have to show to you, that was the gleam of light that came into Job's mind. Old Master Wilcox says, "Whenever thou hast a sense of sin, look to the cross ; and if thou dost see thy sin and dost not see thy Saviour, away with such a seeing of sin ! " And I say so too. Oh, it is the right thing as a sinner to see Jesus, but to see sin only may drive you to despair and to self-murder, like another Judas. To see sin and to see thy Saviour—that is true repentance, evangelical repentance, the repentance that needs not to be repented of. I have heard say that music never sounds so sweet as when it comes over water ; and surely the notes of pardon never sound so sweet to a soul as when they come across the floods of deep soul sorrow. Jesus is precious when you see Him through your tears. I know of nothing that gives such beauty to Christ, or, rather, that doth so give clearance to the eye that it can see the beauty of Christ, as tears in the eyes—the tears of confession of sin.

Oh, to have, then, to-night, just such a confession ! Somebody says, " Well, I wish I could confess my sin ; it would greatly relieve my mind." Dear friend, go and confess your sin. " To whom ? " you ask. Well, not to me. I have got enough in my own heart that is bad, without having anything of yours. No, not to me : I could not stand it. I cannot understand how a priest can make his ear the common cesspool for the parish ; for that is what the man has to do. He just takes in all the draff and sewage of all his congregation into his own soul, and, if he does not become the most polluted creature in the world through it, it is because he was so to begin with. God deliver us from making such confessions. If you have anything to confess of wrong you have done to your fellow-men, go and confess it. And, what is more, go and make restitution.

I heard of a country minister who preached in a barn one night, and on the way home he overtook a man who, apparently, did not want him to walk with him ; but he did, and he noticed that the man had something or other under his smock frock. By-and-bye they came to a cottage; the preacher had to go another way, and at last the man said, " The fact of it is, sir, I am carrying a spade under here which I borrowed from a neighbour and never returned, and therefore practically stole ; and when I heard your sermon I took the spade home. I could not sleep till it was returned."

Now, such a thing as that you are bound to do to your fellow-men. If you have wronged anybody go and set that right, if you expect mercy. But still, the confession of your heart must be to God. Get into your chamber and pour out your sins before God, into the ear of that High Priest who cannot be polluted by what you tell Him because He is incapable of pollution. He will hear it, and, what is more, He will give you an absolution which is worth having. He will effectually cleanse you from every trace of sin.

Thus much upon the confession.

II.

Now, the second part of our subject is an enquiry. When a soul feels its sin, it naturally is led to say, " What must I do to be saved? "

The text says, " What shall I do unto Thee, O Thou preserver of men? " This shows that the questioner was willing to do anything that he could do. But yet he was bewildered, for he asks, " What *shall* I do? " as though he did not know what to do but look this way or that way or the other. " What *shall* I do? " O soul, if God has awakened you, and you do not know the Gospel, it will be little wonder if you are like one in a maze, not knowing which way to go ; and you will cry like those we read of just now, " Men and brethren, what shall we do to be saved? " And it shows, too, that the person using this question surrendered at discretion, for he says, " What shall I do? " as much as to say, " Lord, I make no terms with Thee, no stipulations, no bargains. Only save me. I have sinned. Do what Thou wilt with me, only have mercy on me. Lord, I throw it up. I have done with the fight against Thee now. Only tell me how I may be reconciled, and here stands Thy servant. Do as Thou wilt with me, but have pity on my soul. What shall I do unto Thee, O Thou preserver of men? "

Now, this question may be answered in this way: " You can do nothing at all." It may be so answered. It is not the full answer. It may be so answered, and must be so answered if the meaning of it be, " What shall I do to escape from God? I have sinned: whither shall I flee? Shall I dive into the grave and hope to hide myself in the unfathomable mines of death-shade? Shall I fly beyond the sea, o'er trackless

waves, or shall I, in order to conceal myself, plunge into the
deepest hell, hoping there to escape Thy wrath?" In vain,
in vain, in vain. You cannot escape from God. It was said
of the old Cæsars that all the world was only a great prison
for Cæsar—that he could always find out the offending party.
And so the whole universe is but a great prison for sinners.
God can find you out, and will. You cannot escape from
Him. Oh, then, let the question stand thus: "What shall
I do by way of expiation for my sin? Suppose I were to
suffer?" Years of suffering will make no atonement for your
sin. You may lie on the hard bed, in the hospital, for twenty
years together. No sin will be put away in that way. You
might scourge yourself and wear a hair shirt and put yourself through innumerable torments, but no sin would vanish
so. This bloodstain comes not out with any human washing.
There is only one blood that can fetch out the bloodstain of
sin, and it is the blood of Christ. "What shall I do?"
asks the soul. "Shall I keep the commandments for the
future?" If you do, you will only do what you ought to
do. Pay what you may, it is all due already; and besides,
you will not keep the commandments for the future. You
will continue still to be imperfect and to be sinful. With the
best intentions in the world you will still go astray. It is
hopeless, therefore, for you to attempt to discharge your
debts before God in that way. When Thomas Oliver, the
famous Wesleyan preacher, was converted he had been in his
early days a most graceless man, and had many times robbed
his creditors, but on being converted he set to work to pay
every one. And he did. He discharged all his liabilities in
full, and travelled many miles to pay a man a sixpence that
he had owed to him, in order to be clear. But you can never
clear your debts before God. They are too heavy for any
human payment. There they are; and if you ask, "What
can I do to put away my sin?" our answer is, Nothing: you
can do nothing. And, best of all, there is no need you should,
for there is One who paid the debt; there is One who discharged the liabilities before you were born. And for every
soul that trusts in Jesus his debts were paid on Calvary's
bloody tree, and the receipt, the receipted bill, was nailed up
upon that cross, and is there now; for Christ has "taken

away the handwriting of ordinances that was against us, and nailed it to His cross"; and there it is freeing His people from all charges for ever. Happy is the man that is a believer in Christ.

But take this question again: "What shall I do?" I do not think it is a full answer to say, "You can do nothing." What did Peter say? "Men and brethren, what shall we do?" was the question put to Peter. Did Peter say,

> Sinner, nothing do,
> Either great or small?

No, he did not say that. He would not have spoken an untruth if he had, in the sense we have already spoken of; but still that is not quite the right answer. When the Philippian jailer said to Paul, "What must I do to be saved?" Paul did not say, "Nothing at all." No, he had got something that the man had to do, and it was this: "Believe on the Lord Jesus Christ, and thou shalt be saved." And Peter had a reply to the crowd in the streets. It was, "Repent and be baptised, every one of you." I think Peter must have been a Baptist. Surely he spoke out more plainly than some could very well do who profess to preach the Gospel.

So then, in answer to the sinner's question, "What shall I do unto God?" we reply, Go to your Father and confess your sin. You cannot do less. Tell Him you deserve His wrath. Do you feel you do? If not, do not be a hypocrite. Go and confess that you have broken His law, especially by acts of omission. Make a clean breast of it. Plead guilty. Stand at the bar and say, "Guilty." And when you have done this, you are bidden to repent. That is, there must be a thorough change of mind as to all this. The sin you loved must be hated. That which gave you pleasure must now cause you pain; and you must, by God's strength, turn away from these sins and have done with them. "Repent," said the apostle. And then Paul said, "Believe"; and that, you have been told a thousand times, is to trust. Trust yourself in the hands of Jesus; rely upon Christ, who was the substitutionary sacrifice for sin. Depend upon Him. And then it is added, "Be baptised," for the Gospel, mark you, is: "He that with his heart believeth, and with his mouth confesseth, shall be saved." You must confess Christ as well as believe in Christ. And it is put thus, again, "He that believeth and is baptised shall be saved." There ought to be, there should be, an open declaration before men of that faith which you have in your heart towards God. And it is a small thing, after all, though there be some that kick at it. No doubt some Christians here will tell me to leave it out ; and shall I leave it out to please you? God forbid. I am responsible to someone higher than you ; and as Peter said, " Repent and be baptised, every one of you," so say I the same to every soul here that asks the way of salvation. And as the Master said, " He that believeth and is baptised shall be saved," it is as much as my soul is worth to leave out a single clause of it. I will put it as He bade me put it, and preach it to you thus. Believe on the Lord Jesus Christ, and be baptised in acknowledgment of this, your faith, for there must be the open confession as well as the secret confidence in Jesus Christ.

Now, this is what you are to do; but this still is nothing by way of merit. There is no merit in believing: there is no merit in repenting. The merit lies in Jesus. The power to save lies in the work of the Holy Spirit in your soul. Yet still the Holy Ghost saves nobody while he is asleep, and no man is dragged into Heaven by his ears. We are made willing in the day of God's power. The Holy Ghost does not repent: He has nothing to repent of. We repent, and He leads us to it. The Holy Ghost does not trust. Why should He trust? It is we that trust ; but He works the trust in us.

So, then, as an answer to this question, " I have sinned. What shall I do unto Thee? " the answer is, " Believe on the Lord Jesus Christ, and thou shalt be saved."

III.

But now, finally, we have in our text a title: " O Thou preserver of men."

Ancient saints were accustomed to address the Lord by different titles, and they generally selected names that were suitable to their condition. Now, when a man is sad he looks round upon God to see if there is anything in God's character or God's dealings that would give him hope ; and Job lights on this: "God is the preserver of men." That is to say, "I am a sinner, but I am still alive."

> Lord, am I yet alive—
> Not in torments, not in hell?
> Still doth Thy good Spirit strive,
> With the chief of sinners dwell?

Then, you see, there is a hope. O Thou who hast preserved me up to this day, what hast Thou done it for? I have sinned, but oh, I beseech Thee, save me, for hast Thou not kept me alive for this very purpose? Is it not written, "For the longsuffering of God is salvation"? Lord, by Thy long-suffering look on me.

Now, I know that I am speaking to somebody here that has been shipwrecked. Why were you not drowned as well as others? I remember speaking one day to an officer who rode in the famous charge of Balaclava, and after he had spoken to me about his feelings as he rode along up to the cannon's mouth I could not help saying to him, "My dear sir, surely God saved you, when the saddles were being emptied, because He had some views of sovereign grace on you." I have heard of a man living in America to the age of ninety-three unconverted, and then recollecting a sermon he heard fifty years before; and then God blessed it to him, and he lived three more years to rejoice in the sovereign grace of God. Why did not he die before he was ninety-three? Because God meant to save him, and He kept him alive till He did save him. He has kept you alive, dear friend. You escaped the fever. Yellow fever could not lay you low. In that hospital abroad you could not die because the Lord meant to save you. And He has brought you here to-night, I hope, because, as the preserver of men, He means to hear your prayers and give you His grace in your soul. God grant that it may be so! At any rate the man who has been spared from many perils has good reason to say that word, "Thou preserver of men," and to take hope from it and appeal to the longsuffering of God.

And then, do not you think that Job meant by this, moreover, to speak of the way in which God supplies the daily wants of mankind? We could not live without bread. We could not exist unless we had nutriment for our bodies. And who finds this? It is sent to the whole multitude of the human race by God's good providence. In that sense God feeds us all virtually by making the earth to produce her harvests. O Thou that feedest all mankind, and so dost preserve them, wilt Thou not give crumbs of mercy to a poor starving soul like me? Is not it good pleading? O Thou preserver of men, have pity on me. If Thou art so good even to the unthankful, I, too, a poor soul that have been unthankful, I do pray Thee to preserve me ; and I will be thankful for ever and ever.

And may Job not have meant that it is God who preserves His saints from going down into the pit ; and therefore he says, " O Thou Saviour of men "—(put it so for a moment, for the sense will be synonymous)—" I beseech Thee have pity on me and preserve me." We spoke this morning of a man who said that if ever he was saved he should be the greatest wonder in all Heaven, and the angels would come trooping down to the doors to look at him, and would say, " Here is the strangest man that ever was saved yet." And we said that that would bring all the more glory to God ; and we say it now. If thou art an out-of-the-way sinner, far removed from hope, and the Lord save thee, so much the more will His name be famous throughout eternity. And since He has saved tens of thousands and millions of souls that were once as lost as thee, why, appeal to Him as the preserver or Saviour of men, and beseech Him to save thee.

And now I have this mournful reflection that, though I have tried to put the way of salvation before you, this audience will all be scattered in a few minutes north and south and east and west, and with it every word that I have said will be scattered and forgotten too, save where, here and, there, God's Spirit shall be pleased to make a lasting impression. I do pray it may be so, in many of your souls. Why, there are some of you that I am looking upon now that have been hopeful dozens of times. We have heard about your being awakened ; we have seen you at our various meetings ; or, if we have not heard of it, it has been so. You have been stirred again and again and again, and you have said, " I have sinned " ; but you have never got any farther. It is a very awful thing to be at Heaven's gate and not to enter. I believe every time a man gets washed up almost on shore from the Dead Sea of sin, if he does not get on shore it becomes, humanly speaking, less and less likely that he ever will. Oh, happy are those hearts that yield to the divine impulses early ; but unhappy shall you be if you feel the drawings of God's love to-night and do not come. Oh, that He might draw mightily, that He might lead you now to cry out with an exceeding bitter cry, "My God, I must be reconciled to Thee ; I cannot live under the shadow of Thine anger. I cannot bear to have Thy furbished sword for ever hanging over my devoted head. O God, forgive me ere I go to sleep this night. Speak the word of mercy. Have pity on my guilty soul."

Ah, dear soul, if you feel an agony for God, an agony for salvation, you shall have it ; you shall have it ; you shall have it. The gates of Heaven always open to those that know how to knock hard. If thou canst, knock hard and entreat and cry. "The kingdom of Heaven suffereth violence, and the violent take it by force." God give thee that violence to-night ; and mayst thou this evening say, "I have sinned, but I am pardoned. I can do nothing unto Thee, O Thou preserver of men, but Thou hast enabled me to bring Thy dear Son before Thee, and I do so now, believing in Him, and I am saved." Amen.

XX.

THE MASTER'S SUMMONS.

Arise, let us go hence.—(John xiv. 31.)

YOU will remember that the Saviour had been sitting at the Paschal table, and He had also celebrated for the first time that ordinance in which throughout all time we are bidden to remember Him. After supper, He began to pour out His heart to His people in that memorable chapter which begins with these comforting words: "Let not your hearts be troubled"; and He was continuing in a strain of consolation —most delightful it must have been to them, and I should think no less pleasing to Himself ; for he that makes others happy generally enjoys the operation himself—when just as it were, in the middle of His discourse, having spoken concerning His own obedience to His Father, He seemed to start and say, "Let us go to it at once. A great work is to be done, and a great suffering is to be endured. Let us not tarry. Arise, let us go hence."

Whether He did arise or not is very questionable. Some have thought that He did, and that the next two chapters were mainly spoken on the road to the garden of Gethsemane. But I hardly think so, and, though one cannot tell for certain, it does look from the 18th chapter, at the 1st verse, as if He did not go then ; for the 18th chapter says: "When Jesus had spoken these words, He went forth with His disciples over the brook Cedron, where was a garden, into the which He entered, and His disciples."

Moreover, although it has been said that the chapter about the vine and the branches may have been suggested by the vines through which the Saviour passed on the way to Gethsemane, it does not seem to me as if the chapters read like a conversation on the road. There is such a very deep solemnity about them, a quiet and subdued air, and, withal, they are so deep and so full of mystery. There are such pregnant sentences teeming with meaning, that they do not seem to me to be like the discoursings of one who speaks as he walks along, but rather like the deliberate utterances that would be given forth in a chamber in quiet and peace. Perhaps you have never tried it experimentally, but I have, and I know that preaching out of doors is quite a different thing from preaching indoors, and that what you would say to a congregation outside or in conversation with friends on the road is never so profound as that which you would speak to your own familiar acquaintances in the quiet of a room. It seems to me that the conjecture of a great many commentators and expositors is correct. The Saviour here seems to start in the midst of His discourse, and He says, "Let us go hence!" And then, rising, perhaps, from the place where He had been speaking, He feels there is still more to say, and, keeping His posture of standing, He goes on to say somewhat more of that last impressive discourse which He intended to utter before He was taken from them. However, it is not very important: it will mean just the same, whether He did go or whether He did not. It is an explanation dropped by the way ; it is a sort of sacred interpolation upon the sense indicating, as a chance word will sometimes do, what is going on within. It seems very natural. It is all the better tell-tale of the internal processes which were going on in the Saviour's soul.

It seems to me that these words, "Arise, let us go hence," which, in the original Greek, were only three words, may, first of all, be viewed as our Master's brave watchword, and then, secondly, for all time they may be accepted as His servant's stirring motto: "Arise, let us go hence."

I.

First, then, they are the Saviour's brave watchword. In these words He expressed four things.

And, first, He expressed His desire to obey His Father. The clause preceding read thus: "But that the world may know that I love the Father ; and as the Father gave Me commandment, even so I do. Arise, let us go hence." He was eager to do His Father's will ; but that will was about to be revealed to Him in suffering. O brethren, some of us could willingly enough go to serve the Lord in activity, but to go and serve Him in suffering—we halt, we hesitate, we deliberate. But not so with the Saviour. His sufferings were to be infinitely greater than any that can fall to our lot.

In the garden they were to fetch from His entire body a bloody sweat; they were to consist afterwards of shame and spitting and cruelty and reproach and crucifixion pains, and of death itself. He knew, knew to the full, what it all meant, and, for all that, without the slightest hesitation, He says, " Let us go to it ! If My Father hath mixed for Me a cup full of bitterness and gall, shall I not drink it ? "

And he does not sit till the cup is passed to Him, but He goes towards it. He does not wait until that chalice shall be placed to His lips and the dregs shall be drained forcibly into His throat. Not he ! But He rises up, as though He were going to a triumph. He goes cheerfully and willingly, to be obedient unto death, the death of the cross, that He may do His Father's will. O matchless lesson of patience ! Lord, help us to learn that lesson. " The spirit truly is willing, but the flesh is weak." Pray God help even this poor flesh to glorify Him, if need be, in the way of suffering.

And pray remember, dear friends, that in this suffering, which the Saviour was so willing to endure, out of obedience to His Father, there was one peculiar bitterness. It was this, that His Father would leave Him in it. We can bear pain if we are supported by the presence of God. Even death itself is no longer terrible when Jesus softens the couch by His presence. But, O, beloved, to know that a part of our trial will consist in a sense of soul-desertion—this is terrible ! It must be a solemn abnegation of self-love, a real crucifixion of the spirit, when we can forgo not only all earthly joys, but all Heavenly joys, too, for a time, if we may but endure to the end in obedience, and suffer and perform all God's righteous will. Child of God, would you be willing, if God should bless you to save others, to be without one comfortable look from His eyes by the month together ? Would you be content, if it were needful to qualify you to instruct other saints, to be dragged through the deepest mire yourself, to be made the offscouring of all things, and in the operation to be without any consolation from God ? Perhaps you can say, " Yes "; but if it came to the point, would you act like the Master ? Would you rise up from supper and say, with quiet deliberation, " Let us go to this suffering, be it what it may. If the Lord is glorified by it, then ' March onward ! ' is the

word we hear, and onward will we march, let the road be
rough as it may "?

Remember that it is said in the text that our Lord went
to these sufferings, and especially to the peculiar suffering of
being deserted by His Father, with this motive "that the
world may know that I love the Father." The man Christ
was desirous that beyond all dispute everybody should know
that He loved the Father. And assuredly everybody who
knows the story of the cross knows that. We, beloved, know
that He loves us; but please to notice how He loved the Father.
It was not only out of love to man that Jesus died, but out of
love to God, to accomplish the Father's purpose, to satisfy
the Father's longings, to honour the Father's broken law, to
fulfil the Father's justice and give full channel for the Father's
love. It was for this that Jesus went to the cross, and this
sustained Him: "I shall make all men and angels and devils
know that I love the Father." Oh, that we might have some
such motive as this in our service, that we could say, "It shall
be no question with the world whether I love Christ or not.
They despise Him, but they shall know that I adore Him.
They cast out His name as evil, but they shall know that there
is one who loves every letter of that name and is willing to
sacrifice all things for Christ's sake." Beloved, 'tis a glorious
motive. It sustained the Saviour: may the like motive constrain us to go forward in the path of self-sacrifice, that we
may obey God and make all men, whether saints or sinners,
know that we love the Father. The first thing, then, that we
see in this brave watchword of our Saviour is His desire to
obey God.

The second thing I see in it is this—His readiness to meet
the arch-enemy. Look at the 30th verse: "Hereafter I will
not talk much with you: for the prince of this world cometh,
and hath nothing in Me." Then quick after it comes, "Arise,
let us go hence." Our Lord's conflict in the garden with
Satan was very painful. Who can forget how heavy His
soul was even unto death? And the temptations with which
He was there assailed were peculiarly trying. But since our
Lord knew that He must on our behalf fight with Satan and
overcome him, He did not hesitate to go to the fight. There
were soldiers in the old days, like the Persian soldiers, who
had to be driven to battle with whips. They never won the
victory. But the brave Spartan soldiers stepped each man
into his place in the ranks with as much alacrity as if he were

Q

stepping forward into a marriage ceremony. They rejoiced to fight for their country. Now, our Lord and Master was not driven to the last conflict, but He came forward, a volunteer, for our sake, saying, "Let us go hence." I can only compare Him to that old Nazarite, the ancient hero, the son of Manoah, who, as he went through the vineyard, heard a lion, and it roared upon him, and he turned aside from his father and mother and received the leaping beast and slew it, as though it had been a kid, and flinging down the carcase, left it there filled with honey which by-and-bye should be his delight. So did our Saviour step a little while into that garden of Gethsemane, and there in desperate conflict with the lion of the pit He slew him and left him there overcome ; and from that victory you and I to-night gather sweet refreshment—out of the eater, conquered and slain, cometh honey and sweetness to our soul.

And it seemed so brave of our Master to say, "Let us go hence," as though He took a step or two in advance to meet His adversary. The Son of Man was not afraid of the dragon of the pit. "Let us go hence," said He.

But, thirdly, I think this watchword revealed an intense desire in the Saviour's heart for action. You perceive He is communing with those whom He loved best of any upon earth. The eleven were sitting around Him. His big soul is swelling within Him. He has got a work to do, and He wants to be at it. So He breaks off His conversation for a moment, and says to them, "Let us be at it! Let us go hence." He had just been discoursing with them upon the sweetest of all subjects, speaking about that priceless gift of the Paraclete, telling them of the promised Comforter. He breaks that off. He feels it is not a time for talking. "Henceforth," saith He, "I will not talk much with you, for the Prince of this world cometh." He wanted to act. He feels the pressure of events upon Him. The time has come in which no longer can He use dainty words of love, but He must go to stern deeds of conflict. And it was the communion table, too, that He left, that very table of which He said, "With desire have I desired to eat this Passover with you before I suffer." From this He tears Himself away and all its dear associations and solemn feelings. "Arise," says He, "let us go hence."

Have you never seen a man who wanted to do good feel as though he could break away from Christian ordinances and sweet means of spiritual profit to get away and do good to others—something of that spirit that stirs the war-horse when the battle draweth nigh, when he smelleth the battle afar off, and he says, "Aha! aha!"? In the midst of the trumpets he paweth and waiteth for the conflict, with his soul striving within him. It was so with Jesus. With "that stern joy that warriors feel" when they meet with "foemen worthy of their steel," He longed for the fight, and could give up the joy of fellowship that He might enter into the action, for His soul was hot within Him while He said, "Arise, let us go hence."

But once more, there was a fourth thing which these words indicate, namely, His intense desire to accomplish our redemption. That is the point which to us comes nearest home. What if I say that up to that moment His elect were unredeemed? Many of them had entered Heaven, but it was by virtue of the foresight of the sacrifice that He offered. But suppose He had never authorised that sacrifice? The supposition does not dare to be dwelt upon, even for a single moment; but where would have been the covenant if it had never been ratified? Where would have been the promises if the stipulations on the part of our covenant head had never been fulfilled? Where would your hope have been, and mine, dear brethren and sisters? If there had been no bloody sacrifice, how could poor sinners have been washed from sin? Where would have been the atonement to Almighty wrath for our tremendous guilt? If I may so speak, everything was in jeopardy till that hour. "Will He do it? Will He bear it? Will He hold on till He can say, 'It is finished'? Will He bear the strain? Will He have strength enough? When He passes between the millstones of eternal wrath, will He come out as pure grain, the much finer flour? When He is tested and tried, yea, consumed with fire, will He to the end hold on till all His work is done?" Oh, the Saviour longed to get it through. He wanted to be able to say of His dear children, "I have redeemed them out of the hand of the enemy." He wanted to be able to say of His spouse, "I have paid her debts as her only kinsman; I have redeemed her heritage and have set her free; and the man Jesus, like the man Boaz in Ruth, could not be at rest until His spouse was all His own and there was none to claim her, for He had fully redeemed her. "Arise," said He, "let us go hence," as if He had said to the sheep, "Let the shepherd go and pay the ransom-price for you. Let Me go, and let the sword be sheathed in My bosom, that you, the sheep of My care, may never be touched therewith. Let Me go and bear that you may never bear the whole of the wrath that is due for your sin."

Oh, it is great love, great love, marvellous love, that makes Him step forward with such alacrity and say, "Let us go hence. Let us go to redeem My people, and finish the work which God has given Me to do."

II.

Now, reflect on that, dear brethren and sisters, at your leisure; and now follow me for a minute or two while I use this short expression as the stirring motto for the Church in all time, "Arise, let us go hence."

This should be the motto of every new convert. Do I address some who have lately been saved? You have experienced a change of heart within the last few weeks. Now the very first thing you have to do is to come out from the world. In your ear Christ puts it, "Arise, let us go hence! Come out from among them: be ye separate. Touch not the unclean thing." It does not mean that you are to go out of the world, or that you are actually to leave friends and relatives, but to come away from all their idle and sinful customs, come away from all their pursuits and all their pleasures—come right out. You are a child of God: don't act as the children of Satan do. If you have followed a bad trade, leave it; if you are a member of a corrupt Church, leave it. Your course is plain: separate yourself from them and come straight away and follow your Lord Christ without the camp, bearing His reproach, "Arise, let us go hence," saith He.

But have you been converted for some time? Have you already trodden the path where believers walk with Christ? Bear their cross then still. The Saviour saith, "Arise, let us go hence." You have got one measure of faith; do not sit down and say, " I have got enough faith." No, go for twice as much faith. You do love Jesus: do not say, " I love Him enough "; go hence and love Him more. You have a hope that is bright: don't say, " It is enough for me," but seek to have it brighter still. Remember, as soon as you are satisfied with yourself, you will never grow any more until that satisfaction is gone. Get rid of it: let this be constantly your idea, " Not as though I had already attained, either were already perfect, but I press toward the mark for the prize of the high calling of God in Christ Jesus." O beloved, that is the point to aim at. " Let us go hence," farther on. Advance upon everything that you have done and everything that you have been, from strength to strength, go on, and wrestle and fight and pray—

> Tread all the powers of darkness down,
> And win the well-fought day.

The same motto may be used by Christians when they have got into a state of great enjoyment. Perhaps you have been lately favoured to feed upon the Gospel more fully than ever. You have come here this evening, and you have been very thankful that the Lord has spoken to your heart, and you feel very happy. Dear brother, if you enjoy God's presence at the Communion table (which will be best of all), I hope you will hear like the sound of a trumpet behind you, "Arise, go hence! " Where to? Why, back to that cold Church of which you are a member. Try and throw a live coal into the midst of them and warm them up; back to your family, where there are so few that know the Lord. Tell them what you know, and seek their conversion. Go hence, go hence from the Church and table of God in among the ungodly. Go and weep over them; pray for them and seek their salvation. Oh, it is so very easy to sit down at the table, and to sit and hear Gospel sermons, and sing sweet hymns and hear sweet prayer-meetings and say, " It is glorious—

> My willing soul would stay
> In such a frame as this!

Ah, that is very lazy and very selfish. Every mouthful a man eats—the strength of it should be used afterwards for some good end; and every mouthful of spiritual refreshment a Christian gets should either be spent in the patience of suffering or else in the perseverance of service; and if God gives you a specially good meal as He did His servant Elias, it is because you are to go a specially long journey. He went forty days in the strength of that meal. I say that if you get special food from God, you ought to undertake some special service. Go and do more than you ever thought of doing before. If God has made you strong, don't go on with boy's work: undertake man's work. If you have grown to manhood, do man's work. We want some of those that can be leaders, serjeants in the army of Christ, and if the Lord has made you fit for it, don't be ashamed to take that rank, but come to the very front in the service of your Lord and Master. "Arise, let us go hence."

I cannot resist the feeling that there are some of my brethren that ought to hear that in this way while they are sitting here, if they recollect that one-third of the population of this world live in China, and out of all the millions of China there are very few indeed—they might almost be told upon the fingers—who have ever heard of Christ. Men are wanted to go and tell these people about salvation. We heard a dear friend say the other night that they did not want money so much as men, and that simple-hearted men that love Christ were just what they wanted. Surely there ought to be a stir throughout the Church of zealous young men who would say, "Arise, let us go hence."

Then there are others sitting here—men of business that love their Lord, and they can do something for the nation sometimes; but here are sinners perishing and they never think of doing anything for them. I would the Lord would say in their hearts, "Arise, go hence!"

There came into the Tabernacle some few years ago a young Christian man who was everything that could be wished, but he did not do much for Christ. The sermon touched his heart, and he went back to the town where he lived; began to preach in the street, and at this moment he has one of the largest congregations in a certain town, and has built a large tabernacle which he keeps full. I hope he will occupy this pulpit in two or three Sabbath days to come, and you will see what a man can do in business when God does but quicken him in the work.

III.

"Arise, let us go hence." Is not that a call to those Christians who eat the fat and drink the sweet, but send no portion to hungry souls? "Arise, let us go hence." I should like to sound that in many a village chapel where a few score people meet all the year round to make them-

selves comfortable over a little snug Gospel. Why not get
out in the fields on a summer's day and preach there, or do
as the Methodists do, go up and down the streets singing—
anything to get the people in? If the chapels are empty,
are the ministers to sit still and say, "We can't help it"?
No, if the people won't hear us in chapels, let us preach in
theatres, or anywhere. The people *must* hear the Gospel.
"Go ye and preach the Gospel to every creature" is a command that cannot be fulfilled by preaching good sermons
to empty pews. If you come in here, I thank you for it. It
saves me a deal of trouble, for I have not to go after you;
but if you would not come after me, I would sooner go after
you, by some means or other to get the ears of the people,
that they may hear the Word, for this is the motto of the
Church, "Arise, let us go hence!" out of our chapels, out
of our churches, out of our little snuggeries, down dark alleys
and to little meeting houses, and let us go through all England
and the United States, and pour out our troops just as in
the old crusading days the West poured out its chivalry
on to the East to break the Moslem yoke and set the Gospel
free.

When men can make money and say, "I will go and
preach the Gospel in foreign countries"—when men will step
forward and say, "We could earn good positions in the
Army or Navy or law, but we will take up the lowest position
in the Church for the glory of Christ's name"—then will
the crusading times come back again with true splendour.
O Lord of Hosts, let the Sacred Comforter come into the
hearts of all Thy blood-bought ones, and this shall be; and
a mysterious impulse shall go through the Church like that
which went through the world in former ages when they said,
"*Deus vult*," God wills it, and the Church shall say, "Arise,
let us go hence, far hence unto the heathen."

As for us as a Church, let us always be going hence; let
us break forth on the right hand and on the left; let our
forces be scattered that they may be multiplied; let us invent
every system of work that ingenuity can devise, and use old
systems at the highest possible rate. Let us go hence from
all we have done to do something more. Let us arise—that

means upward. Let us go—that means forward. Let us go hence—that is, let us leave all behind that we have already done and up and away to something more.

I think the day will come when this word, which I have sounded out as a trumpet-note, will come very softly as though it dropped from the harp or dulcimer, to the ear of each one of us. It may be it will in our lone chamber, or it may be as we walk the streets—but it matters not where —Jesus will come and commune with us very sweetly, and as He is talking with us He will say, "Arise, let us go hence!" and in a moment we shall leave this heavy clay behind us and find ourselves in the gloryland. Might we not long for that whisper—"Arise!"—not go alone, but "go with me" —my beloved, my Saviour, my sweet companion—"we will mount together!" Ah, I see some of my dear aged friends longing for that time, and those of us who are younger will go perhaps before the older ones. Who can tell? I never pray "From sudden death, good Lord, deliver me." Is there a greater blessing for a Christian than sudden death —to shut your eyes on earth and open them in Heaven and know nothing about it—just to wake up in glory and ask, "Where am I?" to find, instead of wife and children around you, Seraphim and Cherubim with whom you can join your everlasting song? Oh, 'tis blessed! You might almost say, "Good Master, speak the word now!" "Arise, let us go hence."

God bless you, for Christ's sake. Amen.

MARSHALL BROTHERS LTD.,
Printers. London.